# Strategic CSR Communication

**djøf FORLAG**
JURIST- OG ØKONOMFORBUNDETS FORLAG
LYNGBYVEJ 17, POSTBOKS 2702
2100 KØBENHAVN Ø - TLF. 39 13 55 00

# Strategic CSR Communication

Mette Morsing & Suzanne C. Beckmann (Eds.)

Jurist- og Økonomforbundets Forlag
2006

*Strategic CSR Communication*
First Edition, First Printing

© 2006 by DJØF Publishing Copenhagen

DJØF Publishing is a company of the
Association of Danish Lawyers and Economists

Cover Design: Morten Højmark
Print: Narayana Press, Gylling
Binding: Damm's Forlagsbogbinderi, Randers

Printed in Denmark 2006
ISBN 87-574-1587-0

DJØF Publishing
17, Lyngbyvej
P.O.Box 2702
DK-2100 Copenhagen
Denmark

Phone: +45 39 13 55 00
Fax: +45 39 13 55 55
E-mail: forlag@djoef.dk
www.djoef-forlag.dk

# Contents

6

# CHAPTER 1

# Strategic CSR communication: An emerging field

*Suzanne C. Beckmann,*
*Mette Morsing & Lucia A. Reisch*

*There is a tradition of not talking too much about corporate social responsibility. This is very sympathetic and very Danish, but when taking this stance it is difficult to see the economic potential. One should ask oneself: What is it that we are doing, and how can we use it to improve our image?*

Claus Hjort Frederiksen, Danish Minister of Employment, April 2006[1]

In March 2006, a new business-led European Alliance for Corporate Social Responsibility (CSR) was kicked off by the European Commission COM (2006) 136 final its goal being "to reconcile Europe's economic and environmental ambitions" and hence to follow up on the Commission's plans as outlined in the Green Paper Chapter "Promoting a European Framework for Corporate Social Responsibility" (COM 2001 366) and the following Communication on CSR (COM 2002 347). In these chapters, CSR was envisioned to make a contribution both to the Lisbon Goals of Competitive Markets as well as to the Gothenburg European Strategy for Sustainable Development (COM 2001 264). Accordingly, the Alliance calls EU businesses to "move up a gear" and go beyond minimum legal obligations in order to make Europe a "pole of excellence" in CSR. However, the Alliance may also be seen as the result of intensive corporate lobbying against prior more radical plans of obligatory CSR norms, regulation, and monitoring systems. Whatever stance is taken, it is now clear that in order to bring the CSR case forward in Europe, it will more than ever be necessary for consumer activists, NGOs, policy makers, and especially companies themselves to advance good reasons to engage in voluntary CSR activities and to inform the general public about such endeavours. For all organisations and stakeholders, strategic CSR communication then becomes increasingly important and relevant.

Strategic CSR communication, however, is not a straightforward communication task. In this book we take the point of departure in the corporate managerial perspective and have therefore invited our colleagues to investigate the potentials and challenges for corporate managers, who are increasingly expected to communicate their CSR efforts to a variety of influential and alert stakeholders. While companies acknowledge the necessity to inform their stakeholders about their CSR efforts, they also seem to approach this communication task with some hesitation. Studies have shown how Danish managers are exposed to increased expectations from their stakeholders to engagement in social responsibility, yet they are reluctant to communicate the CSR messages themselves (Morsing, Schultz & Nielsen, 2004). While they want the world to know, they hesitate to communicate about the CSR engagement and rather opt for third party endorsement such as the media or expert assessments. Simultaneously, a proliferation of the concept of CSR is taking place and it is increasingly difficult to know for managers what CSR engagement they are expected to engage in and which CSR issues are strategically rewarding to communicate about. Critical issues and NGO "hot spots" are constantly changing: while companies in "sin industries" such as tobacco, alcohol, petro-chemicals, and pharmaceutical industries previously were typical targets for criticism, today in principle all companies are potential targets, as issues such as child labour, workers' rights or animal welfare emerge and potentially influence *any* globally operating company. Therefore, this book takes a process perspective on communication of CSR, where CSR is not a matter of defining *the* CSR effort or issue once and for all, but rather that CSR entails for the development of a satisfactory relationship with a variety of concerned and potentially influential stakeholders.

In this introductory chapter, we first present the context of increased pressure to not only engage in CSR efforts but also to communicate about this engagement. Then an outline of the historical development of CSR is presented and some of the related concepts are briefly introduced. Following is an empirically based study that delivers a very concrete typology to answer the question of "why" do companies engage in ethics and CSR. Then stakeholder management theory is demonstrated to be a core element in much current CSR theory and practice, and following, we suggest that companies operating in Denmark are facing an "Americanization" of CSR, which implies a quest for more conspicuous, yet sophisticated communication strategies. Finally, we give an overview of the various book chapters in Part I and Part II.

### The business of business is value creation
One good reason to engage in CSR efforts and CSR communication can be found when listening to the market. In the largest global survey of the public's expectations, the Millennium Poll on Corporate Social Responsibility carried out in 1999, over 25,000

13

individuals across 23 countries on six continents revealed that they form their impressions of companies by focusing on corporate citizenship (Environics, 1999). Moreover, two out of three people want companies to go beyond making money and contribute to broader society goals, and over 20 % of consumers report having rewarded or punished companies based on their social performance during the past year. During September 2000, MORI (Market Research and Opinion Research International), on behalf of CSR Europe, interviewed 12,000 consumers across twelve European countries on their attitudes towards CSR. 70 % said that a company's commitment to social responsibility is important when buying a product or service, and one in five would be very willing to pay more for products that are socially and environmentally responsible. While these studies have serious problems with a positivity bias that puts into question the significance of the numbers, they still do show that CSR has turned into a widely accepted norm that triggers socially desired answers. Furthermore, methodologically sounder studies also report significant consumer interest in CSR issues (e.g., for Germany: imug, 2003; Lunau, Ulrich & Streiff, 2003). For the United States, Bhattacharya and Sen (2004) report that almost 80 % of all US consumers do consider CSR an important characteristic for their purchase decision. In Scandinavian countries, according to the Reputation Quotient,[2] more than 90 % of the general public find that corporations should be responsible for more than just their shareholders. In Sweden (Micheletti & Stolle, 2004) and Denmark (Dyhr, 2003; Tobiasen, 2004), the "political consumer"[3] is still perceived as a force to be reckoned with. Political consumers are defined as people who sometimes boycott or buycott products or services for political, ethical, social or environmental reasons. Following Hirschman's (1970) notion that all it takes in some markets is for a small number of consumers to actively voice their dissatisfactions and thereby effectively police an imperfect market, such a core cadre of consumers will be enough to decisively threaten or strengthen a company's and/or a brand's market value (Beckmann & Langer, 2003).

14

In order to react to these voices, many corporations have intensified their efforts to develop, integrate, and communicate their CSR efforts to their stakeholders, mostly via respective labelling and CSR reports, some also via commercials and special events. Others have created forums such as stakeholder dialogues, conferences, and seminars, and have started different transparency initiatives. While critical voices remain and heated debates on the pros and cons of CSR are still going on (see Guthey, Langer & Morsing in this book), there is a growing conviction in management circles that companies will increasingly be assessed on the basis of their social performance, that respective outperformance presents a competitive advantage (e.g., Porter & Kramer, 2002), and that the value creation processes around the world will need to become more transparent and intelligible if they are to be seen as politically legitimate (Elkington, Emerson & Beloe, 2006). Hence, the latest management literature seems to have changed the wording of Milton Friedman's influential classic published in The New York Times in 1971: "the business of business is business" into "the business of business is value creation", one way being engagement in CSR.

**Evolution of the concept of CSR**
Before addressing the ways in which CSR can benefit businesses, the historical development concerning CSR will be briefly described in order to enrich our understanding of this concept. An influential chapter in the readings of CSR by Carroll in 1999, "Corporate Social Responsibility: Evolution of a Definitional Construct" outlines in detail the progression of CSR from the modern era of SR, social responsibility, beginning in the 1950s to how we have come to think of CSR today.

In the 1950s, CSR writings often referred to SR, perhaps because corporations had not yet come to represent a substantial force in the social sector. In this era, managers overwhelmingly thought their responsibilities to society were substantial and far beyond what was covered by their profit-and-loss statements (Carroll 1999). In the 1960s, there were significantly more attempts to define what CSR meant and the CSR literature exploded in this direction. Authors emphasized "social power", the "degree of voluntarism" and made reference to businesses being a "proper citizen" (i.e. Davis, 1960; McGuire, 1963). In the 1970s, the CSR construct was further developed into "corporate citizenship" and understanding the "multiplicity of interests" – the start of what is today known as stakeholder management thinking – began to emerge. Johnson said during this period: "In this approach, social responsibility in business is the pursuit of socioeconomic goals through the elaboration of social norms in prescribed business roles; or, to put it more simply, business takes place within a socio-cultural system that outlines through norms and business roles particular ways of responding to particular situations and sets out in some detail the prescribed ways of conducting business affairs" (Johnson, 1971, p. 51).

This quote also links the ethical and moral ties that are often integrated with the concept of CSR. Yet, the 1970s were also the era of Milton Friedman's famous sentiments and the economic critic of CSR as a 'utility maximizing' endeavour (see Johnson, 1971). CSR scholars fought back with ethical and moral reasoning to the pursuit of CSR without empirical evidence as to its effects. Thus, the 1980s moved away from a definitional focus to begin gathering data and testing the outcomes of actual CSR practices and activities.

In the 1980s, more empirically grounded research emerged. This led to the suggestion of alternative or supplementary themes such as corporate social performance (CSP), stakeholder theory, and business ethics theory. CSP compared to CSR can be thought of as measuring the activities of CSR. CSP "emphasizes the concern for corporate action and accomplishment in the social sphere…With a performance perspective, it is clear that firms must formulate and implement social goals and programs as well as integrate ethical sensitivity into all decision making, policies, and actions" (Carroll, 1991, p. 40). Essentially, CSP stresses the results focus of CSR and the quantification, measurement and evaluation of CSR efforts (Wood, 1991). Nonetheless, CSR and CSP are very similar concepts and are often used interchangeably.

16

In the latter stage of the 20th century, which brings us to today's framework, Carroll concludes that "CSR continues to serve as a core construct but yields to or is transformed into alternative thematic frameworks" (Carroll, 1999, p. 268). The progression of stakeholder theory is an example of this phenomenon and as with most theoretical work, the evolution of concepts is often necessary and highly desirable. Especially as the business context rapidly changes and societal values and norms evolve, theoretical works must continually question the empirical evidence of the past and how relevant it is in this day and age. As scholarly and professional research continues, the stakeholder management and communication literature is a large piece of this writing.

## Recent perspectives on a fuzzy concept

Following the majority of managerial studies and drawing on the above history of the concept, there is a general agreement among marketers, communication scholars, and social scientists that CSR is defined as the organization's status and activities with respect to its perceived societal obligations (Brown & Dacin, 1997). Again: such a definition turns our attention to the perceptions of corporate CSR engagement in terms of how well the corporation is able to engage with its stakeholders, rather than to assessments of individual CSR activities. Hence, from a motivational viewpoint, CSR is about the extent to which a company is prepared to examine and improve its impact on all those affected by its activities and to view its long-term reputation within the context of the social and ecological sustainability of its operations (Frankental, 2001, p. 23). Many authors have highlighted the fuzziness of the concept of CSR (Morsing & Langer, 2006) and the overlaps with concepts such as responsible corporate governance (Kuhndt et al., 2004), the social enterprise,[4] sustainability management (Kaptein & Wempe, 2001), corporate citizenship (Matten & Crane, 2005; Mirvis & Googins, 2006), corporate social responsiveness (Ackerman & Bauer, 1976), and corporate sustainability (Dyllick & Hockerts, 2002).[5] Others have discussed whether the individualistic concept of responsibility can be applied to institutions and corporations at all (Goodpaster & Matthews, 1982). As one re-

17

sponse, business ethics has developed a "modern" dialogue-based concept of responsibility (e.g., Homann & Blome-Drees, 1992): Accepting responsibility means to give answers to inquiries of internal and external stakeholders, to give account for business behaviour, and to develop a culture of transparency, reliability, and trustworthiness in a dialogue on equal terms of sovereign partners.

From a managerial view, CSR can be viewed as the corporate implementation of the concepts of sustainable development and stakeholder management, and herewith as one element of sustainable management (Loew et al., 2004). Multinational institutions (such as IAO, UNO, AI and OECD), stakeholder round tables, industry associations, and corporate initiatives (e.g., the Global Compact) have worked since more than a decade on the ascertainment of this umbrella concept. They have developed indicators, measurement instruments, industry reporting standards (such as AA1000, SA 8000 and ISO 14001), and auditing schemes.[6] In academia, several European research consortia on CSR issues are trying to improve the theoretical foundations of the concept, to further empirical knowledge on CSR practice, and to map out policy recommendations based on that research.[7]

In a nutshell: Beyond conceptual debates, political debates, and management talk, CSR is in practice well entrenched and amply funded today, and most large corporations have accepted to respond to it. The reasons for engaging in CSR and for how to communicate CSR however are rooted in different factors.

### Engaging in values

Paine (2003) distinguishes various "paths to values" that managers may take when orienting themselves to CSR issues and then pursuing action: While some companies may be problem-driven by a crisis or a scandal, others may be motivated by an executive's personal conviction or by a process of logical reasoning as to the benefits of such behaviours (i.e., opportunity-driven). In fact, most firms arrive at a value-oriented management model through a mixture of both positive and negative factors. Moreover, Paine introduces four major clusters and one additional fac-

18

tor that describe the rationale for a shift towards corporate values (see Figure 1).

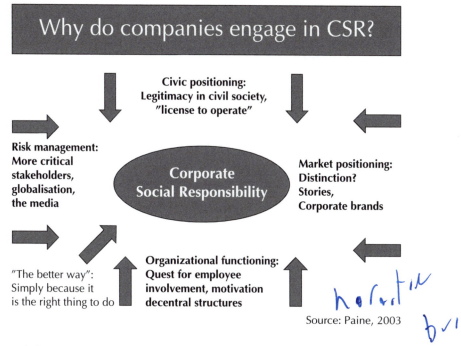

Source: Paine, 2003

While risk management, organisational functioning, market functioning and civic positioning may all be said to belong to "the business case" for CSR, i.e. the arguments that entail a business-economic logic, "the better way" may be categorized as "the normative case", where any manager or employee has a moral obligation to contribute to the improvement of society. While "the normative case" in various ways defined the revitalization of the 1990s, today many studies investigate CSR from a "business case" perspective (Smith, 2003). A study of the development of CSR in the Scandinavian countries confirms this turn towards a corporate "business case" orientation (Morsing, Midttun & Palmås, in press).

1. *Risk management:* By addressing and anticipating various risk factors, managers ideally strive to eliminate certain risks, for example internal misconduct due to employee carelessness, neglect, or illegal behaviour. Individual and corporate misconduct

19

are risks that must be monitored and reduced since they are potential "time bombs" waiting to go off. Misdoings can cause problems of crisis proportions, particularly if discovered by the public (for instance: Enron, Arthur Andersen, Tyco). Risk management through strong organizational values and behaviours can build and maintain a company's image, brand, and employee moral. A value-orientation can also pre-empt the implementation of expensive laws and legal requirements as well as reduce exposure to fines and litigation, so that tangible and intangible benefits are likely to arise. Finally, an executive's reorientation towards values often reflects their company's stage of development. For instance, executives of well-established, large firms may want to *protect* their company's reputation or its brand, whereas smaller and/or entrepreneurial firms are more likely to talk about *building* a reputation or *establishing* a brand.

*2. Organizational functioning:* Executives may rationalize a turn to values as a means for organization building. Rather than a defensive measure this is a positive effort to build a well-functioning organization where values are essential for cooperation, encouraging commitment and inspiring innovation. The purpose is to energize internal and external stakeholders and to exude ideals such as respect, honesty and integrity. These could act to reduce transaction costs, attract and retain employees, and strengthen consumer loyalty.

*3. Market positioning:* A third cluster of themes is a company's desire to position themselves favourably vis-à-vis their competitors. Managers that pursue this orientation focus on the ability of values to shape their company's identity and reputation by building its brands, or earning the trust of customers, suppliers or other business partners, and stakeholders. Although seemingly similar to the organizational functioning rationale, the market positioning focused manager is externally focused. An important point for many of these managers is "what customers and other market actors expect of the products and services they buy and the companies with which they deal" (Paine, 2003, p. 16).

*4. Civic positioning:* Corporate citizenship or civic positioning is the company's standing and reputation in the community.

20

While some manager wish to establish a corporate image as being a progressive force for social betterment, others seek good relationships with non-market or "civic" constituencies such as governments, nongovernmental organizations (NGOs), and local community groups. Still others strive to establish their firm as an overall solid corporate citizen that obeys the law, pays its taxes, and upholds ethical standards to respect the societies in which it operates.

5. *"A better way":* A fifth concept is simply "a better way" to conduct business that does not require corporate justification for its practice. For this group of managers, the very idea of values evokes something worthwhile in and of itself (Paine, 2003, p. 23). There is little rationalizing about risk management, organizational functioning, or corporate reputation. The orientation is largely towards responsibility, humanity, and citizenship.

## Management studies on CSR and stakeholder outreach

As shown above, engaging in values is motivated by different factors. Yet, they are all based on a perception of the firm as a part of a political-social-economic network with more or less intense exchange relations with external (e.g., consumers, community, government, competitors) and internal (e.g., employees, owners) groups that assert their claims as regards information, resources, programmes, and products. This perception is mirrored in the "stakeholder management approach" (Carroll, 2003; Donaldson & Preston, 1995). Stakeholders are defined as any group who affects or is affected by the achievement of the firm's objectives (Freeman, 1984).

Stakeholders employ a combination of four basic strategies to implement their concerns: the mobilization of public pressure via mass media; of political pressure via political parties and institutions; of market forces via "exit and voice" strategies; and of pressure on the corporate actors themselves. The need for a strategic stakeholder outreach also depends on the degree of "public exposure", i.e., in how far the corporation touches upon public interests in its business behaviour and, vice versa, in how far it is affected by actions that are carried out in the public interest, such as regulations. According to Dyllick (1992), the important determinants of public exposure are: sensitive industry sector, large company size, high degree of internationalization, strong market orientation, closeness to end consumers, and a high brand value. And the higher the public exposure of a company, the more important is a genuine CSR strategy and stakeholder dialogue.

A key role is that of the NGOs that have become more professional and less dogmatic. As regards CSR, NGOs have lately taken opinion leadership and cooperate closely with international organisations such as UNO or OECD (see also Georg in this book). Attitudes of companies and NGOs are changing, and business-NGO partnerships are increasingly considered and initiated (Schiller, 2005, see also Marsden & Andriof, 1998 for a typology of NGOs and hence potential partners in such alliances). Moreover, the media and consumer organisations fulfil their self-assumed role as "CSR watchdogs" and increasingly use their agenda setting power in the public discourse. The media, in particular, plays an important role both as a platform and a multiplier (Reisch, 2001). As a consequence of this constellation, the tolerance level for companies that do not comply with CSR standards is decreasing. The higher their brand equity, the more vulnerable are companies to become the object of "name and shame campaigns". These, in turn, can lead to the loss of reputation, of image and brand value, and hence the loss of sales and of employees' motivation and loyalty. According to analysts, social equity has been shown to have a measurable and increasing influence on sales and brand equity – and herewith on corporate value (social equity is measured, for instance, by commercial consultancies such as www.goodbrand.com's GoodBrand Social Equity Index™. The financial risk involved in this power of media-NGO alliances has long been recognized by financial institutions. Banks and insurances were – together with ethical rating agencies and consumer organizations – among the first to actively call for reliable and systematic CSR information and auditing procedures. Today, the financial community is rather a "friend than a foe" (Echo Research, 2003) of CSR practices worldwide.

22

It has been argued that CSR as a corporate management approach can only be successful if it is a "business case" (Smith, 2003). There is an ongoing debate on whether CSR practices contribute to the bottom line or not (e.g. Capaldi 2005; Margolish & Walsh, 2003). While a key complaint of critical voices is that CSR hurts financial performance – or at best does not matter – recent research shows the opposite. An award-winning meta-analysis (Orlitzky, Schmidt & Rynes, 2003) looked at 52 studies over 30 years, finding a statistically positive correlation between CSR and financial performance. According to the authors, these two factors mutually reinforce each other due to improved managerial competency and improved corporate reputation. Similarly, Hopkins, (2003) has compiled evidence of a positive relationship between the overall quality of management of a firm and, interestingly, the way it treats its critical stakeholders. For the future, he expects that corporations will increasingly perform in-depth benefit-cost analysis of CSR and that they will engage in stakeholder outreach more systematically.

However, the question of "how" this outreach will take place and how corporations will communicate with their stakeholders will differ depending on cultural norms and institutional framework. This is where intercultural management studies come into play.

## The "Americanization" of Danish CSR approaches

As has been detailed elsewhere (Morsing, 2003; Morsing & Beckmann, 2006), the traditional Danish approach to CSR is a rather "silent strategy". Yet, while the crave for demonstration of conspicuous CSR activities is in Europe traditionally regarded as an American phenomenon of corporate philanthropy (Matten & Moon, 2004), we see Danish companies increasingly engaging in visible activities and policies with an equal conspicuous orientation as a consequence of stakeholders' expectations and quest for transparency. We argue that this turn towards an "Americanization" of Danish CSR practices emphasizes CSR as a competitive advantage, thus making CSR a locus of distinction with an emphasis on the individual corporation. This is in contrast to the

23

continental state-defined approach, in which CSR is embedded in the regulatory and institutional framework, and in which CSR has been much less a matter of companies' individual discretion. As such Danish companies are forced to develop and articulate a CSR approach different from their traditional and institutionally embedded CSR approach, since such an approach is difficult to articulate in terms of corporate distinction and, moreover, does not fulfil stakeholders' crave for more visible substantiated CSR efforts (Morsing & Thyssen, 2006).

Traditionally, corporate social responsibility as a visible strategy is regarded in Denmark as a particularly American phenomenon, reflecting American traditions of self-help and minimum or at least indirect government, which has resulted in an emphasis on community involvement, stringent legal frameworks, shareholder driven corporate governance, voluntary corporate contributions and corporate philanthropy, i.e. giving back to society some of the wealth the company has created thanks to society's inputs. However, this does not imply that Danish or European businesses have been socially irresponsible. As a matter of fact there is evidence demonstrating the contrary, namely that European businesses are "more susceptible to social pressure both from government officials and from other forums to behave "responsibly"" (Vogel, 1986, p. 50), and that European businesses have been much more of a partner of the state in working towards societal goods (Matten & Moon, 2004). This may be seen as a reflection of the continental predominantly state-defined welfare societies, which we claim is particularly outspoken in Northwest Europe, including Scandinavia.

While the notion of CSR derives first and foremost from the United States resulting in a predominant definition of CSR as a voluntary corporate policy, CSR as a voluntary corporate policy is fairly recent and still a fragmented phenomenon in a Danish context. With other scholars we suggest that the key reasons that CSR has not been exposed to the same extent of "corporate talk" in Denmark as in the US, is that the legal and institutional framework in Denmark has already included and institutionalized many of the issues that arise as CSR. Further, Danish models of trust and authority relations differ from those that prevail in the more liberal USA (Matten & Moon, 2004; Schwartz, 1992). In a Danish state-defined model of capitalism, formal institutions integrate and embed the social responsibility of companies (i.e. laws, regulation, mandatory requirements), and in Denmark companies or business associations such as for example the Confederation of Danish Industries (Dansk Industri), The Confederation of Danish Employers (Dansk Arbejdsgiverforening), and The Danish Confederation of Trade Unions (LandsOrganisationen) usually have participated with other social and political stakeholders in the design, review and re-design of such systems. This has contributed to making the obligations legitimate in most corporations, and have also contributed to the emergence of less formal institutions, values, attitudes, customs or traditions which locate the role of the corporation in society much closer to societal goals and agendas than is found in the American system (Matten & Moon, 2004).

Thus CSR of Danish corporations has to a much lesser extent been a question of companies' individual discretion than in US corporations. The social responsibilities of Danish business have been played out in a context with more deeply embedded relationships between business, society and the state, which has been influenced by the role of the state in risk sharing, less strong influence on capital markets, and regulation of labour markets such as the role of trade unions and industry associations (Midttun & Dirdal, 2004).

An analysis of the traditions for social responsibility in North America and Europe has lead to a distinction between explicit and implicit CSR (Matten & Moon, 2004). *Explicit CSR* refers to corporate policies that lead companies to assume responsibilities for selected areas of interest of society. "Explicit CSR would normally involve voluntary, self-interest driven policies, programmes and strategies of corporations to address issues perceived by the company and/or its stakeholders as part of their social responsibility" (Matten & Moon, 2004, p. 341). Explicit CSR represents a specific focus on the corporation and hence emphasizes the imperatives and drivers for social responsibility influencing corporations; and the tools for social responsibility that corporations can deploy. This special focus on the corporation can be encouraged by corporations themselves, but also other business drivers such as public policy and government ideology, business associations and societal representatives.

*"Implicit CSR* refers to a country's formal and informal institutions through which the corporations' responsibility for society's interests are agreed and assigned to corporations" (Matten & Moon, 2004, p. 342). Implicit CSR normally comprehends values, norms, and rules, which often result in mandatory requirements for corporations to address issues, which are perceived as appropriate and reasonable obligations put on corporate actors by social, political and economic interests upon corporate actors. As such, implicit CSR is embedded in the business-society-government relations within a political system in a way that we refer to as state-defined, which is particularly outspoken in the Scandinavian countries. It may result from strong norms, which all parties recognize and in which all participate, and which may "inform regulation whose legitimacy is confirmed by its democratic context or prevailing approach to policy-making, such as participatory consensus-seeking practices" (Matten & Moon, 2004, p. 343). In such a context a strong system of social capital is expected to develop around the design and implementation of the norms and the regulation. Interestingly, prior research found that European companies are more prone to describe their CSR engagement in a broader social context, while their US counterparts focus on the corporation as the centre of CSR activities (Maignan & Ralston, 2002). In Figure 2, the relation between explicit and implicit CSR approaches is depicted.

26

**Figure 2:** "Implicit and Explicit CSR"
(Source: Matten & Moon, 2004)

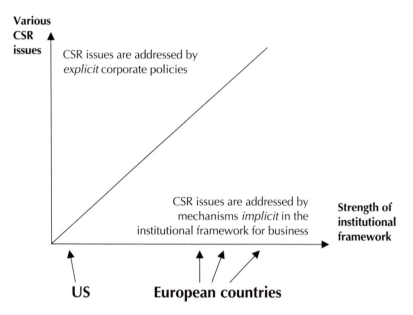

Explicit and implicit CSR both deal with social issues in the relations of companies and their stakeholders. Though they represent competing approaches, there is presumably a balance between explicit and implicit activities, but we suggest that one assumes dominance. In Europe – and hereby Denmark – the implicit approach is dominant, while in the US the explicit approach is customary.

Matten and Moon suggest that there has been a recent move from implicit CSR towards a more explicit form of CSR in Europe, and we argue that the current demand for more conspicuous demonstration of CSR initiatives posed on Danish companies is an indication of this move. We see Danish companies engaging in activities and policies with a similar orientation as the North American corporations not so much built on a heritage of voluntarism, but as a result of new expectations from stakeholders, i.e. encouraged by the institutional framework of Danish companies. It is evidenced for example by the growth of a large number of

27

business associations and business networks with the declared goal of promoting CSR, by the emergence of a CSR consultant industry, and by the more explicit status of CSR within companies in terms of CSR professionals, CSR departments, code of conducts, CSR policies, sustainability reports and CSR as part of the corporate branding efforts. Also the investment community, the media, and business education have demonstrated a growing interest in analyzing CSR as an autonomous phenomenon.

This turn towards an "Americanisation" of Danish CSR practices brings a new focus on CSR as a potential competitive advantage. It makes CSR a locus of distinction and carries a focus on the individual corporation's CSR efforts that is not state-defined. Instead of accepting being embedded in a neutral state-defined value context, corporations are to make their CSR activities part of their individual strategic identity focusing on distinction. This forces Danish companies to develop and articulate a CSR approach different from their traditional inherent and implicit approach, which is difficult to articulate and demonstrate, to fulfil stakeholders' crave for more substantiated CSR efforts. A turn towards an explicit approach to CSR implies a sharpened and strategic demonstration of the CSR efforts, and hence a closer look at with whom, when and how to communicate.

## What to expect from this book

This book addresses the reader who takes a critical interest in issues of strategic CSR communication. The book contributes with a multi-disciplinary perspective to reflect the challenges of the increased quest for strategic CSR communication in a Danish managerial context. We acknowledge that Danish companies cannot choose any longer: increasingly they have to handle an "explicit" as well as an "implicit" CSR approach in terms of strategic communication. However, we argue that Danish companies need to address the demands for explicit CSR communication strategies in a new and more subtle way than their US counterparts: while they need to inform stakeholders about their CSR commitment, they should be careful not to disregard their contex-

28

tually bound traditions for stakeholder participation and close interaction with representative of the state and civil society.

To address these issues we have invited colleagues to share their experiences and reflections concerning more general aspects of strategic CSR communication and specific stakeholders. Hence, the book is divided into two parts.

**Part I** sets the scene for strategic CSR communication. Key questions are raised and mainstream assumptions about CSR communication are conveyed and challenged. While corporate CSR engagement is encouraged and increasingly expected, interestingly, a strong criticism is voiced from the politically Left as well as from the Right. From the Left, Joel Bakan, in his book and film "The Corporation", emphasizes that CSR is window dressing that enables companies to continue unethical practices and to resist government regulation. From the Right, The Economist, drawing on arguments from liberalist thinkers such as Milton Friedman and Adam Smith, has argued that CSR is a waste: it distracts companies from their core roles of producing goods and services and making profits (Marsden, 2006). While companies want to communicate themselves as socially responsible and legitimate actors, such criticisms simultaneously shape a challenging scene for the corporate communicative efforts.

In the chapter by Guthey, Langer and Morsing it is argued that although CSR by liberalist thinkers is accused of being "merely a management fashion", it should not be dismissed as such: CSR may indeed be productive as a management fashion. Vallentin shows how different views of public opinion can serve as useful tools for understanding corporate social responsiveness, and he reflects on how companies may create and analyze contemporary awareness of public opinion. Kjær demonstrates how CSR in terms of the relationship between business and society is staged by the business news. In particular, Kjær advocates critical attention to how "business in society" is constructed by analyzing the interests and motives behind the presented issues: who is setting the scene, and who claims to speak on behalf of which stakeholders: "the public", "the industry", "the nation" "the market", or? Langer raises the issue of ethicality in his analysis of stealth marketing, as com-

29

panies try to influence increasingly sophisticated stakeholders by continuously developing different and cleverer communication tools. Finally, Morsing and Schultz argue that while the public may encourage CSR activities they may be reluctant to listen to the CSR message and therefore suggest three communication strategies for companies to carefully consider as they engage in communicating CSR activities to potentially skeptical audiences.

**Part II** explores the challenges of communicating CSR vis-à-vis different stakeholders. While CSR and ethics have often been argued as driven by the politically concerned consumer, who is assumed to require information about corporate decisions and actions, the contributions acknowledge, yet challenge this assumption. While consumers are still one of the drivers of the corporate CSR agenda, other important stakeholders have conspicuously appeared on the political stage. Increasingly, investors, NGOs and B2B customers ask companies to document and communicate their CSR efforts. To complicate things further, companies are encouraged to engage in CSR efforts, while CSR communication is not always appreciated by stakeholders. Often companies are perceived as self-complacent, self-absorbed or even distasteful as they stage themselves as benefactors to a good cause, trying to look good while drawing on other people's misery.

Beckmann demonstrates that only little knowledge has been produced so far about consumers' motives, perceptions and actual behaviours in response to CSR activities and communication, and she argues that studies on the impact of CSR information on consumers have brought mixed results and thus calls for more research. Along the same lines, but based on a German CSR project, Reisch suggests a number of venues to approach a broader audience of stakeholders, as she raises the question on whether consumers should be approached as a separate target for CSR information at all. Georg discusses the opportunities for companies to engage in partnerships with NGOs to promote understanding and dialogue. But she also points at the potential risks for both parties in engaging in close communicative relations. With the case of IKEA, Andersen demonstrates how companies are prompted to request documentation from suppliers with regard to social and environmental behaviour, as the boundary between company and supplier is blurring in the eyes of the public. While integration of suppliers in the corporate communication process is emphasized as a driver of corporate CSR communication by Andersen, Hockerts points our attention to investors as another driver. He argues that investors show growing interest in assessing companies on other assets than purely financial indicators, as they see CSR as a strategic element of companies' competitive advantage. Finally, Ellerup Nielsen and Thomsen focus on the discursive strategies employed by companies in their social reports. Based on an empirical study they suggest that two CSR discourse orders seem to prevail social reporting, and they discuss the managerial implications as companies strive towards sending consistent messages.

We have asked all authors to pose three critical questions for reflection, hoping that they will challenge conventional and stimulate alternative thinking about CSR communication and in particular about *strategic* CSR communication.

## Acknowledgements

Like all editors of anthologies, we depended on the authors' engagement, deliveries and willingness to play along the lines of the scene we have chosen to set for strategic CSR communication. Therefore, we first and foremost wish to thank all authors who have contributed by not only analysing the various perspectives on strategic CSR communication but also to challenge them. We also want to thank Cheryl Iseli, who has provided very useful editorial assistance for the introductory chapter. Furthermore, each contribution has benefited from the readings and discussions with students enrolled in the CBS executive Master of Corporate Communication in 2005. Their constructive comments spurred revisions and adjustments, and we thank them all sincerely for engaging in this effort so productively.

## References

Ackerman, R. W. & Bauer, R. A. (1976). *Corporate social responsiveness: The modern dilemma.* Reston, VI: Reston Publishing Company.

Beckmann, S. C. & Langer, R. (2003). Consumer-citizen boycotts: Facilitators, motives and conditions. In: *Proceedings of the 32nd European Marketing Academy (EMAC) Conference.* Glasgow: University of Strathclyde.

Bhattacharya, C. B. & Sen, S. (2004). Doing better at doing good: When, why, and how consumers respond to corporate social initiatives. *California Management Review,* 47(1), 9-24.

Brown, T. J. & Dacin, P.A. (1997). The company and the product: corporate associations and consumer product responses. *Journal of Marketing,* 51 (January), 68-84.

Capaldi, N. (2005). Corporate social responsibility and the bottom line. *International Journal of Social Economics,* 32(5), 408-423.

Carroll, A. B. (1991) The pyramid of corporate social responsibility: Toward the moral management of organizational stakeholders. *Business Horizons* 34(4), 39-48.

Carroll, A. (1999) Corporate social responsibility. Evolution of a definitional construct, *Business and Society* 38(3), 268-295.

Carroll, A. B. (2003). *Business and society: Ethics and stakeholder management.* Ohio: South-Western Educational Publishing.

Commission of the European Communities (2001). *Communication from the Commission concerning a sustainable Europe for a better world: A European Union strategy for sustainable development.* Brussels: EC, COM (2001) 366 final.

Commission of the European Communities (2002). *Communication from the Commission concerning Corporate Social Responsibility: A business contribution to sustainable development.* Brussels: EC, COM(2002) 347 final. COM (2006) 136 final.

Davis, K. (1960). Can business afford to ignore social responsibilities? *California Management Review,* 2, pp. 70-76.

Dickinson, R. & Carsky, M. L. (2005). The consumer as economic voter. In: R. Harrison, T. Newholm, & D. Shaw (Eds.). *The ethical consumer.* London: Sage.

Donaldson, T. J. & Preston, L. E. (1995). The stakeholder theory of the corporation: Concepts, evidence, and implications. *Academy of Management Review,* 20(1), 65-91.

Dyhr, V. (2003). CSR as a competitive factor in a consumer perspective. In: M. Morsing & C. Thyssen (Eds.). *Corporate values and responsibility – the case of Denmark,* pp. 281-286. Copenhagen: Samfundslitteratur.

Dyllick, T. (1992). *Management der Umweltbeziehungen. Öffentliche Auseinandersetzungen als Herausforderungen.* Wiesbaden: Gabler.

Dyllick, T. & Hockerts, K. (2002). Beyond the business case for corporate sustainability. *Business Strategy and the Environment*, 11(2), 130-141.

Echo Research (2003). *CSR 3: Corporate Social Responsibility and the financial community – friends or foes?* Report prepared by Echo Research, Surrey, UK.

Elkington, J., Emerson, J., & Beloe, S. (2006). The Value Palette: A tool for full spectrum strategy. *California Management Review*, 48(2), Special Issue on Strategies for Corporate Social Responsibility, 6-28.

Environics International, Ltd., The Prince of Wales Business Leaders & The Conference Board (1999). *Millennium poll on corporate social responsibility: Executive briefing*. Toronto, Canada: Author.

Frankental, P. (2001) Corpoarte social responsibility – a PR invention? *Corporate Communications*, 6(1), pp. 18-23.

Freeman, R. E. (1984). *Strategic management. A stakeholder approach*. Marshfield, MA: Pitman.

Garriga, M. & Mele, D. (2004). Corporate social responsibility theories: Mapping the territory. *Journal of Business Ethics*, 53, 51-71.

Goodpaster, K.E. & Matthews, J.B. Jr. (1982). Can a corporate have a conscience? *Harvard Business Review,* January-February

Hirschman, A. O. (1970). *Exit, voice, and loyalty. Responses to decline in firms, organizations, and states.* Cambridge, MA: Harvard University Press.

Homann, K. & Blome-Drees, F. (1992). *Wirtschafts- und Unternehmensethik.* Göttingen: UTB.

Hopkins, M. (2003). The business case for CSR: Where are we? *International Journal of Business Performance Management*, 5(2/3), 125-140.

Johnson, H. L. (1971). Corporate social responsibility revisited, redefined. *California Management Review*, pp. 59-67.

Kaptein, M. & Wempe, J. (2001). Sustainability management. Balancing conflicting economic, environmental and social corporate responsibilities. *The Journal of Corporate Citizenship*, 2 (Summer), 2001, 91-106.

Kuhndt, M., Tuncer, B., Snorre Andersen, K., & Liedtke, C. (2004). Responsible corporate governance. An overview of trends, initiatives and state-of-the-art elements. *Wuppertal Chapters No. 139.* Wuppertal: Wuppertal Institute of Climate Environment Energy.

Loew, T., Ankele, K., Braun, S., & Clausen, J. (2004). *Bedeutung der CSR-Diskussion für Nachhaltigkeit und die Anforderungen an Unternehmen.* Final Report. Berlin: future e.V. & IÖW.

Lunau, Y, Ulrich, P., & Streiff, S. (2003). *Soziale Unternehmensverantwortung aus Bürgersicht: eine Anregung zur Diskussion.* Bericht des Instituts für Wirtschaftsethik an der Universität St. Gallen, im Auftrag der Philip Morris GmbH, München, St. Gallen: IWE-HSG.

Maignan, I. & Ralston, D. A. (2002). Corporate social responsibility in Europe versus the US: insights from businesses' self-presentations. *Journal of International Business Studies*, 33(3), 497-515.

33

Matten, D. & Moon, J. (2004). A conceptual framework for understanding CSR. In: A. Habisch, J. Jonker, M. Wegner, & R. Schmidpeter (Eds.). *Corporate Social Responsibility across Europe*, pp. 335-356. Berlin: Springer.

Matten, D. & Crane, A. (2005). Corporate citizenship: Toward an extended theoretical conceptualization. *Academy of Management Review*, 30(1), 166-179.

Margolish, J. D. & Walsh, J. P. (2003) Misery loves companies – rethinking social initiatives by business. *Administrative Science Quarterly*, 48, 268-305.

Marsden, C. (2006). In defence of corporate responsibility. In: Kakabadse, A. & Morsing, M. (Eds.) *Corporate social responsibility. Reconciling aspiration with application.* pp. 24-39. London: Palgrave MacMillan.

Marsden, C. & Andriof, J. (1998). Towards an understanding of Corporate Citizenship and how to influence it. *Citizenship Studies*, 2(2), pp. 329-352.

McGuire, J. W. (1963) *Business and society.* New York: McGraw-Hill.

Michelletti, M. & Stolle, D. (2004). Swedish political consumers: Who they are and why they use the market as an arena for politics. In: Boström, M., Føllesdal, A., Klintman, M., Micheletti, M. & Sørensen, M. (Eds.). *Political consumerism: Its motivations, power, and conditions in the Nordic countries and elsewhere.* Proceedings from the 2$^{nd}$ International Seminar on Political Consumerism, Oslo, August 26-29, 2004, pp. 145-164.

Midttun, A., & Dirdal, T. (2004). Nordic industry and CSR: Frontrunners or discrete societal partners? Chapter for The European Academy of Business in Society – 3rd Annual Colloquium *The challenge of sustainable growth: Integrating societal expectations in business:* September 27 & 28, 2004.

Mirvis, Ph. & Googins, B. (2006). Stages of Corporate Citizenship. *California Management Review*, 48(2), Special Issue on Strategies for Corporate Social Responsibility, pp. 104-126.

Morsing, M. (2003). Conspicuous Responsibility: Communicating Responsibility – to Whom? In: Morsing, M. & Thyssen, C. (eds.), *Corporate Values and Responsibility – the Case of Denmark*, pp.145-154. Copenhagen: Samfundslitteratur.

Morsing, M., Schultz, M. & Nielsen, K. U. (2004). Social ansvarlighed giver ikke automatisk respekt. *Ledelse i Dag*, November, pp. 32-40.

Morsing, M. & Beckmann, S. C. (2006). Virksomhedens sociale ansvar: Danske CSR traditioner i lyset af angelsaksiske og kontinentale CSR traditioner. In: Djursø, H. T. & Neergaard, P. (Eds.). *Social ansvarlighed: Fra idealisme til forretningsprincip*, pp. 115-126. Århus: Academica.

Morsing, M. & Langer, R. (2006). CSR communication in the business press: Advantages of strategic ambiguity. In: *Proceedings of the 11th International Conference on Corporate and Marketing Communications.* Ljubljana/Slovenia: Faculty of Social Sciences, University of Ljubljana.

Morsing, M. & Thyssen, O. (2006). *CSR and the normalization of hypocrisy.* CBS: Working paper.

34

Morsing, M., Midttun, A. & Palmås, K. (in press) Corporate social responsibility in Scandinavia – a turn towards the business case?. In: May, S., Cheney, G. & Roper, J. (Eds.): *The Debate over Corporate Social Responsibility*, London: Oxford University Press.

Orlitzky, M., Schmidt, F. L. & Rynes, S. L. (2003). Corporate social and financial performance: A meta-analysis. *Organization Studies*, 24(3), 403-441.

Paine, L. S. (2003). *Value Shift. Why Companies Must Merge Social and Financial Imperatives to Achieve Superior Performance*. New York: MacGraw-Hill.

Porter, M. E. & Kramer, M. R. (2002). The competitive advantage of corporate philanthropy. *Harvard Business Review*, 80(12), 56-69.

Reisch, L. A. (2001). The new media: A resource for sustainable consumption? In: L. Michaelis (Ed.). *Report from the Expert Workshop on The Media: A resource for sustainable consumption*, 8-9.01.2001, Oxford Centre for the Environment, Ethics and Society, June 2001, Mansfield College, Oxford, (UK).

Schiller, B. (2005). *Trends in NGO-business partnerships*. Ethical corporation report. Ethical Corporation Online (www.eldis.org). London: Eldis.

Schwarts, S. (1992). Universals in the content and structure of values: Theoretical advance and empirical tests in countries. In M. P. Zanna (Ed.), *Advances in experimental social psychology*, Vol. 25, pp. 1-65. Orlando, FL: Academic Press.

Smith, N. C. (2003), Corporate Social Responsibility: Whether or How? *California Management Review* 45(4), 52-73.

Tobiasen, M. (2004). Political consumerism in Denmark. In: Boström, M., Føllesdal, A., Klintman, M., Micheletti, M. & Sørensen, M. (Eds.). *Political consumerism: its motivations, power, and conditions in the Nordic countries and elsewhere*. Proceedings from the 2nd International Seminar on Political Consumerism, Oslo, August 26-29, 2004, pp. 113-144.

Vogel, D. (1986). *National Styles of Regulation: Environmental Policy in Great Britain and the United States*. Ithaca, NY, London: Cornell University Press.

Wood, D. J. (1991). Corporate social performance revisited: A conceptualization based on organizational literature. *Academy of Management Review*, 4, 359-368.

## Notes

1. cited in: *Rønn, L.: Pral: Samfundsengagement betaler sig. Jyllandsposten. 24.04.2006.*
2. See
   *www.reputationinstitute.com/main/index.php?pg=res&box=reputation_quoti ent* for details.
3. Following the discussion on corporate citizenship, this phenomenon has also been termed "consumer citizenship" (Dickinson & Carsky, 2005) or "participatory consumerism".

4. See e.g., the Social Enterprise Alliance and their publication Stanford Social Innovation Review (*www.ssireview.com*).

5. For an overview of theories see Garriga and Melé (2004). For a historical view on how these different concepts developed and how they are linked up with each other and CSR see Loew et al., 2004.

6. For instance: CSR Europe (*www.csreurope.org*); ILO (www.ilo.org); the Global Compact (*www.unglobalcompact.com*); AI (*www.webamnesty.org*); OECD Guidelines (*www.oecd.org/daf/investment/guidelines*); the Global Reporting Initiative (*www.globalreporting.org*).

7. For instance: "Rhetoric and realities: Analysing corporate social responsibility in Europe" (RARE) (*www.rare-eu.net*).

# PART I

# Setting the CSR Communication Agenda

# CHAPTER 2

# Corporate Social Responsibility is a Management Fashion. So What?

*Eric Guthey, Roy Langer and Mette Morsing*

*We have to recognize that popular movements in management like reengineering, TQM and Excellence, while essentially transitory in nature, are nevertheless important areas to research. This is because they tell us a lot about managers and management… As we demystify the rhetoric of the management gurus, we can selectively learn from that rhetoric how to make our accounts more plausible to the audience of practicing managers who need to hear what we have to say.*

Brad Jackson, 2001.

"One of the biggest corporate fads of the 1990s – less overpowering, no doubt, than dot.com mania, but also longer-lived – was the flowering of "corporate social responsibility," *The Economist* declared in 2004. "Greed is out. Corporate virtue, or the appearance of it, is in." (2004c). Over the last ten years, the magazine has consistently dismissed CSR as a fashionable "scam," which despite its "vague" and "fuzzy" ideas has become "an industry in its own right," with all the trappings and excesses of other management fashions.

It may seem odd that a publication so openly devoted to promoting the interests and ideology of free enterprise should highlight the commercial successes of CSR as proof of its bankruptcy. But *The Economist* is not alone. The practice of dismissing CSR and other forms of corporate social engagement as mere fashion has become very fashionable itself. So fashionable, in fact, that even many *advocates* of corporate social engagement have internalized it. They often bring up the fashion critique themselves as a means of defending their cause against it. "CSR's time has come, and it is not just a management fad," insists Sandra Macleod, Chief Executive of Echo Research, on the CSRWire Website (CSRWire, 2005). "We take a great care in ensuring that it is not just a fad," says Romesh Sobti, India Representative for ABN Amro Bank NV. "The CSR initiatives are actively mapped by the managing board, inventoried, monitored, and a sustainability report is generated." (Indian NGOs.com, 2005).

Such denials merely serve to reinforce the point that CSR and other forms of corporate social engagement are indeed management fashions. As we detail in this chapter, they exhibit all of the central defining characteristics, including the repeated protest that they are *not* fashions. But if either critics or cheerleaders take CSR's status as a management fashion as grounds for dismissing it, then they misunderstand the nature and significance of both management fashions and corporate social engagement. Corporate social initiatives highlight *the fundamentally social nature of management.* They also highlight the tensions that can arise between these social dynamics, on the one hand, and *the economic imperative to maximize shareholder wealth* in the most efficient manner possible on the other (Margolis & Walsh, 2003).

Strikingly similar tensions dominate debates over management fashions. Individual fashions invariably promote themselves as *the* way to improve the bottom line. But a closer look at the fashion phenomenon reveals how concern for the bottom line competes for managers' attention with a variety of other social networks, dynamics, instincts and commitments, some of them even quite "irrational" in the conventional sense of that term. The fashion perspective also drives home the point that the very notion of what is rational and efficient changes with regularity, because it is constructed in social contexts which themselves are not predicated on pure economic logic or rational efficiency. A closer look at these tensions can provide insight into how communications practitioners can better understand the complexities of these two linked phenomena. In fact, such an in-depth understanding of CSR as a management fashion is mandatory, if communicators want to engage successfully in strategic CSR-communication.

Clearly, addressing the debate about CSR as a management fashion is of utter importance, as being branded as a fad or fashion means – at least for some – that CSR is worthless and not to be taken seriously. The challenge of this paper is, in other words, to proof the value of the CSR-concept not just *despite* it might be a management fashion, but even *because* it is a management fashion. Clearly, this is an issue of utmost importance for practitioners and researchers engaged in CSR, but also for other stakeholders, such as public decision makers and consumer advocates. Hence, the three key questions we address in this paper are: Is CSR a management fashion – and if so, why? What does it mean to be a management fashion and what implications does it have? And finally, which consequences can be sketched out for the strategic communication of CSR, if CSR is a management fashion?

Towards this end we begin by presenting the central themes of the fashion critique of CSR. Then we move on to consider what it means to call something a management fashion by reviewing key research into the subject. We confirm the suspicion that CSR is a management fashion by summarizing our survey of the appear-

41

ance of articles about CSR in the Danish press over a 10-year period. This kind of study has become the standard method for identifying management fashions, but it does not tell us how they function in the daily lives of managers and communications professionals. To understand these dynamics better, we turn to Watson's (1994) description of the *double control dilemma* facing management practitioners. This concept brings the tensions inherent in CSR and management fashions down to a personal level. As every manager knows, tensions between the profit motive and personal values can never be completely resolved. But a better understanding of the double control dilemma can make clear how CSR and management fashions function not only to exacerbate such tensions, but also to help alleviate them, or to channel them in more productive directions. We will conclude with a discussion of the implications of our argument for communications professionals.

### The Fashion Critique of CSR – *The Economist's* Obsession

*The Economist* launched its campaign against CSR, sustainability, and other such business initiatives to address social problems at least ten years ago with the claim that corporate efforts to stop the evils of child labor were perhaps laudable but certainly misguided. (*The Economist,* 1995) Since that article the magazine has pursued its own version of sustainability – sustaining its assault on corporate social initiatives in more than 30 articles, including several survey sections and special reports devoted to the topic (cf. 2000a, 2002a, 2002b, 2004a, 2004b, 2005a, 2005b). *The Economist's* complaint rests on the assertion that corporations can and should be expected to fulfill just one responsibility: to maximize profits and shareholder value. The magazine justifies this free market conviction by paraphrasing Adam Smith. "In their economic lives, people behave as though they had no regard for the public good," the magazine explains. "Yet the outcome, through the operation of the invisible hand, serves the public good better than any social planner could ever do." Because they fail to see this, *The Economist* concludes, "advocates of corporate

42

social responsibility...start with a basic failure to understand why capitalism works." (2001a)

Despite this fundamental misunderstanding, the magazine explains, "charities, non-government organisations and other elements of what is called civil society" have managed to force corporations to bow to their demands. As a result, *The Economist* concludes, CSR has become "the tribute that capitalism everywhere pays to virtue." The corporate world has given itself over to CSR, the magazine recounts, with executives cramming their speeches full of references to social obligations and whole departments charged with managing the CSR function. In virtually every article about CSR, *The Economist* likes to point out that responsibility itself has become big business. "Consultancies have sprung up to advise companies on how to do CSR, and how to let it be known that they are doing it. The big auditing and general-practice consulting firms offer clients CSR advice (while conspicuously striving to be exemplary corporate citizens themselves)," *The Economist* complains. "There are executive-education programmes in CSR, business-school chairs in CSR, CSR professional organisations, CSR websites, CSR newsletters and much, much more." (2005e). Most often *The Economist* parodies all of this frenzied activity in order to dismiss it as little more than "a cosmetic treatment." In one article the magazine ridicules companies under consideration for a sustainability award for "falling over themselves to compete for an ethical Oscar," mixing a "collection of clichés, laced with breathless examples of consultancy-speak such as 'triple bottom line' and 'blended value.'" (2002d). In another it says that "The human face that CSR applies to capitalism goes on each morning, gets increasingly smeared by day and washes off at night."

If CSR indeed generates all this business, it may seem puzzling that *The* Economist is so opposed to it. But in an article endorsing the views of author and economist David Henderson, the magazine goes further, charging that CSR is a particularly "unwelcome fashion" because it can do so much more harm than good. Aside from being "intellectually wrong," the magazine agrees with Henderson, CSR "also promotes policies that are directly welfare-

43

reducing." Adherence to the principles of CSR raises costs and therefore prices, the magazine explains, and these costs naturally get passed on to society at large. CSR also favors increased government regulation and uniform international standards, *The Economist* adds, which place an unfair burden on less developed countries in a decidedly "non-uniform" world. (2001a)

*The Economist's* indictment of CSR as an "unwelcome fashion" has followed the script provided by its critique of management fashions in a more general sense. Over the years the magazine has used strikingly similar terms to charge that management fashions are mostly ineffectual, because they are just for show, and that they also do more harm than good. A 1997 *Economist* survey of the consulting industry elaborated on these two complaints. "The first is that fads fail to deliver," the magazine explained. "Re-engineering programmes are launched with great fanfare, only to fade out as employees get bored and managers move on to the next thing. Many consultancies are guilty of introducing so many fads simultaneously that managers have no chance of implementing them." But the second complaint was that management fashions are more than just ineffectual – they do actual harm by "distracting time and attention from the real business of management" and prompting "the wrong kind of action." "The fashion for de-layering caused companies to get rid of middle managers whose experience and connections are irreplaceable," *The Economist* recalled. "The cult of empowerment encouraged banks such as Barings to hand too much power to junior rogues." (1997). *The Economist* maintained that these shortcomings had become widely recognized, and that the resulting backlash against management fashions already had begun to lead to their decline. The magazine therefore predicted that serious companies soon would lose interest in "off the shelf remedies" and the gurus who peddle them. "Expect a lot more companies to do their own in-house consulting in future," *The Economist* concluded. "It will be known as 'management'."

Predictions are a risky business. *The Economist* made these particularly erroneous predictions before the dot.com boom, the new economy craze, and e-business all took the corporate world

44

by storm, and before several other previously existing fashions (notably reengineering and knowledge management) got their second or third wind. Clearly, the magazine interpreted the inevitable churn of individual management fashions – the manner in which management techniques go in and out of style – as evidence that all management fashions were on their way out once and for all. But churn is actually one of the mechanisms that drives the management fashion process forward. In the next section, we will explore some of the central features of the management fashion phenomenon.

**What Are Management Fashions?**
The term management fashion refers to the way that companies and the people who work for them seem eager to adopt and hype every next organizational improvement program in a lemming-like manner, and then drop it for yet another one without any real sense of follow-through. "The last big idea was shareholder value, sparked by Alfred Rappaport's 1986 book *Creating Shareholder Value* remarked *The Times* of London in 2004. "Rewind ten years and the dominant management mantra was re-engineering. Fast forward to the present day and a new acronym has become the height of fashion: corporate social responsibility." (Dearlove, 2004)

Bain & Company's annual "Management Tools Survey" provides a clear illustration of the churn of management fashions. Since 1993 the consulting firm has tracked the popularity of 25 tools among 500 companies around the globe in order to "provide managers with the information they need to identify, select, implement and integrate the tools that will improve bottom line results." Bain explains that the survey helps managers "sort facts from fictions," because "in the absence of data, groundless hype makes choosing and using management tools a dangerous game of chance." The 2001 survey announced a decline in the use of all the management tools measured, and concluded that executives were turning a cold shoulder in particular to "new economy" tools" in favor of "classic, tried-and-true" management tools that can address "fundamentals of cost and corporate direction." But in 2000 the survey had declared just as earnestly that managers were too busy with the serious business of trying to understand the development of e-business and the rapid pace of change in the new economy to allow themselves to get distracted by balanced scorecards or CRM. After the dot.com bubble had burst, Bain would trumpet its 2003 survey with the headline "New Economy Tools Bite the Dust."

So according to Bain, in 2000 e-business and the new economy *were* the basics, and everything else was a distraction and a "bandwagon" for "quick and easy growth." Within a few years, however, e-tools themselves had become just another distraction away from "the basics," which now included balanced scorecards and CRM. These inconsistencies stem from the ultimately futile attempt to maintain a clear distinction between management fashions on the one hand and "the real business of management" on the other. For this same reason Bain carefully avoids using the word "fashion" in connection with its survey. In fact many people, especially in consulting firms and business schools, still feel uncomfortable around the "F" word. They think that to call a management tool a "fashion" or a "fad" is to imply that it isn't serious, that it doesn't work, and that anyone who uses it isn't focused like a laser beam on improving bottom line results to the exclusion of everything else. Such critiques create, of course, special problems for corporate communicators. If even management itself does not believe in the value of engaging in corporate social responsibility due to mistrust in its value for the corporation, the firm's opportunities to engage in cause related marketing or social marketing are severely limited. This cuts the firm off from marketing its' product to potentially interested consumers to whom such an engagement is of interest. This also makes it generally difficult to communicate the firms' points of view to stakeholders, hence making it vulnerable to all kind of criticism.

Such disdain for the fashion label reflects the general assumption that "the real business of management" consists exclusively of the rational and efficient pursuit of profit. *The Economist*, the Bain survey, and many others would like to avoid the stigma of the fashion label in order to maintain the appearance of managerial rationality. But in his influential research on management fashions, Abrahamson has argued that management fashions are

46

*precisely about* the appearance of rationality, efficiency, and progress. Abrahamson begins from the assertion that management fashions differ in significant ways from aesthetic fashions in clothing or hairstyles. While aesthetic fashions only have to appear modern and appealing to the eye, he says, *management fashions have to appear both rational and progressive.* That is, they have to appear like efficient ways to reach important management objectives, and they have to appear new and improved, that is, better than the older ways of doing so. If they would not promise bigger shareholder revenues, they simply would not become management fads and fashions.

Organizational stakeholders expect managers to act rationally and efficiently, Abrahamson points out, but "in many contexts...it is ambiguous not only what constitutes important ends for managers to pursue, but also what are the most efficient means to pursue these ends." Faced with this problem, managers have to try at least to look like they know what they are doing. In Abrahamson's words, they must seek to conform to social norms of rationality and progress. "Together, norms of managerial rationality and progress create the need for a flow of management techniques that organizational stakeholders believe are rational, at the forefront of management progress, and that managers can adopt in order to appear in conformity with these norms."

According to Abrahamson's definition, management fashions share three basic characteristics: 1) their transitory and collective nature, 2) the central role played by management fashion setters, and 3) a tight connection to norms of rationality and progress. To find these management techniques, Abrahamson says, managers look to the community of what he calls "management fashion setters." These include the business press, consultants and management gurus, and business school professors, all of whom signal to managers whether they think a given management technique will lead to rational management progress. According to Abrahamson, management fashion setters get their ideas by keeping close tabs on the emergent needs of managers as they begin to experience performance gaps between currently fashionable techniques and the tasks they are expected to perform. But the appearance of what counts as rational management technique cannot remain stable for too long, or progress will not seem to occur. Abrahamson therefore defines a management fashion as "*a relatively transitory collective belief, disseminated by management fashion setters, that a management technique leads rational management progress*" (Abramson 1996).

### Tracking Management Fashions

Abrahamson has illustrated the transitory and collective nature of management fashions by employing the now-standard technique of tracking the appearance of press and business print media articles about the fashion in question and plotting them on a graph over time. Holding up the example of quality circles, for example, he has noted that the appearance of articles about this technique rose rapidly in the mid-1980s only to drop off precipitously a few years later. The graphic depiction of this phenomenon renders a bell-shaped curve that has become a staple element of management fashion research (Figure 1).

**Figure 1:** Print media indicators of quality circles, 1977-1986 (Source: Abrahamson, 1996)

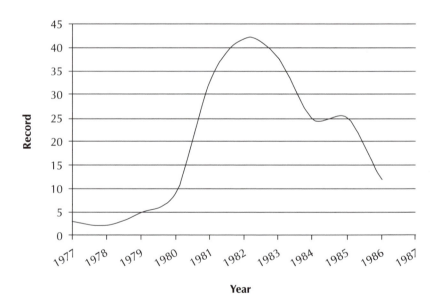

The first step towards confirming CSR's status as a management fashion according to Abrahamson's definition, then, would be to uncover the same pattern of attention paid to the subject in the print media. Towards this end, we tracked the appearance of articles about CSR in four Danish newspapers over a ten-year period. The four newspapers used in the analysis are *The Daily Børsen, Berlingske Tidende, Jyllands-Posten* and *Politiken.* The first is a strictly business focused daily, while the latter three are regarded as the leading daily newspapers in Denmark. They have a combined weekday circulation of over 485,000. Figure 2 represents the results of a search for articles on CSR in these four newspapers from 1995 through 2004. The search rendered an initial 3078 articles, but 42 % of these were eliminated as false hits. During this ten-year period, then, these four newspapers published a full 1788 articles that reported on CSR either partially or in full. What stands out is the striking resemblance between the appearance of CSR as an object of concern in the Danish press and the appearance of articles on quality circles as presented by Abrahamson, as well as the appearance of other management fashions in other studies. Danish print media interest in CSR rose very rapidly from the end of 1995 until it spiked in the middle of 1997. There followed a relative decline in interest over the next two years, followed by a resurgence of articles about CSR. While the number of articles did not remain at that level, results through 2004 show a slow and steady increase in print media interest.

**Figure 2:** Total number of articles about CSR in *Børsen, Jyllands-Posten, Berlingske Tidende,* and *Politiken,* 1995-2004

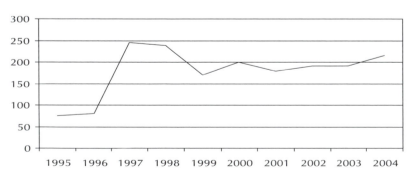

Buhr and Grafström (2004) have used a similar method to track references to CSR in *The Financial Times* during an overlapping period of time, with similar results. But as Abrahamson has argued, the appearance of such rapid, bell-shaped surges in the popularity of management techniques is not sufficient grounds for calling them management fashions, because a variety of factors could explain such results. "We should label these swings 'management fashions' only when they are the product of a management-fashion-setting process involving particular management fashion setters-organizations and individuals who dedicate themselves to producing and disseminating management knowledge" (Abrahamson, 1996). Returning to our survey, we tracked references to institutional actors in the articles surveyed to specify the management fashion setters responsible for the process of disseminating and popularizing CSR in Denmark. Over one third of all references were to companies and consulting firms. Reference to government clearly takes the second place, while experts and analysts, industry and employer organisations, other political references and single persons are all equally represented. Unions and employer organisations do not receive much mention and consumers receive almost none at all.

Over the ten year period, the interplay between the two most common references – private firms and government agencies and officials – tells a lot about the way that CSR caught hold in Denmark. The Danish government functioned initially as the most significant element of the management fashion setting community with respect to CSR. Over time, however, the government's role has diminished, while references to the involvement of private firms in the CSR phenomenon has grown. This trend can be explained by reference to the initiatives taken by the Danish Ministry of Social Affairs, starting in 1994, to foster an "inclusive labor market" under the general campaign heading "It Concerns Us All". The campaign set off an avalanche of CSR events and initiatives such as conferences, network establishment and new models for partnerships and resulted in raised awareness on a broad societal level. More importantly, proponents of CSR emphasized

50

that engaging in CSR made good sense for both companies and society at large, as both parts would benefit from it and progress.

The shift in references in CSR discourse from government to private firms changed the way the topic was discussed in Denmark. A content analysis of the 1788 articles surveyed shows that the reasons or motives most commonly cited for engaging in CSR shifted over the ten year period from an emphasis on social reform and well-being to an emphasis on the proper functioning of business organizations and the market position they stood to gain from participating in CSR. As the management fashion took hold in Denmark, norms of rational management progress came to dominate the discourse, and the emphasis on social reform gave way to appeals to managerial efficiency and the bottom line as justifications for the dissemination of CSR practices.

**Figure 3:** The three reasons for participating in CSR most often cited in *Børsen, Jyllands-Posten, Berlingske Tidende,* and *Politiken,* 1995-2004

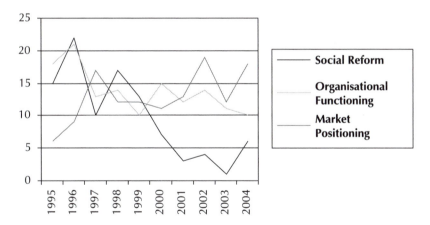

In sum, our analysis reveals that CSR indeed is a management fashion, as media coverage of CSR matches Abrahamson's three criteria for management fashions: 1) sharp bell-curve indicates reveals a rapid increase in CSR, 2) government agencies and private firms are playing a central role as management fashion setters, and 3) engagement in CSR is motivated by (mutual) benefits for both companies and society at large in terms of progress. (Even though our analysis confirmed a shift in attention towards different and competing rationales for CSR-engagement.) Our argument is supported by simultaneous research conducted by Zorn and Collins (forthcoming), who likewise conclude that CSR indeed is a management fashion.

### CSR, Management Fashions, and the Double Control Dilemma

These competing rationales for adopting CSR point towards the recurring tension we mentioned at the beginning of this chapter between social purposes and profit motives. As Margolis and Walsh point out, corporate social initiatives inhabit and exemplify this tension. "Companies are increasingly asked to provide innovative solutions to deep-seated problems of human misery," they point out, "even as economic theory instructs managers to focus on maximizing their shareholders' wealth." (2003) Meanwhile, the authors add, most scholars who study corporate social engagement have tried to argue that this tension doesn't exist, and that corporate social initiatives actually contribute to the bottom line. These scholars have "typically sought to reconcile corporate social initiatives with seemingly inhospitable economic logic" by trying to make a positive correlation between social and financial performance. Stakeholder perspectives try a slightly different approach, insisting that companies must answer to a variety of internal and external constituencies in order to do business. But after a review of existing research, Margolis and Walsh conclude that stakeholder theory's "preoccupation with instrumental consequences" has produced an alternative that also "accommodates economic premises yet sidesteps the underlying tensions between the social and economic imperatives that confront organizations." With the financial bottom line as the ultimate yardstick in either instance, the authors argue, the end result has been to reinforce the assumption that the only legitimate function of the corporation is to pursue profit.

> "The assumption that the primary, if not sole, purpose of the firm is to maximize wealth for shareholders has come to

dominate the curricula of business schools and the thinking of future managers, as evidence from a recent survey of business school graduates reveals. (Aspen Institute, 2002) Investigating corporate social initiatives presents a rich scholarly opportunity in part because the economic account suggests that there should be no so such initiatives to investigate in the first place."(Margolish & Walsh, 2003)

Scholars will never establish an air-tight connection between CSR and the bottom line, Margolis and Walsh argue. Instead, they should claim the tension between social obligation and profit as the starting point of an expansive agenda for research into the "pressing descriptive and normative questions" raised by corporate social engagement. Only by embracing this tension rather than smoothing it over, they make clear, can organizational research hope to make sense to practitioners, who themselves struggle with this same tension every day.

Watson has argued that an understanding of this same tension can help make sense of management fashions, particularly on the personal level of how they affect managers' daily lives. Corporate social initiatives and management fashions more generally don't always clash with bottom line concerns. But when they do, managers and communications professionals can find themselves caught in the horns of what Watson calls the "*double control dilemma*" – the difficulty that those in managerial authority can experience, when trying to balance control over both their organization and their own personal lives and values. "Every manager has a responsibility, by virtue of his or her appointment as a member of the control apparatus of the corporation, to contribute to the performance of the organization as a whole," explains Watson. "But, at the same time, they need to control their own personal lives and identities and to make sense of the work they are doing, both on behalf of the employing organization and in terms of their own personal and private purposes and priorities." (1994) This is a constant challenge for managers, he explains further, because everything about their position and authority conveys the idea that they are the people who are in control. But

53

since the world and the business environment in particular are such fickle and unpredictable environments, they actually don't feel that they are in control of their circumstances most of the time.

According to Watson, this is where management fashions come in to play. Often times managers who adopt the latest techniques, he says, "are trying to exert control simultaneously on behalf of the employing organization and over their own lives by using these ideas and actions *to make sense of their own lives and their place in the scheme of things.*" Slathering after the newest fashion just to keep up with the Jones-es is a very human and social impulse, one that may seem like opposite of the calculated and strategic action the proverbial rational management professional would take. But in Watson's view such behavior can turn out to be adaptive for both the individual manager and the organization as a whole. Management fashions become a problem, says Watson, when the means become the end – that is, when organizational members get so wrapped up in the jargon and the details that they forget why they adopted the practice in the first place. They also become suspect when it seems like certain individuals are simply using them to advance their career. But it doesn't have to be that way. "Personal and corporate control dimensions of managerial work can indeed be in tension," Watson allows, "but can, equally, be managed together to the mutual advantage of both individual and the wider organization." (1994)

Watson is not simply arguing that fashions can contribute to the bottom line if managed properly. Instead he is arguing for a different approach to management based on his underlying concept of *strategic exchange.* Organizations do indeed exist to turn a profit, agrees Watson, but they exist to serve a variety of other purposes as well. In fact, if they don't fulfill these other functions – including legal, social and even moral functions – they won't be able to continue to turn a profit for long. Watson argues that "economic goals can be pursued only through the orchestrating of social cooperation and the exercise of political skills and moral insight." (Watson, 1994) The task of managing an organization therefore consists of a series of exchanges and trade-offs. Manag-

54

ers must strategically negotiate and exchange with a variety of individuals and groups – both inside and outside the organization – towards the end of achieving a balance of these many interests.

The fashion perspective takes seriously the possibility that managers adopt TQM, CRM, BPR, or even CSR not simply because it works best, but also because everyone else is doing it, or even because everyone else is talking about doing it. For Watson, this highlights the fact that social pressures compete with economic imperatives for managers' attention, and that human needs – even human insecurities and weaknesses – motivate managerial decisions just as often as efficiency, rationality, or profit maximization. Managers are not simply rational agents whose every next step is determined by their contractual obligation to advance in the most efficient manner the financial interests of their principals. Attention to management fashions can provide an important reminder that managers' actions are quite naturally influenced by a variety of other social networks, dynamics, instincts and commitments, some of them even quite "irrational" in the conventional sense of that term. From this perspective, management fashions can help managers deal with the double-control dilemma by advancing the interests and addressing the concerns of a variety of different organizational constituencies at once. Even more so than other management fashions, CSR and corporate social initiatives address themselves to the tensions that can arise between these competing interests. While *The Economist's* fashion critique recognizes the tensions between social motives and profit motives raised by corporate social initiatives, the conclusions it draws about them are dead wrong. CSR and management fashions more generally are not mere distractions from the "real business of management." They are precisely what management – that is, the task of orchestrating productive social cooperation in organizations through the balancing of a variety of interests – is all about.

### Discussion and Implications for Communications Professionals

In this paper, we empirically confirm that in Denmark, as elsewhere, CSR is indeed a management fashion. As we readily admit, this is not a terribly original or productive argument *per se*, unless we follow up with the important question: So what? Our answer to this question is that being a management fashion does not automatically disqualify a concept such as CSR, as *The Economist* and other critics strongly imply. Their critique of CSR builds on the assumption that the only business of business is directly to pursue corporate revenue, and that any alleged distraction from this singular goal, such as taking social responsibility, should be abandoned.

In response, we contend that such critique is based on a fundamental misconception of what business and management is about. Based on Watson's ideas on the double control dilemma and strategic exchange, we contend that such critique is based on a functionalist understanding of management and a short-sighted approach to how shareholder value can be increased. The fashion critique fails to recognize that organizations do not merely exist to increase profits, but that they simultaneously serve a number of legal, social and moral functions. Imbalances between these different corporate functions are not exceptional, in fact they are rather common. Managers and communications professionals face these tensions every day. Sound management practice is not about neglecting some of these functions in order to focus on just one of them. In fact, this would create even bigger imbalances. Indeed, sound management requires the orchestration of these various functions in a balanced manner that contributes ultimately to the improvement of the corporate bottom line.

But what are the implications of this insight for communication practitioners? First of all – following Margolis and Walsh – we argue that attempts to reconcile CSR with economic logic by showing the bottom line value of investment in CSR-initiatives are likely to fail. The reason for such failure is simply that Chief Financial Officers (CFO) – who tend towards number crunching, economic premises, and skepticism to CSR – so far have not been able to develop a sufficient method for isolating and measuring the potential profitability of CSR. From a research perspective, then, the bottom line value of CSR can only be assessed for the time being by investigating the tension between social obligations and profit making. For communication practitioners, however, this is barely sufficient.

56

Corporate communicators who see the positive opportunities of CSR even if they can't point at tangible financial benefits typically face the same problem – how to respond when the CFO demands to know: What do we get out of it? How (meaning *how much?*) will an engagement in corporate social responsibility or in associated areas such as corporate sponsorship or cause related marketing contribute to the bottom line?

**Where do we go from here?**
Rather than answering questions about whether and how a firm's engagement in the CSR management fashion should be communicated to stakeholders, we have argued that communication practitioners should be aware of the slippery assumptions behind the charge that CSR is "nothing but a management fashion," and to realize the productive aspects of management fashions. Our discussion has pointed to at least three implications with regard to the issue of strategic CSR-communication. These three implications relate to an awareness of change processes, an awareness of context, and an awareness of the potential collaborators that can help a company deal with both change and context. As our empirical analysis of the Danish media coverage of CSR confirmed, values change and trends can develop rapidly, thus requiring a constant vigilance in order to trace them. Second, our analysis supported the idea that successful management fashions reflect and connect both to broader cultural ideas and to norms of rationality and progress, as in the case of the relationship between the rise of CSR and the reform of the Danish labour market. Third, for these reasons, corporate communicators have to keep their eyes open in their social networks, not just to identify trends, but also to spot potential allies with whom they can collaborate to keep track of existing trends, or even to collectively initiate new ones. It is our sincere hope that these learning points will provide a sound foundation for corporate communicators when assessing the relationship between management fashions and the ever-changing opportunities to engage in strategic CSR-communication.

Hence, we suggest the following questions for reflection:

- In what ways does CSR become productive as a management fashion?
- Who are the CSR trendsetters? Are they the same across industries?
- How does CSR as a management fashion influence the ways that companies represent themselves and communicate with stakeholders about their CSR activities?

## References

Abrahamson, E. (1996) 'Management fashion', *Academy of Management Review*, 21, 254-85.

Buhr, H. & Grafström, M. (2004) "Corporate Social Responsibility Edited in The Business Press – Package Solutions with Problems Included". *Paper presented at 20th EGOS Conference*, Ljubljana, 1-3 July 2004.

CSRWire (2005) "Echo Research: In Corporate Social Responsibility – BP and Body Shop lead the way." *CSRWire* (http://www.csrwire.com/page.cgi/echo.html)

Dearlove, D. (2004) "Wanted: the Next Big Thing." *The Times (London)*. April 29. p. 8.

Jackson, B. (2001) Management Gurus and Management Fashions. London: Roctledge.

Margolish, J.D. & Walsh, J.P. (2003) Misery loves companies – rethinking social initiatives by business. *Administrative Science Quarterly*, 48, 268-305.

*The Economist* (1995) "Consciences and consequences." Vol. 335/7917. Jun 3. p. 13.

*The Economist* (1997) "Survey: Management Consultancy. " March 22. p. S1-S20.

*The Economist* (2000a) "Business ethics: Doing well by doing good." Vol. 355/8167. Apr 22. p. 65.

*The Economist* (2001a) "Finance And Economics: Curse of the ethical executive." Vol. 361/8248; Nov 17. p. 102.

*The Economist* (2002a) "Business: The acceptable face of capitalism? Face value."Vol. 365/8303. Dec 14. p. 73.

*The Economist* (2002b) "Special Report: Lots of it about – Corporate social responsibility." Vol. 365/8303; Dec 14. p. 74.

*The Economist* (2002c) "Business: Irresponsible; Ethical reporting." Vol. 365/8300; Nov 21. p. 74.

*The Economist* (2004a) "Business: Profits and poverty; Face value." Vol. 372/8389; Aug 21. p. 62.

*The Economist* (2004b) "Business: Bluewashed and boilerplated; Corporate social responsibility." Vol. 371/8380. Jun 19. p. 73.

*The Economist* (2004c) "Business: Two-faced capitalism; Corporate social responsibility." Vol. 370/8359; Jan 24. p. 59.

*The Economist* (2005a) "Special Report: The biggest contract – Business and society," vol. 375/8428. May 28, 2005. p. 87.

*The Economist* (2005b) "Survey: Profit and the public good." Vol. 374/8410. Jan 22. p. 15.

*The Economist* (2005c) "Survey: The good company." Jan 22. Vol. 374, Iss. 8410; p. 4.

Indian NGOs.com (2005) "Interview with Mr Romesh Sobti, Country Representative – India, ABN AMRO Bank N.V." (http://www.indianngos.com/issue/microcredit/interviews/romeshsobti/fullinterview.htm)

Watson, T.J. (1994), "Management "Flavours of the Month": Their Role in Managers' Lives", *International Journal of Human Resource Management*, Vol.5 (4), pp. 889-905.

Zorn, T. and Collins, E. (forthcoming): Is Sustainability Sustainable? CSR, Sustainable Business, and Management Fashion.

CHAPTER 3

# Corporate Social Responsiveness and Public Opinion

*Steen Vallentin*

*One should …not be surprised to see our contemporaries so pliant before the wind of passing opinion, nor should one conclude from this that characters have necessarily weakened. When poplars and oaks are brought down by a storm, it is not because they grew weaker but because the wind grew stronger.*

Gabriel Tarde, The Public and the Crowd, 1901

## Introduction

This chapter poses the question: *"What does it mean for companies to be responsive to public opinion – particularly with regard to CSR?"* The question is asked on a conceptual level as opposed to a practical one. Hence, it focuses on clarifying the meaning of corporate responsiveness towards public opinion. It does not providing a case study of how public opinion can actually have an impact on corporate affairs but points to the need for conceptual clarification of this particular relationship.

In the CSR literature, the ideal of corporate adherence to public opinion is expressed in notions of business functioning by public consent and public ownership of business (Carroll, 1999). This is in accordance with the meaning given to public opinion in classical political philosophy emphasizing the ideal of popular sovereignty (Glasser & Salmon, 1995; Splichal, 1999). Instead of resorting to a normative idealization of public opinion along such lines, however, this chapter argues for a more empirically inclined and analytical approach, emphasizing the managerial pragmatics of responsiveness and corporate communication. Instead of approaching public opinion as an abstract, philosophical principle of responsibility that companies ought to adhere to, the chapter focuses on the more tangible, social manifestations of public opinion and emphasizes the usefulness of the concept in making sense of corporate social responsiveness.

In terms of capturing the dynamics of corporate social responsiveness, public opinion may, on the one hand, be considered a narrow concept in that it focuses our attention mainly on the popular, and some would say superficial, aspects of responsiveness. Public opinion refers to the mass mediated dimension of responsiveness, to public debates and representations of opinions that can be more or less insightful and qualified. It refers to results of market analyses, public agenda setting by mass media, and mobilization of opinions by public interest groups. Unlike public policy, public opinion is not a regulatory force. It can influence but not determine corporate decisions (or public policy decisions for that matter).

On the other hand, as the chapter will show, public opinion as a concept embodies variety. It provides a multifaceted point of departure for reflections on the relationship between business and society. The concept has an analytical potential, which rarely comes to the fore in the business literature, including fields such as CSR and corporate communication. In terms of concept development and theoretical reflection, public opinion has mainly been explored in the fields of political philosophy, political science, and sociology. While, for instance, references to public interests and opinions are legion in the CSR literature, public opinion is mostly used as a tacit notion, its meaning being more or less taken for granted. It is a concept that has attracted little attention in and of itself. It has not been subjected to more rigorous exploration and has not really served an analytical purpose. The main contribution of this chapter is to provide a conceptual and analytical approach to public opinion. It presents a typology of views, covering the dominant traditions within public opinion theory, which provide different means of framing public opinion from the corporate point of view – each view embodying a certain philosophy of responsiveness. The chapter shows how different view of public opinion can serve as useful tools for understanding corporate social responsiveness.

The chapter does not claim to present a fully developed analytical framework. It provides a preliminary outline and positioning of what might be called 'a public opinion approach to corporate social responsiveness'. It argues for the relevance and scope of this approach and suggests some possible research directions.

First, the contribution of the chapter is positioned with regards to the classical distinction between corporate social responsibility ($CSR_1$) and corporate social responsiveness ($CSR_2$). This is followed by a brief discussion of the concepts of public policy and public opinion as they relate to corporate social responsiveness. Next, the typology of public opinion is presented using two sets of distinctions: a realist and a constructivist understanding of public opinion, and, secondly, a distinction between an 'inside-out' and an 'outside-in' (corporate) view of public opinion. The result is a typology of public opinion views presented in a two-by-two matrix. In the next sections, the four views are presented individually. The conclusion reflects on the further prospects of approaching corporate social responsiveness from the point of view of public opinion.

## Responsibility, Responsiveness and Public Opinion

It was William C. Frederick (1978/1994) who originally made the distinction between an abstract and often vague and elusive philosophical-ethical concept of *corporate social responsibility* (CSR$_1$) and a more practical and instrumental concept of *corporate social responsiveness* (CSR$_2$). While the fundamental idea of CSR$_1$ is that "business corporations have an obligation to work for social betterment" (p. 151), CSR$_2$ refers to "the capacity of corporations to respond to social pressures" (p. 154). And whereas the debate about CSR$_1$ tends to be moralistic and based on "speculative generalities" about *why* companies should be socially responsible, CSR$_2$ provides a more pragmatic and analytical view of *how* companies actually respond to tangible forces in their social environment (p. 155).

CSR$_2$ promises a more tangible and feasible, i.e. realistic (in a managerial sense), approach to the question of the role of business in society as it focuses on the social technologies, tools, techniques and procedures by which companies respond to social pressures (Frederick 1978/1994, p. 159). CSR$_2$ not only calls for specialized skills in areas such as stakeholder management, public relations and public affairs; it also relies on "the ability of general managers to factor social impacts into their business decisions" (Black & Härtel, 2004, p. 127; see also Epstein, 1987). Moral vagueness is thus replaced by a research agenda with a clearly defined area of empirical concern. In the words of Strand (1983, p. 90): "Organizational adaption to the social environment is not a normative question that is debatable – it is an area of scientific study."

The emergence of CSR$_2$, however, has not led to a displacement of CSR$_1$. CSR$_2$ has been considered an unsatisfactory replacement because it fails to provide any real guidance in terms of positive values (Frederick, 1986). While providing an action

64

counterpoint to the principled reflection of $CSR_1$, $CSR_2$ promotes no specific values-based philosophy of response (Frederick 1978/ 1994; Carroll 1979; Frederick, 1986; Wood, 1991). The $CSR_2$ approach sidesteps the issue of defining the content and meaning of corporate social responsibility in more exact terms (Frederick 1978/1994, p. 160). Also, bearing in mind that an effective response can be about "fending off, neutralizing or defeating" social forces aiming to lead the company in a direction thought to be desirable for society in general (Frederick, 1986, p. 132), being responsive is not necessarily synonymous with being responsible (Wartick & Cochran, 1985, p. 763).

It follows that responsiveness should not be considered a replacement for responsibility. Rather it provides an alternative, complementary research strategy. A strategy that is particularly well suited to the study of certain forces in the broad field of CSR. Although the force of public opinion may conceivably be approached from the point of view of $CSR_1$, this chapter argues that it makes more sense to approach it as a matter of $CSR_2$. The argument is that public opinion is too elusive and transient a phenomenon to provide a sound basis for formulating a principle of corporate responsibility. To claim that corporate policy (and thus corporate responsibilities) should, strictly speaking, be based on public opinion, would be an expression of misguided populism. However, it makes good sense to argue that corporate policy, in one way or another, should be responsive to public opinion.

The following discussion of the relationship between public policy and public opinion will help to further clarify the implications of approaching corporate social responsiveness from the latter vantage point.

### Public Policy vs. Public Opinion

The notion that business and management are "affected with the public interest" (Drucker, 1986) has been articulated most succinctly in *the principle of public responsibility* (Preston & Post, 1975; Frederick, 1978/ 1994; Oberman, 1996; Wartick & Cochran, 1985; Wood, 1991), which defines corporate responsibilities in terms of public policy and emphasizes the institutional embeddedness of business. Although public opinion is often mentioned in the same breath as public policy and is considered to be one of the main drivers of public policy it is important to maintain a clear distinction between the two concepts. Although their meanings may overlap, it makes a considerable difference whether corporate social responsiveness is approached from one or the other vantage point. The following discussion focuses on the classical view of public policy and public responsibility presented by Preston and Post (1975).

Preston and Post argue that the most significant impact that society exerts on business is through the realm of public policy. Although criteria of managerial success and failure are established both by market forces and public policy, the former is subservient to the latter as market exchange mechanisms are themselves a product of public policy. The public policy process is a large-scale institutional factor, which supposedly permits corporate social responsiveness to become an operational reality with significant and broad effects (Frederick, 1978/1994). There is, however, a tendency for public policy to be defined either in very narrow or very broad terms limiting the operational value of the concept. If public policy is defined in terms of legislative action and direct governmental activity only, the principle of public responsibility will be too narrowly conceived as there is a tendency for the law to lag behind changing social values (Logsdon, 1996; Preston & Post, 1975; Wartick & Cochran, 1985). Public policy, in this narrow sense, does not necessarily address many issues that confront, or may potentially confront, companies in social policy areas (Jones, 1980). Legality does not ensure legitimacy. Therefore, it is imperative for Preston and Post to avoid a narrow and legalistic interpretation of the term *policy* (1975). They emphasize that public policy may be made explicit in law and other formal acts of governmental bodies but that it can also manifest itself in implicit policies that are not formally articulated or enforced. Public policy includes the letter as well as the spirit of the law – and the societal values and commitments reflected in that spirit (see also Oberman, 1996).

66

A problem with the broad conception of public policy, in operational terms, is that public responsibility effectively becomes synonymous with social responsibility considering that it becomes difficult to distinguish public policy from the fabric of society and from social change in general (Wartick & Cochran, 1985, p. 761). Another factor limiting the operational value of the broad conception of public policy is its idealized character. Preston & Post define public policy as an inclusive, deliberative process through which "the members of society – individuals, organizations, and interest groups – identify issues of public concern, explore conflicting view points, negotiate and bargain, and – if a resolution is reached – establish objectives and select means of obtaining them" (Preston & Post, 1975, p. 2). Public policy is "the means by which society as a whole articulates its goals and objectives" (p. 101), it refers to "widely shared and generally acknowledged principles directing and controlling actions that have broad implications for society at large or major proportions thereof" (p. 56). The public policy process reflects "general societal commitments and shared values" (p. 12). As Oberman (1996, p. 468) points out, the implicit theme here is "social control through value consensus". Building on a structural-functionalist paradigm, Preston and Post tend to emphasize integration and consensus while disregarding conflict and coercion (ibid., p. 470).

Although the contribution made by Preston and Post is usually considered to be a reflection of $CSR_2$, they clearly venture beyond the limitations of this approach as Frederick (1978/1994) has articulated it. They formulate a broad and consensual principle of public responsibility, which, ultimately, fails to be more operational than other principles of $CSR_1$. This chapter sticks more closely to the responsiveness agenda in the sense that it, as mentioned, reflects on modes of corporate social responsiveness while sidestepping the challenge of formulating a normative principle of responsibility.

Preston and Post (1975, p. 11) argue that "*policy* is a more precise and formal concept than mere public opinion, attitude, or belief". They continue: "These latter forces, when sharply defined and powerfully represented, may bring about changes in public policy itself; more frequently, they reflect recognition of policy goals already established and implemented". On the face of it, it is hard to disagree with the first part of the statement. Public opinion is a more fleeting and transient force than public policy; it carries less institutional weight. For the purposes of this chapter, however, the first part of the statement can be read as a challenge: to provide a more precise and formal conceptualization of public opinion. Instead of reducing public opinion to 'mere opinion', the analytical substance of the concept must be clarified and made explicit from the corporate point of view. While public opinion only provides a partial, non-comprehensive view of corporate social responsiveness (as opposed to the more totalizing concept of public policy), it has considerable scope because it makes it possible, as the chapter will show, to arrange and integrate many theoretical elements that are often treated separately (cf. Husted, 2000). With regards to the second part of the statement, public opinion should not just be regarded as a reflection of 'something else'. It can be a force in itself, one that is not dependent on the promise or threat of government intervention to have an effect on companies. Public opinion has meaning above and beyond the realm of public policy.

## Conceptualizing Public Opinion

Since the aim of this chapter is not to provide a normative, consensual idealization of public opinion, but to emphasize the managerial pragmatics of responsiveness and corporate communication, it is important to remain focused on the tangible, social manifestations of public opinion – as opposed to its ideal function and character. A brief overview of the main, sociologically inclined definitions found in public opinion theory will serve as a point of departure. Glynn et al. (1999, pp. 17-24) provide an operational starting point by distinguishing between five overlapping, yet distinct, definitions:

*1) Public opinion as an aggregate of individual opinions*
According to this definition, public opinion is a simple sum or distribution of individual opinions, which is measured through the use of surveys and opinion polls. This is the province of commercial market analyses.

*2) Public opinion as a reflection of majority beliefs*
Here, public opinion is regarded as the equivalent of social norms. The basic idea is that people tend to conform to the majority opinion among their significant others. Public opinion thus emerges as those opinions "in the sphere of controversy that one *can* express in public without isolating oneself" (Noelle-Neumann in Glynn et al., 1999, p. 18).

*3) Public opinion as a reflection of group interests*
Public opinion is considered here not so much a function of individual opinions and expressions hereof as a reflection of the cultivation and communication of opinions by interest *groups*. The power dynamics and conflicting nature of public opinion formation are emphasized. This 'action theory of public opinion' points to the mobilization of opinions by public interest groups as well as other forms of social activism.

*4) Public opinion as media and elite opinion*
This definition questions whether public opinion is really a reflection of the opinions and interests of the general public or of mobilized publics. It suggests that public opinion is more a projection of the agendas of powerful elites such as commercial media, companies, politicians and political parties, as well as other resourceful special interests. 'Public opinion' thus emerges as a rhetorical device that is used to legitimate arguments and fortify positions in public debates. And public opinion formation is portrayed as being highly amenable to domination and manipulation by resourceful elites.

## 5) Public opinion as fiction

This definition goes a step further than definition '4' by emphasizing the phantom-like nature of public opinion. Here, the basic idea is that 'public opinion' is a term that is used so freely in the media and in public debates that it seems almost meaningless. If the term is used indiscriminately, without qualitative or quantitative evidence to support it, does it have any value at all? This represents the most radical view of public opinion as a mere image constructed and manipulated by elites to support political agendas (Glynn et al., 1999, pp. 17-24).

Now, these are five general definitions of public opinion with broad societal relevance. In order to apply these definitions in the context of corporate social responsiveness a change of perspective is needed so as to emphasize the corporate point of view. But first an ordering and preliminary translation of the various definitions is called for.

The first step will be to turn the five definitions into four. Definitions 4 and 5 can arguably be turned into one as they are essentially variations on the same theme, emphasizing the constructed and manipulable character of public opinion. The second step will be to equip the different views with proper headings in order to capture the particular approach to corporate social responsiveness they each entail. Definition 1 will be termed *the market view* as it points to corporate uses of the tools of market analysis and essentially frames public opinion as a market force. Definition 2 will be termed *the social control view* as it shows how public opinion can be a constraining force silencing opposition to dominant ideas. Definition 3 will be termed *the mobilization view*. With its focus on the mobilization of opinions by interest groups, particularly those of civil society, this view points to corporate challenges relating to stakeholder management. And, finally, definition 4/5 will be termed *the strategic enactment view*. This view shows how companies are not just subject to the influence of public opinion (as suggested by the social control view); public opinion formation is also subject to the influence of resourceful companies making their presence felt publicly through various means of corporate communication with the aim of creating and/or maintaining an opinion climate that is supportive of their particular activities and goals. The social constructionist view emphasizes the ability of companies to engage in public agenda setting and to influence/co-create public opinion through corporate communication. In other words, it points to the enacted dimension of public opinion. More so than the other translations, which are relatively straightforward, this latter one has an interpretative bias in that it emphasizes corporate agency at the cost of other relevant issues related to viewing public opinion as a reflection of elitist public discourse. As suggested, the strength of this bias is that it provides a good counterpoint to the social control view.

The third and final preliminary step in ordering and translating the views will be to fit them into a two-by-two matrix. This is done using two sets of distinctions: First, a distinction between a realist and a constructivist understanding of public opinion, and, secondly, a distinction between an 'inside-out' and an 'outside-in' (corporate) view of public opinion. Concerning the first distinction, I will argue that the market view and the group view are, strictly speaking, realist in the sense that they, respectively, describe public opinion in terms of concrete research data (measured opinion) or concrete behaviors (mobilized opinion). With regards to the other side of the distinction, I will argue that the social control view and the social constructionist view are constructivist in the sense that they regard public opinion not as a concrete, clearly identifiable object but as a more amorphous reflection of social processes of construction which the company must respond to and/or take part in on the level of its overall corporate communication strategy. Concerning the second distinction I will argue that the market view and the social constructionist view both emphasize the corporate side of public opinion formation, i.e., how public opinion to a certain extent is a product of corporate communication ('inside-out'), whereas the group view and the social control view both regard public opinion as a force that is brought to bear on companies from the outside, from the surrounding environment ('outside-in'). The result is a two-by-two matrix shown in Figure 1.

**Figure 1:** Corporate Views of Public Opinion

|  | 'Inside-out' | 'Outside-in' |
|---|---|---|
| Realist | The Market View | The Group view |
| Constructivist | The Social Constructionist View | The Social Control View |

Next, the insights of the four views in terms of corporate social responsiveness will be given a more elaborate treatment. The different
views should be considered as distinct but not mutually exclusive.

**The Market View**

The market view represents the predominant, or even hegemonic
definition of public opinion (Herbst, 1995). It refers to uses of surveys and opinion polls, i.e. – from the corporate point of view –
the tools of market analyses and environmental scanning. The
market view must be considered the most basic, routine and
common way for companies to relate and respond to public opinion. Market analyses form an integral part of companies' endeav-
ors to make sense of their environment by providing a continuous
stream of information about public sentiments concerning corporate affairs. In its purest form, when the numbers are taken at face
value, this view is realist because public opinion is regarded simply as a statistical distribution of research data. It provides an 'inside-out' view because the results of market analyses are highly
dependent on the questions asked and the response options given
to respondents. Results of market analyses necessarily have a corporate bias. They are always, in spite of technical claims of objec-
tivity, a reflection of the instrument with which they have been
measured. Corporate uses of surveys are an instance of companies producing 'their own public opinion' which may then, if
necessary, be used to counter opinions put forward by other societal actors, such as journalists and representatives of NGOs.

For companies, the strength of this view lies in its institutionalized status and the fact that it is an integral part of traditional market thinking. With CSR on the agenda, focus may change from

market positioning to civic positioning in a broader sense (Paine, 2003), but the difference between viewing markets as aggregates of individual preferences and choices and viewing public opinion as an aggregate of individual opinions is minimal. Being responsive to public opinion means taking account of statistical distributions of preferences, expectations and demands of individuals, sampled from the general public or from segments hereof (i.e. publics). Parallel to this, sales figures can serve as a reflection of public sentiment. Responsiveness is perceived in terms of market forces.

Public opinion appears as something that is continuously measured and analyzed in order to make sure that the company is aligned with public demands and expectations concerning its products, services, actions, decisions, brand(s), values, image, reputation – and CSR-policies. Through the use of surveys, the sentiments of particular constituencies or of the general public can be measured. However, by turning public opinion into an internally produced representation of opinions, i.e., a passive measurement, this view fails to capture the active and potentially disruptive aspects of the concept. The market view is shrouded in a safe, albeit potentially treacherous (and thus risky), air of predictability as the questions asked in market analyses are necessarily reflections of what is already known and what has already been experienced. In light of these limitations, the group view provides some important complementary insights.

**The Mobilization View**
The mobilization view represents the action theory of public opinion. It provides an antidote to the atomistic view of sociality and public opinion provided by surveys and polls. It focuses not on the individual but on the power dynamics of the cultivation and communication of opinions by various interest groups/publics. Unlike the market view, the mobilization view emphasizes the spontaneous, voluntary and potentially disruptive mobilization of opinions in society; not how opinions can be measured but how they come to make a difference in regard to companies and corporate decision-makers. The mobilization view thus points to the non-market aspects of public opinion. According to this view, public opinion is one of the social and political forces that shape the interactions be-

73

tween companies and stakeholders outside, but in conjunction with, markets (Mahon, Heugens & Lamertz, 2004, p. 171; Baron, 1995 and 2002). It is a realist view because it associates public opinion with concrete behaviors in the form of mobilized public interests, and it is an 'outside-in' view because it emphasizes how external publics can influence corporate decision-making.

The mobilization view emphasizes that society is more than a mere aggregate of disparate individuals with an equal share in the formation of public opinion. According to this view, the formation of public opinion is an organic process reflecting power differentials and the functional composition of society, where interests are organized in and by groups primarily. The group is the dominant means of expressing and influencing public opinion. By "expression of public opinion" is meant "bringing the public opinion to bear on those who have to act in response to public opinion" (Blumer, 1948, p. 73). If no active influencing is taking place, no public opinion has been established concerning a particular issue. No interest – no public opinion – is considered real unless it manifests itself in group action (Olson, 1971, p. 119). Such action may be more or less organized. It can include everything from demonstrations and happenings minutely orchestrated by NGOs to less synchronized and more or less effective consumer boycotts.

What defines the mobilization view is its rejection of the notion of 'the general public'. According to this view, the only way for companies to meaningfully relate to the public is to interact and/or communicate with particular stakeholders, publics, or constituencies. The mobilization view describes the emergence of stakeholder groups representing public interests and bringing them to bear as 'opinions of publics' (Grunig, 1979). Being responsive to public opinion means taking account of stakeholder interests, particular those of civil society. It is not all corporate stakeholders who can legitimately claim to speak on behalf of or to represent the public interest. The mobilization view has a particular eye for the spontaneous and voluntary mobilization of opinions by NGOs/social activists and the need for companies to take the risk of civil society interference into account in their actions, decisions, policies and corporate communication. In

74

the terminology of Grunig (1979), being responsive to public opinion becomes a matter of dealing with latent, manifest and active publics through communication and dialogue, interaction and partnerships (see Mitchell, Agle & Wood, 1997, for a more elaborate theory of stakeholder identification and salience; see Renn, Blättel-Mink & Kastenholz, (1997) for a discussion of levels of public empowerment in corporate decision-making).

**The Social Control View**

Compared to the market view and the mobilization view, the social control view describes public opinion as a less tangible, albeit still very real, social force. It describes public opinion as a reflection of the predominant opinion climate at a particular place and time, which serves as a court of judgment on the individual (Noelle-Neumann, 1979).

In her theory of 'the spiral of silence', Noelle-Neumann (1984) suggests that people are equipped with a 'quasi-statistical' organ that allows them to perceive with great subtlety the development of opinions in their social environment. Focusing on the fear of isolation as a social psychological force, she argues that it is more important for people to avoid isolation than to express their own judgments and concerns in public. Particularly when it comes to controversial, socially contested issues, people tend to conform to the majority opinion among their significant others. Public opinion is thus regarded as the equivalent of social norms; the values and beliefs of the majority come to serve as its basis. People don't want to get stuck supporting the 'wrong' opinion that is losing momentum and going out of style. Metaphorically speaking, people want to be on the bandwagon of the winning worldview.

Public opinion can then be defined as those opinions "in the sphere of controversy that one can express in public without isolating oneself" (Noelle-Neumann, 1979, p. 150). Public opinion represents not the voice of reason, not a rationally formed consensus but the voice of the majority or the voice of a loud minority being perceived – via mass media – as the majority. This view of public opinion is thus closely related to notions of 'the tyranny of the majority' (Tocqueville, 1969) and 'the silent majority' (Bryce, 1995).

75

Public opinion becomes similar to the concept of fashion. It creates conformity by silencing opposition to dominant ideas; it establishes priorities and confers legitimacy (Noelle-Neumann, 1979).

When applied to companies, their managers and their communication strategies, this view resembles the new institutionalism in organization theory (Powell & DiMaggio, 1991; Scott, 1995; Scott & Christensen, 1995) with its emphasis on the isomorphic – 'outside-in' – processes through which organizations become more homogeneous. According to institutional theory, organizations deal with uncertainty by modeling themselves after other organizations (i.e. their significant others) (DiMaggio & Powell, 1983). In order to increase their legitimacy and survival prospects, organizations ceremoniously adopt practices and procedures defined by prevailing rationalized myths of successful management (Meyer & Rowan, 1977). In managerial terms, drawing also on the spiral of silence theory, corporate leaders do not want to get caught supporting an outdated management philosophy and therefore will tend to be very sensitive to changes in management fashions, CSR being a prime example. Even if corporate managers find CSR to be populist and inefficient nonsense, they may ceremoniously conform to CSR standards, because they perceive the climate of public opinion to be such that it is the only legitimate thing for them to do. And if they do not conform to CSR standards, they have little interest in being very outspoken about it.

In terms of corporate social responsiveness and corporate communication, the social control view has a distinct air of political correctness about it. Being responsive to public opinion, according to the social control view and with regards to CSR, means taking account of prevailing social norms and either aligning, if only ceremoniously, corporate policy with them in a particular organizational field or keeping silent about the corporate non-commitment to CSR. As a case in point, CSR is in many ways a debate – or a controversy – without an active corporate opposition. On the side of companies, advocates promoting politically correct views of corporate responsibilities dominate the CSR debate. There may be a majority of companies that are not particularly concerned about or involved in CSR but, if that is the case, they remain largely a silent majority.

## The Strategic Enactment View

Whereas the social control view emphasizes how corporate leaders are subjected to the constraining force of public opinion, which hinders a free public exchange of opinions and ideas, the strategic enactment view points to the ability of resourceful companies to subject the public agenda to corporate interests. The basic premise of the latter view is that public opinion formation is dominated by powerful elites through the mass media – with companies themselves being among the most powerful elites. The difference between the two views is similar to the distinction between an institutional and a strategic view of corporate legitimacy. The former "emphasizes the ways in which sector-wide *structuration dynamics* generate cultural pressures that transcend any single organization's purposive control", whereas the latter "emphasizes the ways in which organizations instrumentally manipulate and deploy evocative symbols in order to garner societal support" (Suchman, 1995, p. 572). In line with the strategic view of corporate legitimacy, the strategic enactment view of public opinion emphasizes how companies can affect (what is being perceived as) public opinion through corporate communication ('inside-out'). The size of corporate marketing and public relations budgets allow companies to dominate public talk about their activities as they are often able to more or less drown out other voices with corporate messages giving a corporate spin to particular issues. In this respect, companies co-create the "external" reality to which they claim to be responsive (Christensen & Cheney, 2000, p. 262). After all, no one is more concerned about corporate activities than companies themselves and considering the resources they have at their disposal in getting the corporate message across through various media, other more critical voices with the public interest in mind, like representatives of NGO's, will often have a hard time reaching and convincing a wider audience about the salience of their cause.

The strategic enactment view emphasizes that public opinion formation is a mass mediated game of representation which resourceful companies can themselves take part in staging through corporate communication. Public opinion in part appears as a

77

mediated projection of the corporate agenda – regardless of what occupies the general public. This view is all about the corporate ability to create and/or maintain (the impression of) a favorable opinion climate. The central message is that companies are not simply at the mercy of public opinion – public opinion is to be enacted. This view thus poses a challenge for corporate communication managers who are employed to master the symbolic game of corporate legitimacy. It involves a pragmatic understanding of the usefulness of tools like surveys, stakeholder models, and politically correct views of CSR as means of representation that can be – and are being – used strategically to legitimize the actions, decisions and policies of the company.

**Conclusion**

The chapter has provided a broad outline of 'a public opinion approach to corporate social responsiveness'. As emphasized, such an approach can only claim to provide a partial, non-comprehensive view of corporate social responsiveness. There are other social forces driving corporate activities and commitments in the field of CSR, some of these are related to the public policy arena whereas others have to do with the demands placed on companies by other companies in business networks. The public opinion approach focuses on the popular dimension of the business-society relationship. Going against the tendency to reduce public opinion to 'mere opinion' or to take its meaning for granted, the contribution of the chapter has been to provide a conceptualization which attaches specific meanings to the concept in a systematic way. The chapter has shown how the concept of public opinion, as a sensemaking tool, can encompass several philosophies of responsiveness. From the reactive stance of the market view, to the more defensively inclined mobilization view, the accommodating mode of the social control view and the proactivity of the strategic enactment view (cf. Wilson, 1975; Carroll, 1979). It has shown how the concept of public opinion can be used to cover a broad range of themes relating to corporate social responsiveness – from uses of market analyses to stakeholder management and corporate communication strategies.

78

## Where do we go from here?

As stated above, the chapter does not claim to present a fully developed analytical framework. It provides a preliminary outline and positioning of a particular approach to corporate social responsiveness. Further research in this direction can either suggest alternative ways of approaching public opinion, using other distinctions and other definitions, or contribute to strengthening the suggested approach. The approach needs strengthening in a number of areas, including elaboration of the theoretical assumptions underlying each of the views as well as a more elaborate construction of the overall theoretical framework. Theoretically, the chapter has focused on relating the overall CSR discourse to public opinion theory on a general level. Further theoretical work may focus on relating public opinion, in more conceptually and empirically specific ways, to research developments in fields such as corporate communication, stakeholder management, issues management, and reputation management, as well as modern, contextual organization theory (the new institutionalism in particular). Empirically, the explanatory relevance of the suggested views needs to be tested in case studies and, also, the relations between the different views need to be explored. A key question, considering that the suggested views of public opinion are not mutually exclusive, is how they can be combined analytically.

Other pertinent questions are:

- Can the suggested views be regarded as indicative of particular phases in the development of corporate social responsiveness (at the level of individual companies)?
- Can they be regarded as indicative of particular phases in the development of issues (cf. issues management)?
- Is the typology a useful tool for analyzing corporate views and awareness of public opinion?

These are just some of the questions the suggested approach to corporate social responsiveness may lead to.

# References

Baron, D.P. (1995). Integrated Strategy: Market and Nonmarket Components. *California Management Review,* 37/2, 47-65.

Baron, D.P. (2002). *Business and its Environment, 4th ed.* Upper Saddle River, NJ: Prentice Hall.

Black, L.D. & C.E.J. Härtel (2004). The five capabilities of socially responsible companies. *Journal of Public Affairs,* 4/2, 125-144.

Blumer, H. (1948). Public Opinion and Public Opinion Polling. In: Katz, D. et al. (Eds.) (1954). *Public Opinion and Propaganda – A Book of Readings,* pp. 70-78. New York: Holt, Rhineheart and Winston.

Bryce, J. ([1888] 1995). *The American Commonwealth.* Indianapolis: Liberty Fund.

Carroll, A.B. (1979). A Three-Dimensional Conceptual Model of Corporate Social Performance. *Academy of Management Review,* 4/4, 497-505.

Carroll, A.B. (1999). Corporate Social Responsibility – Evolution of a Definitional Construct. *Business & Society,* 38/3, 268-295.

Christensen, L.T. & Cheney, G. (2000). Self-Absorption and Self-Seduction in the Corporate Identity Game. In: Schultz, M., Hatch, M.J. & Larsen, M.H. (Eds.). *The Expressive Organization,* pp. 246-270. Oxford: Oxford University Press.

DiMaggio, P.J. & Powell, W.W. (1983). The Iron Cage Revisited: Institutional Isomorphism and Collective Rationality. In: Powell, W.W. & DiMaggio, P.J. (Eds.) (1991). *The New Institutionalism in Organizational Analysis,* pp. 63-82. USA: The University of Chicago Press.

Drucker, P. (1986). *The Frontiers of Management – Where Tomorrow's Decisions Are Being Shaped Today.* USA: Dutton.

Epstein, E.M. (1987). The Corporate Social Policy Process: Beyond Business Ethics, Corporate Social Responsibility, and Corporate Social Responsiveness. *California Management Review,* 3, 99-114.

Frederick, W.C. (1978/1994). From $CSR_1$ to $CSR_2$ – The Maturing of Business-and-Society Thought. *Business & Society,* 33/2, 150-164.

Frederick, W.C. (1986). Toward $CSR_3$: Why Ethical Analysis is Indispensable and Unavoidable in Corporate Affairs. *California Management Review,* 28/2, 126-141.

Glasser, T.L. & Salmon, C.T. (Eds.) (1995). *Public Opinion and the Communication of Consent.* USA: The Guildford Press.

Glynn, C.J., Herbst, S., O'Keefe, G.J & Shapiro, R.Y. (1999). *Public Opinion.* USA: Westview Press.

Grunig, J.E. (1979). A New Measure of Public Opinions on Corporate Social Responsibility. *Academy of Management Journal,* 22/4, 738-764.

Herbst, S. (1995). On the Disappearance of Groups: 19th- and Early 20th Century Conceptions of Public Opinion. In: Glasser, T.L. & Salmon, C.T. (Eds.). *Public Opinion and the Communication of Consent, pp.* 89-104. USA: The Guildford Press.

Husted, B.W. (2000). A Contingency Theory of Corporate Social Performance. *Business & Society*, 39/1, 24-48.

Jones, T.M. (1980). Corporate Social Responsibility Revisited, Redefined. *California Management Review*, 22/3, 59-67.

Logsdon, J.M. (1996). Just a Classic – Assessment and Reflections on Private Management and Public Policy. *Business & Society, 35/4*, 454-459.

Mahon, J.F., P.P.M.A.R. Heugens & K. Lamertz (2004). Social networks and non-market strategy. *Journal of Public Affairs*, 4/2, 170-189.

Meyer, J.W. & Rowan, B. (1977). Institutionalized Organizations: Formal Structure as Myth and Ceremony. In: Powell, W.W. & DiMaggio, P.J. (Eds.) (1991). *The New Institutionalism in Organizational Analysis*, pp. 41-62. USA: The University of Chicago Press.

Mitchell, R.K., Agle, B.R. & Wood, D.J. (1997). Toward a Theory of Stakeholder Identification and Salience: Defining the Principle of Who and What Really Counts. *Academy of Management Review*, 22/4, 853-886.

Noelle-Neumann, E. (1979). Public Opinion and the Classical Tradition: A Re-Evaluation. *Public Opinion Quarterly*, 43/2, 143-156.

Noelle-Neumann, E. (1984). *The Spiral of Silence – Our Social Skin*. USA: The University of Chicago Press.

Oberman, W.D. (1996). Preston, Post and the Principle of Public Responsibility. *Business & Society*, 35/4, 465-478.

Olson, M. (1971). *The Logic of Collective Action – Public Goods and the Theory of Groups*. USA: Harvard University Press.

Paine, L.S. (2003). *Value Shift*. USA: McGraw-Hill.

Powell, W.W. & DiMaggio, P.J. (Eds.) (1991). *The New Institutionalism in Organizational Analysis*. USA: The University of Chicago Press.

Preston, L.E. & Post, J.E. (1975). *Private Management and Public Policy*. Englewood Cliffs, NJ: Prentice Hall.

Renn, O., Blättel-Mink, B. & Kastenholz, H. (1997). Discursive Methods in Environmental Decision Making. *Business Strategy and the Environment, 6*, 218-231.

Scott, W.R. (1995). *Institutions and Organizations*. USA: Sage Publications.

Scott, W.R. & Christensen, S. (Eds.) (1995). *The Institutional Construction of Organizations – International and Longitudinal Studies*. USA: Sage Publications.

Splichal, S. (1999). *Public Opinion – Developments and Controversies in the Twentieth Century*. USA: Rowman & Littlefield Publishers.

Strand, R. (1983). A Systems Paradigm of Organizational Adaptations to the Social Environment. *Academy of Management Rewiew, vol. 8*, 90-96.

Suchman, M.C. (1995). Managing Legitimacy: Strategic and Institutional Approaches. *Academy of Management Review*, 20/3, 571-610.

Tarde, G. (1901). The Public and the Crowd. In: Clark, T.N. (Ed.) (1969). *Gabriel Tarde – On Communication and Social Influence*. USA: The University of Chicago Press.

Tocqueville, A.d. ([1848] 1969). *Democracy in America*. USA: Doubleday & Company.

Wilson, I. (1975). What One Company is Doing About Today's Demands on Business. In: Steiner, G.A. (Ed.): *Changing Business-Society Interrelationships*. Los Angeles: Graduate School of Management, UCLA.

Wartick, S.L. & Cochran, P.L. (1985). The Evolution of the Corporate Social Performance Model. *Academy of Management Review,* 10/4, 758-769.

Wood, D.J. (1991). Corporate Social Performance Revisited. *Academy of Man-*

# CHAPTER 4

# Business news and the definition of business and society

*Peter Kjær*

*As business has become a major focus of everyday life,
the role of the business journalist has become
increasingly more important to both media and society.*

Chris Roush, 2004

## Introduction

In 1956 a newspaper editor considered the news coverage of business firms: "In the coverage of [individual firms], news must be selected with great care by the editorial staff, since not every piece of news is fit to print, and to a large extent firms must enjoy the same protection as private lives. That greengrocer Petersen closes his shop or goes bankrupt is no more important to the press than him getting the flu, dying or entering into holy matrimony" (Møller, 1956, p. 48).

The quote reminds us of the fact that more news has become fit to print today. Needless to say, the ups and downs of particular business firms have become newsworthy, as has almost every other aspect of business. And just as important, we now expect private lives, including illnesses or marital status to play a role in business news, at least occasionally. A case in point was the media coverage in 2003 of the private economy, family history and sexual stamina of Erik Sprunk-Jansen, the CEO of the Danish pharmaceutical company Lundbeck. Here the business press questioned the private financial transactions of Sprunk-Jansen and described in great detail private company parties and excursions, private consumption, statements about the CEO's private love life, and so on.

The 1956-quote highlights an important aspect of all news reporting, including business news, namely that any news item involves taking up a relation to society, implicitly or explicitly. It involves particular distinctions between what is accessible and newsworthy – and what is irrelevant and hidden from view, and it also involves certain framing conceptions of the relevant community to which this issue is important etc. The quote suggests that, at the time of writing, the boundary lines were in fact quite clear, and that the "we" addressed by the reporter was a general public, interested in common affairs. In fact, the author, Poul Møller, goes on to state that individual firms may become interesting news items when they influence great number of people as employees, when they influence the level of prices in the country as such, or when they, as monopolies, "possess a power that concerns the welfare of the country".

84

As such business news always implies a conception of corporate social responsibility – of the place of business in society, but the definition of "business" as well as "society" varies over time. In 1956, the official side of business was the only side relevant to the press, and the society implied was largely that of the Danish nation state. The question is what "business" and "society" has become in the news today? Apparently, more than just official business has become newsworthy, but what has become the focus of attention and for whom?

In this chapter my empirical emphasis will be on how changes in business news content over the last 50 years. The analysis will not relate to standard definitions of corporate social responsibility but opts for a broader sense of the term emphasizing how actors conceive of the role of business in society. Corporate social responsibility, in this broad sense, simply means how news texts, i.e. journalists and their sources, represent the relationship between firms and the community in which they operate.

Such an analysis will not allow us to determine whether or not the press enhances responsible corporate behavior (or whether the press itself is a responsible member of society), but it will suggest how the press, in its news coverage, constitutes a particular semantic arena in which actors may engage in communication about the interconnection between society and corporate action. Hopefully such an exercise will prove fruitful, not least from a perspective of strategic CSR communication, because it makes it possible to highlight the particular communicated nature of business and of the relationship between business and society today.

In the following I first briefly describe how I will approach the study of content changes empirically. I then describe how the content of business news has developed in quantitative terms, i.e. what have been the preferred themes in the news, and in qualitative terms, i.e. how business and society have been represented in news about business. Finally I summarize my findings and relate them to the practice of strategic CSR communication.

85

## Method

My analysis will combine a quantitative and a qualitative approach to news content about business. Traditionally, the preferred method for the study of media content was quantitative content analysis. Through the measurement and systematic coding of large quantities of media texts, it was believed that one might be able to discover some of the underlying patterns in news coverage e.g. in terms of the topics dealt with, the preferred genres or the overall tone of news reports.

A quantitative approach necessitates the development of rather formalized indicators of content. The advantage of the approach is that it allows analysts to describe variation in particular content features rather precisely. The weakness, however, is that formalization makes it difficult to consider the concrete meaning of media texts, and how any text is part of a particular context or situation in which a certain news item makes sense. Thus the coverage of SAS economic difficulties may appear to be constant in terms of overall themes (e.g. competition, lay-offs, return on investment) and tone, but statements may mean something radically different just after the "9-11"-terrorist attacks compared to what they meant just after SAS' being fined 250 million crowns by the EU competition authorities a few months earlier (Kjær & Langer, 2005). Therefore many media scholars combine qualitative and quantitative approaches, using quantitative analysis in the first mapping of a body of texts and then qualitative analysis in a closer study of selected media texts. Qualitative analysis here implies a reading of content items that attempts to discern the frame of meaning of individual texts through a process of interpretation and comparison of textual elements and their mutual relations. In the following my emphasis will be on how news texts represent issues and events as newsworthy, and "frame of meaning" here means the framing conceptions that give meaning to particular events and actions in a text (see also Ekecrantz, 1997; Gavin, 1998; Risberg et al., 2003; Tienari et al., 2003).

The quantitative part of the analysis of business news in the following builds on a database that describes content features in two Danish dailies, "Berlingske Tidende" and "Børsen" between 1960 and 2000 (see Kjær, 2005). "Berlingske Tidende and "Børsen represent two important segments of the national print media: the all-round quality newspaper with national circulation and a broad editorial orientation – and the more specialized niche newspaper that caters a more select audience within a more limited area of interest. The period between 1960 and 2000 was selected for study because the field of business journalism has become a distinct journalistic sub-field in that time-span. From the mid-1960's a process of innovation and expansion commenced resulting in the development of ideals of critical business reporting, the creation of new formats and genres in business journalism, and an overall expansion of business news in terms of outlets, readership and journalists dedicated to the field (Kjær & Langer, 2005).

The original database includes one week's content in each newspaper in 1960, 1970, 1980, 1990 and 2000. A total of about 9000 content items (news articles, editorials, commentary, small notes, tables and illustrations) were coded, using a code sheet that coded content in relation to 30 variables, ranging from size and text type to themes and sources.

My analysis in the following will focus on data concerning the years 1960, 1980 and 2000. This limits the data set to 5352 content items.[1] The analysis involves only two variables: economic content and theme "Economic content" is a measure made up of a series of indicators allowing for more or less restrictive definitions of economic content in the sample (which contains all edited content). Economic content includes articles in economic sections and supplements and articles that have economy as the primary or secondary theme. Articles that are not oriented towards economic issues at all (e.g. film reviews or sports) or articles in which economic issues play only a minor role are viewed as "Non-economic". The variable of "Theme" deals with the subject matter of economic articles, in terms of the different issues pertaining to economic activity that the article describes: production, labor relations, investment, economic policy etc. The measure thus allows us to see how economic coverage has evolved since 1960.

87

The quantitative analysis is supplemented by a qualitative analysis of a much more limited sample of texts. Here articles from "Berlingske Tidende" from one week in 1960, 1980 and 2000 have been selected for closer study. From each year, the ten largest articles dealing particularly with business were sampled and subjected to a reading that emphasized the types of news stories that were characteristic of each year – by considering how news stories place events and issues in context (in space and time), how the articles deal with the issues they describe (as problems, conflicts, solutions etc.), and finally how the actors and their mutual relations are described. I here consider how news stories involve particular framing conceptions of the firm and its place in society.

The analysis is presented as three historical *snapshots* of business news in 1960, 1980 and 2000. The snapshots will allow for an identification of the general changes that have occurred in business news since 1960 – but not for a more detailed appreciation of the development of the business press over time. The snapshots will focus narrowly on themes and typical stories in the news, and will not consider other aspects of content that have also changed – such as the size of articles, the use of various sub-genres, the use of sources, and the visual presentation of the news.

## Modernizing business, modernizing society

In 1960 the business press in Denmark was very limited in size – in almost any dimension. Apart from periodicals connected to trade associations and employer federations, "Børsen" was the only outlet with general circulation that emphasized business and economy, but its circulation only amounted to 7.400 copies per day in 1960. Interestingly, however, as the following table shows, less than 50 % of all content items in "Børsen" had business and economy as its primary or secondary focus. In terms of space, only about 20 % of the edited space of the newspaper was taken up by business and economy articles. The remainder of the newspaper was preoccupied with general news, politics, world events etc. In "Berlingske Tidende", which had a much larger circulation (163.000 copies on weekdays), the share of economic content was even smaller.

**Table 1:** Economic content as share of total volume and space in Berlingske Tidende and Børsen 1960

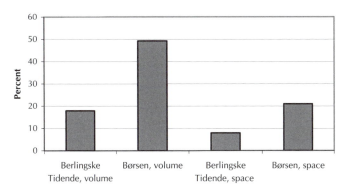

While the two newspapers differed in terms of how much attention they paid to economic issues in general, they were quite similar in terms of how they prioritized among different themes in the news:

**Table 2:** Dominant themes in economic news 1960

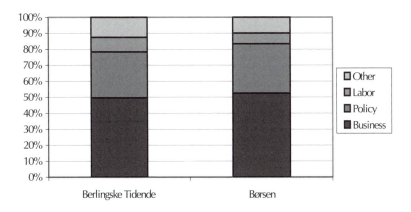

Table 2 shows how both newspapers dedicated about half of their economic content to business news, i.e. to articles about products and production, markets and investment. Similarly both newspapers dedicated another 25-30 % of the content to policy issues, e.g. macro economic policy that made up the most important political theme in both newspapers, and less than 10 % percent to issues having to do with labor relations. The category of "other" almost exclusively dealt with legal matters, e.g. trials, economic crime, and questions of legal liability.

The typical large news article in "Berlingske Tidende" in 1960 presented a story of yet another step taken by a company, an industry or an organization to modernize or rationalize production, distribution or marketing:

*"Trial run of giant diesel engines at B&W.* On Wednesday Burmeister & Wain will conclude the trial run of the first out of six 10 cylinder diesel engines of the 84-VT2BF-180 (..) While the '84, which is its pet name among the Christianshavn professionals, is being packed and shipped to one of the leading personalities in Norwegian shipping, ship owner Sigval Bergesen JR, B&W has now seriously inaugurated its new 28-meter tall and, 23-meter wide, and 90-meter long testing hall" (November 17th, 1960).

In stories of individual firms, as in the quote above, firms were vigorously pursuing strategies of technical development, specialization and rationalization. In stories that involved groups of firms or other actors, such as chambers of commerce or business associations, one also stressed the constant quest for rationalization and market expansion – overcoming obstacles through planning and rational decision-making. Mostly quests were successful, in the end. Only a few articles defined more problematic situations: failing exports, weak demand for particular products or industrial conflict. In the first two cases, the causes were depicted as externally given and simply called for rational adaptation to changed circumstances, whereas the case of industrial conflict necessitated a different set of responses (see below).

Although there were examples of conflicts, the issues depicted in news articles in 1960 were mainly described not as conflicts of

90

interest but as challenges to actors in the quest for rationalization and progress. In a story of a small aviation company, the entrepreneur had to convince people of the potentials in aviation in modern society; in a story about the economic prospects of the cooperative movement in Denmark, the highly decentralized structure seemed to be an obstacle to planned changes. Other stories carried traces of a more mythical conflict of man against nature as was evident in stories about how coastal areas were reclaimed from the sea or how a large new diesel engine was being tested (the quote above). In each case challenges were overcome through rational argumentation, planning or scientific experimentation. In a few spectacular cases conflicts had evolved. In a story about a strike in a number of Danish slaughterhouses, the chapter listed a series of direct confrontations over rationalization, working hours and management. However, the article also mentioned how the existing labor market institutions would resolve the conflict.

The actors of the 1960-articles were often collectives: a group of concerned actors developing industrial plots; a group of engineers testing new technology; the cooperative movement developing its retailing stores; the fishing industry; carrot producers; Denmark...The pronouns "one" and "we" were used extensively so as to signal the communal nature of the enterprise. In most cases these collectives engaged in grand projects of industrial modernization. There were, once again, exceptions to this rule: the article on the slaughterhouse strike did not describe just one collective, but the collective of workers facing management, which appealed to the employer association. In all the other examples the collectives were depicted as responsible members of society engaging jointly in the process of economic development.

In 1960, the frame of meaning constituted by business news articles seemed to be one that situated business as part of a collective pursuit of industrial modernization, where obstacles were typically associated with the past – or something outside the direct control of the agents involved (the world economy) – and dealt with through rational argumentation, planning, scientific experimentation. In this world, business became newsworthy only insofar as it faced the same challenges as the rest of society. Society was ever-present as a largely unproblematic frame in the context of which the actors engaged in economic activities, it was the *inside*, sometimes challenged or threatened by the *outside* of "nature" or "the world economy", and in fact mostly economic actors appeared as socially responsible actors just by doing what they did. Conflicts were rarely explicit and were usually relegated to particular authoritative arenas outside the sphere of business.

In sum, the representation of business and society in the news implied clear boundary lines both between the inside and outside of business, and the inside and outside of society. Private business affairs were typically not considered, whereas the public side of business, i.e. its contribution to the progress of society, was worthy of consideration.

### Business and society in peril

In 1969-70, "Børsen" was reorganized and re-launched as a modern business daily focusing more wholeheartedly on business news and on critical reporting. Although the initial response from the side of business was somewhat lukewarm, the new concept caught on and "Børsen" began increasing its circulation reaching new audiences outside its traditional sphere of operation. Thus by 1980 its daily circulation had gone up from less than 7.000 to 31.000 copies. Gradually, other media actors followed suit and began prioritizing business news and developing a more distinct journalistic orientation. The all-round newspapers expanded their business pages, and soon a number of business magazines were launched to cater a new emerging business oriented audience.

This development was reflected in the relative volume of articles and in the space taken up by economic content in "Berlingske Tidende" and "Børsen":

92

**Table 3:** Economic content as share of total volume and space 1980

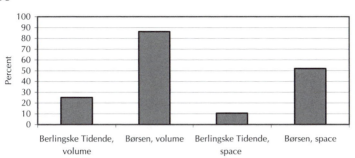

In "Børsen", the share of economic content had increased from less than 50 % to more than 85 %. Similarly the space taken up by economic content had more than doubled. Both trends indicated that "Børsen" had abandoned its all-round orientation and had become a specialized newspaper in the business and economy field. In "Berlingske Tidende", there was a more limited increase in economic coverage, suggesting that the newspaper had not yet become part of the new orientation towards business journalism.

Thematically, "Berlingske Tidende" shows an interesting trend towards an increased emphasis on policy themes and labor relations, and the share of business-oriented articles actually decreased from 1960 to 1980:

**Table 4:** Dominant themes in economic news 1980

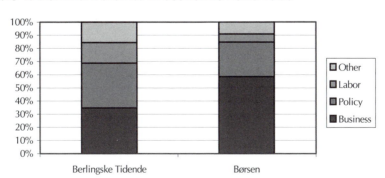

"Børsen" increased its share of business-oriented articles, but only by a few percent, and here policy also remained an important theme in economic articles. In both newspapers, the thematic category of "Other" still contains a significant number of articles on legal issues, although they are now complemented by articles of a broad variety of subjects (consumer issues, pollution etc.).

The typical large 1980-article was a story of how actors, companies, industries etc. struggled to survive in a crisis-ridden economy: "*Furnace producers threatened after giant sales.* Many of the firms that, in the fall of 1979 saw their chance of getting out of economic difficulty by throwing themselves into the production of wood furnaces have already closed down, and the rest are deeply threatened. Wood furnaces did not become the life-saver the manufacturers in distress had hoped for when the great demand emerged about a year ago" (November 12, 1980).

In contrast to the 1960-stories of progress, the future was bleak and resistance was strong: Agricultural producers pursued strategies of concentration to survive, but faced austere market conditions and internal opposition. Retailers issued a credit card to combat a bank initiative that would entail new costs in the retail sector. A small garment factory struggled for new orders, but faced unfair international competition, while a large IT-producer desperately needed public procurement. And the government passed new legislation that only increased the uncertainty in the affected industry. To be sure there were some successes as new business opportunities appeared, such as wood burning furnaces, corporate head hunting or private pension schemes, but each of these opportunities seemed to involve new potentials for opportunistic behavior and conflict.

Most articles in 1980 involved conflicts, and whereas the few conflicts that were considered in 1960 could be seen as somewhat irrational – as obstacles to progress, as the resistance of the "past" – conflicts had become a pervasive feature of news in 1980. Almost every news story involved a conflict of interests – between large and small producers, banks and retailers, new and old producers, domestic and foreign producers, the interests of firms and the interests of individual managers, or the interests of

94

banks and the interests of consumers. The problem, however, was that there were no straightforward solutions. Most conflicts had to be fought out, in the market or sometimes politically, but there was no guarantee that a resolution was at hand, even in the long run. Thus even when political intervention occurred, the outcome might be new conflicts – which was the case when the government attempted to change legislation on mortgage loans.

In 1980 we find challenged collectives. Whereas the 1960-articles occasionally mentioned outsiders and opponents to the on-going modernization process, the struggle between big and small was at the forefront in 1980. Big business entities pursuing grand schemes of expansion and concentration clashed with (usually) smaller entities with divergent interests: individual firms seeking to survive, established businesses seeking to uphold quality standards, or common people being lured by the promises of "easy money". In a few cases roles were reversed somewhat: sometimes the state was pitched as the leviathan unwittingly, perhaps, hurting business and the general public with its bureaucracy or its lack of attention. The only actor seemingly representing society as a whole was the occasional expert that spoke out against certain harmful practices or trends.

In 1980, the frame of meaning of business news situated business in the tragic position of having to pursue one's interests, and attempting to survive in a hostile environment that was characterized by fierce opposition, unjust competition and arbitrary regulation – and where small actors seemed to be fighting a losing battle against big business and, sometimes, government. In this situation, it became problematic for firms to find their proper place in society, probably because there were several competing versions of society in which businesses were struggling to find their place (see also Pedersen et al., 2000) for a similar interpretation of political journalism). The air of frustration in many news reports was indicative of a sense of loss: Someone ought to act responsibly, but almost nobody seemed to be able to do so. There ought to be unified society, but it seemed to have been lost. In this representation of business and society, the boundary line between the inside and the outside of the firm was maintained, in the sense that journalists did not look into the internal operations of companies, but were mainly concerned with the external activities of firms and businesses. At the same time, the relationship between business and society was being challenged, both in the sense that business activities were being problematized as irrational, opportunistic or in conflict with other interests, and in the sense that the actions of other social actors, including the state were also being brought into question.

### Strategizing in financial markets

Many observers describe the 1990s as the heyday of the business press. During the 1980s both "Jyllands Posten" and "Berlingske Tidende" successfully introduced special business sections, and several business and management magazines and newsletters were also introduced with some success. The new emphasis on business news seemed to resonate well with policies of fiscal restraint combined with a deregulation of financial markets in the mid-1980s. Around 1990 a series of business scandals as well as a growth in private pension schemes and investment funds contributed to the popular appeal of business news leading to renewed interest in the field among all-round newspapers that had not prioritized business before. Even national radio and television stations began to include business in their regular programming. By the mid-1990s, the market for business news seemed to be almost overcrowded, but nevertheless the production of business news has since then spread to new channels or technological platforms as existing media have supplemented their old platforms with internet platforms, and several new dedicated web-based business information services have evolved, providing instant information and analysis, especially in the field of finance.

As table 5 shows, "Børsen" maintained its clear prioritization of economic content, and even increased the relative volume of economic content compared to 1980:

96

**Table 5:** Economic content as share of total volume and space 2000

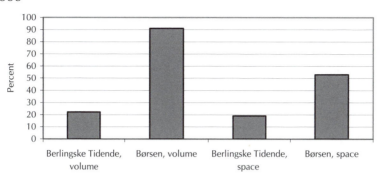

"Berlingske Tidende" dramatically increased its economic coverage in terms of space so that by 2000 almost 20 % of the total edited space was taken up by economic coverage. The fact that the relative number of articles did not expand in "Berlingske Tidende" can be explained by the increasing importance of what can be termed "economic information", tables, lists, indexes and so on, which were typically lumped together in the coding process.

In terms of themes, "Berlingske Tidende" now prioritized business themes at the expense of policy and labor:

**Table 6:** Dominant themes in economic news 2000

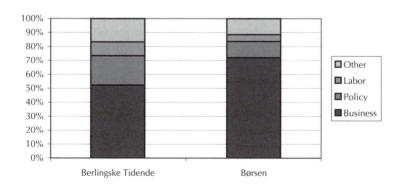

97

"Børsen", in turn, further increased its focus on business, from about 60 % in 1980 to more than 70 % in 2000, primarily at the expense of policy whose share was almost cut in half.

If one breaks down the theme of "business" into "production", "sales and marketing" and "finance and investments", it turns out that while there was a relative balance between production/sales and finance in 1960 and 1980, the dominance of finance in 2000 was overwhelming: In "Berlingske Tidende" two-thirds of the business articles had a finance theme, while almost three-fourths of "Børsen's" business articles had a finance theme. Articles in the "Other"-category still comprised several articles on legal issues, but now moral/ethical issues also surfaced as a small but nevertheless detectable theme in 3-4 % of all articles.

Not surprising, the typical large news article in 2000 was concerned with finance: *"Framfab going up.* Danish web success. The Danish division of the Internet consultancy firm Framfab expects a twenty-fold increase in profit and a four-fold increase in turnover by the end of the year. Contrary to the mother company, the Danes know how to make money" (November 15, 2000).

In 2000, the idea of growth seemed to have been securely reinstalled but in part without the broader promises of progress of 1960. In 2000 all firms, as a matter of fact, did their best to develop and exploit market opportunities – usually as measured by stock value or shareholder value. Some market opportunities came from new ideas carried forth by entrepreneurs, while others emerged with structural changes in particular industries that made mergers and acquisitions a profitable strategy of expansion. New opportunities were even created by political decisions. In 1980, political decisions were largely something that hindered (or should have hindered) business development, while in 2000 political decisions created new opportunities by changing property rights or by sanctioning particular behaviors.

Even in 2000, issues were described as conflicts, but not so much conflicts of interest as conflicts of interpretation. Several stories on individual companies detailed how management expectations collided with judgments offered by "the market", a metaphor which almost always stood for stock market analysts –

98

or, more rarely, key investors: a bio-tech firm thus faced criticism for being "intransparent", while the large Danish telephone company, Tele Danmark's move into the Swiss market triggered a "reluctant" market reaction. Sometimes the conflict was not just a conflict between firm and market but between entrepreneurs (amateurs) and experts (professionals), where the entrepreneur had visions, innovative ideas etc., while experts either were insightful or just plain skeptical. How were such conflicts to be resolved? In most cases they were not, but it was assumed that "the market", i.e. the investors, would prove who was right or wrong. In one case, an article described the rise and fall of a business entrepreneur that had been skilled in maneuvering in the market, but he had ultimately misjudged the situation and now faced bankruptcy. In a few cases other options seemed possible: continued negotiations, court settlements or government intervention. Mostly, however, conflicts of interpretation remained open – to be resolved through the financial markets.

In 2000, stories usually revolve around the "strategist", be it an entrepreneur or an established business corporation, seeking to exploit business potentials. These strategists were not alone, but always faced challenges from "the market": investors, competitors, consumers, and stock analysts. In this context, the state was no longer seen as a barrier to the market but an agent that created or expanded the market, and even represented the interests of "the market", as in the case of intransparency in the insurance industry. Whereas the problem for actors in 1960 was one of overcoming obstacles to modernization, and in 1980 one of surviving in an unjust world, the problem in 2000 seemed to be one of communication: of showing "the market" that one was a credible strategist. Communication seemed to take different forms: direct negotiations (in the case of real estate take over or in a case of conflict in the insurance industry), public displays of responsiveness (in a case that involved the public utility company Nesa or in case of the Carlsberg Breweries or simply "transparency", i.e. making oneself open to scrutiny by "the market" (in the case of a biotech firm).

The frame of meaning of business in the news in 2000 was one that emphasized business strategists in conflicts of interpretation with "the market" – forcing them to communicate by entering into negotiation processes, engaging in responsive symbolic action or by becoming transparent. In contrast to the conflict-ridden and challenged collectives of 1980, order seemed to have been reinstalled, but in contrast to the world of 1960, the news stories no longer implied society as a pre-given frame of reference. That place had been taken over by "the market", and instead responsiveness had become part of conflicts over interpretation – as a way of communicating with the market to restore confidence and reputation. Within this frame of meaning it became possible to problematize both external and internal business activities, or rather, the distinction ceased to be meaningful. Personality traits, managerial styles, internal power struggles were newsworthy, if they were interesting to the market, and apparently the concerns of the market knew no formal limits. Thus even broader social concerns could be construed as interesting from a market perspective: the interests of consumers, the environment, the need for regulation of competition, etc.

**Discussion**

The three historical snapshots illustrate a dramatic transformation of business news, and of the ways in which business and society are represented in the news.

Not only has there been a significant expansion in economic news. Within the general category of economic news, "Business" has become a key theme, and within the category of "Business", "Finance" has become a dominant frame of reference. Thus there has been a shift of attention from economy broadly conceived towards more specific business-oriented themes, suggesting not only that business firms are seen as interesting in and of themselves but also that business journalists and editors have come, increasingly, to equate "economy" with "business" and "finance."[2]

Comparing the two newspapers, the niche nature of "Børsen" stands out in 1980 and 2000. "Børsen" seems to be more focused on a limited number of themes,[3] while "Berlingske Tidende" is

100

concerned with a broader variety of issues, including economic policy issues. However, the two newspapers show a similar trend in terms of the shifting balance between economic policy and business between 1980 and 2000.

This entails that business has become visible in a way hardly imagined 30 or 40 years ago. Whereas the emphasis, in 1980, on macro economic problems made national policy makers, and economic policy institutions such as the Ministry of Finance etc. highly visible, the recent emphasis on business and finance, has put firms firmly in the media spotlight.[4] Similarly, as suggested by the introductory quote from 1956, the aspects of business firms that are made visible have also changed from an emphasis on external activities such as products or market strategy towards a growing emphasis on internal aspects such as management styles, personalities and intra-organizational conflicts.

If we consider in more detail the ways in which journalists frame their stories about business, we find that one has moved from frames of meaning in which firms were represented as embodying larger social interests in their "normal" economic activities, towards a situation in which firms are represented as autonomous entities engaging not with nature (outside society) nor competing ideals of society, but rather with "the market" as something that in many ways *stands in* for "the public", "government" or other entities representing the whole of society, and which motivates the continuous scrutiny of business activity.

On the one hand, this can be seen as a kind of closure in business news, in which a financial frame or a market frame excludes other interests and aspects of society from news stories. On the other hand, it also suggests how the news has become an arena, among others, in which struggles of interpretation are played out. While the "business of business" is increasingly interpreted within a financial frame of meaning, the legitimacy of concrete corporate activities is being routinely challenged – at least in the larger business news articles, and subject to continuous definition. However, the problem with these challenges to corporate legitimacy is that legitimacy is no longer conferred by established institutions such as the Public, Science or the State (see also Tsoukas,

101

1999), but by a more transient constellation of concrete and abstract actors speaking and acting in the name of "the market". Thus attempts to restore legitimacy may prove to be a confusing game of revolving mirrors, and may subject corporate behavior not to the test of whether it conforms to any particular social norms or values, but to speculations as to the expected reactions of "the market". In such a world, corporate legitimacy, or indeed corporate social responsibility, is no longer a question of civic virtue or of adhering to established social norms but a question of perceived confidence and risk. In this situation, socially responsible behavior involves not so much a relation between an actor and a given society, as it involves particular types of communication in which one invokes "societal interests" or "responsibility", and thereby contributes to defining them. In other words, business news has become a political arena in which various actors, such as journalists, stock market analysts, and corporate communicators struggle over the definition of both business and society.

From the perspective of strategic CSR communication, the expansion of business news thus involves new challenges as well as new possibilities.

Communicating strategies of corporate social responsibility with- and through the media may be an uphill battle since the dominant news frame in business coverage is not oriented towards broader social or policy issues, and since the "society" or "community" to which one may attempt to appeal has become increasingly difficult to pinpoint. Thus while there is rarely any doubt that firms like Carlsberg Nesa or Tele Danmark (TDC) are expected to responsive, it is less clear whether they should relate to "Denmark", to "the Public", to "the costumers" or to "the investors".

However, it is also this latter aspect, which opens up a field of *strategic* communication in the sense that CSR communication today must engage actively with the definition of the business of business in society, and hence also with the definition of society.

CSR communication is not just a question of informing the public of the good deeds performed by a responsible corporation. CSR communicators have engage strategically with a variety of

102

stakeholders (including the media) and actively seek to convince them not only of how particular activities are "good" and how the firm relates to particular visions of community. In addition, facing "the market" one also has show how this makes good sense as a business strategy.

## Where do we go from here?

In the Introduction, I deliberately chose a broad definition of corporate social responsibility that made possible an analysis of how news texts deal with the place of business in society. In doing so, I also suggested that *any* news text concerned with business takes up a relation to a broader community. Mostly, however, such relations are taken for granted either because 'society' has simply been viewed as a given or because broader social relations are made invisible by an overwhelming emphasis on financial aspects. In this context, strategic CSR communication is not so much a question of adding something radically new to news reports but rather a question of engaging with, articulating and redefining something that is always already there.

*Hence, the following questions for reflection are derived from this chapter:*

- What are the typical issues being considered in the journalistic coverage of the field of business in question?
- What "wholes" are these issues related to, e.g. "the public", "the industry", "the nation", "the market"? Who claims to speak on behalf of these "wholes"?
- When communicating about CSR activities, whose conceptions of society does one relate to – and attempt to change?

## Acknowledgements

The research presented in this chapter has been carried out as part of two research projects: "The Rise of the Nordic Business Press" funded by the Joint Committee for Nordic Research Councils for the Humanities and the Social Sciences, and the "PRO-MEDIA Project" funded by the Danish Social Science Research Council.

## References

Davis, A. (2000) "Public relations, business news and the reproduction of corporate elite power", *Journalism* Vol. 1(3), 2000, pp. 282-304

Ekecrantz, J. (1997). "Journalism's discursive events and socio-political change in Sweden 1925-87" *Media, Culture and Society*, 19(3).

Fligstein, N. (1990). *The Transformation of Corporate Control*, Cambridge MA: Harvard University Press.

Gavin, N. (1998). *The Economy, Media and Public Knowledge*, London and New York: Leicester University Press.

Kjær, P. (2005). "The evolution of business news in Denmark 1960-2000: context and content". *CBP-Working Chapter*, Copenhagen Business School.

Kjær, P. & Langer, R. (2005). "Infused with news value: Management, managerial knowledge and the institutionalization of business news", *Scandinavian Journal of Management*, Vol. 21(2), pp. 209-233

Møller, P. (1956) "Pressen og erhvervslivet" in *Avisen i dag*, Copenhagen: Berlingske Forlag.

Pedersen, O. K., Peter K., Esmark, A., Horst, M. & Carlsen, E. M. (2000). *Politisk Journalistik*. Århus: Forlaget Ajour, 2000

Risberg, A., Tienari, J. & Vaara, E. (2003). "Making Sense of a Transnational Merger: Media Texts and the (Re)construction of Power Relations". *Culture and Organization* 9/2, 121-137.

Risberg, A., Tienari, J. & Vaara, E. (2003). "Making Sense of a Transnational Merger: Media Texts and the (Re)construction of Power Relations". *Culture and Organization* 9/2, 121-137.

Tsouchas, H. (1999). "David and Goliath in the Risk Society. Making Sense of the Conflict Between Shell and Greenpeace in the North Sea", *Organization* 6(1), 1999, pp. 499-528.

## Articles from "Berlingske Tidende" 1960, 1980 and 2000

- "Danfly i vækst" [Danfly expanding], November 14, 1960
- "Gode nyheder for dansk handel med belgierne" [Good news for the Danish trade with the Belgians], November 14, 1960
- "Industriby i Køge Bugt" [Industrial city in the Bay of Køge], November 15, 1960
- "Kæmpe-dieselmotorer prøvekøres på B&W" [Trial run of giant diesel engines at B&W], November 17, 1960
- "Brugsforeningernes omsætning 1500 mill." [1500 million turnover in Coops], November 18, 1960
- "Ingen nye ordrer" [No new orders], November 18, 1960

- "Roulunds Fabrikker solgt til A.P. Møller-rederierne" [Roulund Factories sold to A.P. Møller Shipping], November 18, 1960
- "Strejker og nedsat tempo på en række svineslagterier" [Strikes and slowdowns in a number of slaughterhouses], November 19, 1960
- "Danmark rammes af USA's spareplan" [Denmark hit by US cut down plans], November 19, 1960
- "Det handler om gulerødder" [It's all about carrots], November 20, 1960
- "Spillet om storgrossisten" [The game over the giant wholesaler], November 10, 1980
- "Magasin og BP med nyt fælles konto-kort [Magasin and BP introduce new credit card], November 11, 1980.
- "Brændeovns-fabrikanter truet efter kæmpesalg" [Furnace producers threatened after giant sales], November 12, 1980
- "Lille fabrik kæmper for uniforms-ordrer" [Small factory struggling for uniform orders], November 12, 1980
- "Regnecentralen får råd: Pas på pengene" [Advice to Regnecentralen: Look after the money], November 12, 1980
- "Slagteri-samarbejde for at klare krisen" [Slaughterhouse cooperation to handle crisis], November 13, 1980
- "100.000 kr. for et hoved" [100.000 crowns for a head], November 13, 1980
- "Mangel på konkret viden om nye låneregler" [Lack of concrete knowledge about new mortgage rules], November 13, 1980
- "B&W Skibsværft får ekspert som formand" [Expert new chairman of B&W Shipyard], November 15, 1980
- "Professor: Pengeinstitutter vildleder om pensioner" [Professor: Banks mislead on pensions], November 16, 1980
- "Aktiemarkedet er skeptisk over for Bioscan" [The stock market is skeptical towards Bioscan], November 13, 2000
- "Tele Danmark på milliardopkøb" [Tele Danmark buying for billions], November 14, 2000
- "Nesa bøjer sig for kundekritik" [Nesa yields to customer criticism], November 15, 2000
- "Framfab på optur" [Framfab going up], November 15, 2000

- "Den rigtige idé" [The right idea], November 16, 2000
- "Norden bejlere løbet over ende" [Norden suitors outrun], November 17
- "Dyremoses milliarder" [Dyremose's billions], November 19, 2000
- "Det sidste salg" [The last sale], November 19, 2000
- "Carlsbergs hektiske år" [Carlsberg's hectic year], November 19, 2000
- "Ingen udsigt til gennemsigtighed på markedet for forsikring" [No view to transparency in the insurance market], November 19

## Notes

1. The total volume of coded content in "Berlingske Tidende" was 1248 items in 1960, 1152 items in 1980, and 1608 items in 2000. The total volume of coded content in "Børsen" was 417 items in 1960, 297 items in 1980, and 630 items in 2000.
2. For a critical analysis of the spread of financial journalism, see Davis (2000). For a broader discussion of the rise of a "financial conception of control" within the field of management, see Fligstein (1990).
3. At the same time, Børsen also seems to pursue an all-round strategy in its *business* coverage, meaning that it attempts to cover a large variety of industries and businesses, while Berlingske Tidende is more selective in its selection of newsworthy industries and firms.
4. This observation is supported by a study of agents and sources in the news showing that the share of economic news stories in "Berlingske Tidende" and "Børsen" that depicted firms as the dominant agent rose from between 38 % and 44 % in 1960 and 1970 to between 58 % and 74 % in 2000 (Kjær 2005).

106

# CHAPTER 5

# Stealth marketing communications: Is it ethical?

*Roy Langer*

*Some of the clients that I can't speak about ...
talk about the fact, you know, this kind of marketing
needs to stay undercover. And they pay us
a lot of money to keep it that way.*

*David Elias, CEO of marketing company "Soulkool" in CBS' 60 minutes, July 25, 2004*

## Introduction

**A Kiwi ad hoax**

In January 2006 New Zealand advertising agency DDB launched a publicity stunt for the girly website nzgirl.com on "The Big Day Out", which is an event and music concert day, where up to 40.000 teenagers enjoy entertainment, bands and each other. DDB succeeded in generating intense gossip and lots of media coverage about the campaign. A nzgirl-spokesperson describes how they did it: "[W]e did tell a few key people that we had flown a helicopter over the Big Day Out with a naked guy hanging underneath it. Unfortunately the guy had slipped and fell about 5 ft to the ground. He wasn't badly hurt, just lost a testicle (we never thought you'd believe this part)."

Of course, the whole campaign was a hoax. It never happened. Problem is, the Civil Aviation Authority started an air accident investigation with tax payers' money. DDB and nzgirl blamed the media for this; the media accused them in turn of keeping the story alive by refusing to confirm that the incident was faked. On the nzgirl-website, visitors even could download a movie-clip which showed how a man fell on to a barbed wire fence and was writhing in pain.

The campaign was certainly a creative and cost-effective bait-and-tease campaign, which is one form of stealth marketing. DDB's previous campaigns for nzgirl – including light planes flying overhead towing banners reading "Scott Kelly has got a small dick" and "Josh Short likes it with a strap on" – earned the company even a controversial Gold Lion award at the Cannes Lions International Advertising Festival. Flushed with their success in creating a buzz through guerrilla marketing, DDB pushed the envelope one step further in 2006 in their attempt to create an urban myth. Advertising creative director Paul Catmur defended the campaign with the following words: "My view of commercial creativity has for some time been 'whatever it takes'..."

**Figure 1:** An example of a bait-and-tease campaign (Langer, 2006a)

The nzgirls.com-bait and tease campaign displayed in figure 1 is one example for the increasing use of what is called stealth marketing (also synonymously called undercover marketing). Stealth marketing seeks to create a buzz by initiating word-of-mouth communication (WOM) among potential consumers about products and services. It is celebrated by certain PR, advertising and marketing practitioners and researchers as being a cost-effective alternative to traditional promotion tools, and is sometimes even declared as "the only future marketing has" (Ahmed, 2000) by prescribing "how to reach consumers surreptitiously" (Kaikati & Kaikati, 2004).

It is, however, also one of the most debated and contested communication tools in current corporate promotion tool kits, as consumer advocates and others question its ethics and social responsibility (see Figure 2 for recent examples).

**Recent concerns about stealth marketing**

In 2005 the *Writers Guild of America* (WGA) and the *American Screen Actors Guild*, supported by the associate dean of the *USC Annenberg School for Communication*, launched a campaign against product placement integration. They complained that placement practices hurt their artistic integrity and that they aren't paid for helping to sell the products placed in movies and TV shows. In a *White Paper* (cf. p. 132, 2005), they urged a code of conduct or regulation by the Federal Communication Commission (FCC) that includes disclosure at the beginning of each movie and TV program of the advertising that has been woven into the script and that limits on the use of such advertising in children's programming. WGA-president P.M. Verrone motivated the campaign as follows: "The weaving of paid-for product advertisements into the storylines of television and film raises serious ethical questions. The traditional standards and practices governing commercial product placement are increasingly being swept aside in favor of product integration and branded entertainment. In their race to the bottom line to create the so-called new business model, network and advertising executives are ignoring the public's interest and demanding that creative artists participate in stealth advertising disguised as a story." (*http://www.wga.org*)

In April 2006, Wisconsin-based consumer advocacy group Center for Media and Democracy (CMD) published the report Fake TV news: Widespread and Undisclosed, in which they exposed an epidemic of fake news infiltrating local TV-broadcasters across the U.S. In a 10-month investigation CMD captured 77 TV-stations (i.e. 80 % of the stations reviewed) actively disguising sponsored content by presenting non-edited corporate video news releases from companies including General Motors, Intel and Pfizer as news. CMD-Senior researcher D. Farsetta comments: "It's shocking to see how product placements moves secretly unfiltered from the boardroom to the newsroom and then straight into our living rooms. "The report was accompanied by a formal complaint to the FCC. (*http://www.prwatch.org*)

But it is not only professional associations and consumer advocacy groups, who express concerns: Even *The Financial Times* (March 17, 2006) expressed its concerns about the increased use of undercover marketing, resulting in a mixture of marketing promotion and entertainment – and also politics – in the media when reporting that British celebrity chef Jamie Oliver admitted accepting £15.000 from Heinz as part of a product placement deal in which he agreed to include an up-market version of baked beans on toast on the menu at this restaurant. Oliver's different roles as a TV-chef and entertainer as well as a spokesman for UK-supermarket-chain J Sainsbury (earning £ 1 million) display the blending of promotion and entertainment – and even politics, as Oliver's engagement to improve the quality of food in government schools resulted in that UK politicians from Tony Blair on down scrambled to show their concern about the topic.

**Figure 2:** Recent concerns about stealth marketing

Obviously, and as it is the very purpose of stealth marketing to apply covert means in the attempt to create consumer awareness, it is difficult to assess the exact amount of stealth marketing campaigns and how many covert messages we as consumers are exposed to. However, and thanks to consumer advocacy groups, journalists, researchers and whistleblowers who have disclosed an increasing number of covert campaigns, there is mounting evidence for the growth of stealth marketing. Previously quoted Writers Guild of America estimates that product placements in the U.S. increased in general by 44 % in 2005, hereof by 84 % in American TV-programs alone, representing more than US-$ 1 billion in revenue. And although stealth marketing appears to be more common and widespread in the U.S., studies have recorded and verified the increased use of stealth marketing in other countries, such as Denmark (Langer & Nielsen, 2002; Langer, 2003) and Germany (Baerns, 2003).

Communication practitioners should therefore know about and be able to assess stealth marketing. Despite of the misleading "marketing" in the term, stealth marketing refers to practices that are of interest for *all communication practitioners*: as the examples above already indicated, stealth marketing is as much about

110

PR and strategic communication as it is about advertising and marketing. Stealth marketing is also relevant and of interest for various other stakeholders, such as *CEO's and other managers* (as stealth marketing disclosed is a threat to corporate reputation and influences consumers' perception of the firm and its products, cf. (Folkes & Kamins, 1999), *consumers and consumer advocacy groups* (the primary target of stealth marketing), *politicians and public authoritiesn* (who are supposed to regulate and protect markets and consumers), *professional associations* (not just of marketers, advertisers, PR- and other communication practitioners – but also of journalists, artists, actors and other professions, whose professional values are affected and whose professional ethic is challenged by stealth marketing), *public institutions and mass media* (being the location of stealth marketing) – and "*ultimately to every citizen who participates in mass communication*" (Baerns, 2003, p. 104, my emphasis).

Despite of the importance of stealth marketing for its many stakeholders, only one study specifically addressing it has been published in an international journal so far (Kaikati & Kaikati, 2004). Stealth marketing is often not clearly distinguished from other concepts, such as buzz marketing and guerrilla marketing. In order to increase our understanding of, what we actually refer to, when speaking about stealth marketing, *the first objective* of this chapter *is to offer a sound definition and typology of stealth marketing* that is based on an overview of current communication practices and reflective rigour.

(Kaikati and Kaikati's, 2004) descriptive presentation of stealth marketing praised the concept as marketers "should attempt to create 'zap-proof formulas by relying on more subtle messages that are harder to avoid". The lack of critical reflection by Kaikati and Kaikati has been criticised (Huba, 2005). Hence, *the second objective* of this chapter *is to assess stealth marketing in terms of its ethics and social responsibility.*

Assessing the ethics and social responsibility of strategic corporate communication plans appears to be of utter practical importance for communication, PR, advertising and marketing professionals, as critiques of the ethics and social responsibility of a firms' communication can be costly, both in terms of the firms reputation and literally in terms of the money spent on communication campaigns that might fail. Hence, *the third objective of this chapter is to present a framework for how marketers and other communication professionals can look at their prospective marketing communication plan and practice in order to determine whether it is ethically sound and social responsible.*

I will begin by defining stealth marketing and present a typology of and examples for stealth marketing. As stealth marketing involves boundary spanning communication practices beyond traditional demarcations between corporate and marketing communication (including PR and advertising) and marketing, in what follows, the ethics of stealth marketing will be approached broadly by drawing on insights from both communication and marketing research. In the third section of the chapter I present a periodical overview of basic approaches, modern extensions and future orientations in marketing communication ethics. Based on this overview a framework for assessing the ethics of communication practices is presented and applied in the fourth section when addressing the question of whether stealth marketing is socially responsible and ethically sound. Finally, the fifth section of the chapter discusses implications of this assessment for research and communication practice.

## A definition and typology of stealth marketing

Stealth marketing is not an entirely new communication practice. For instance, in 1929 the founder of modern Public Relations practice, Edward Bernays, won national ink and thrilled his tobacco client by staging a march of cigarette-puffing debutantes at New York's annual Easter Parade. Of course, Bernays did not reveal his tobacco client, but launched the march as part of the women rights and liberation movement: women smoking cigarettes in public was thus framed and perceived as an expression of equality of males and females.

Although covert product placements in Hollywood movies have been common since the 1940s, covert product placements for tobacco boosted since the 1970's, as tobacco ads were booted

112

from TV-channels in the U.S. Hence, the tobacco industry sought and found salvation by going under radar with the help of Hollywood. Between 1978 and 1988, Philip Morris products alone appeared in about 200 movies. In 2006, cigarettes made appearance in several films nominated for best picture at Academy Awards, including Oscar-winning "Brokeback Mountain" and "Capote".

However, today's communication professionals face much greater difficulties to cut through the clutter compared to the challenges Bernays faced in the 1920s or the tobacco industry since the 1970s: Consumers are increasingly resistant to traditional and conventional promotion messages and techniques, which diminishes the effectiveness of conventional mass media advertising. Media-savvy consumers have become increasingly resistant and inaccessible due to ad avoidance (e.g. TV-zapping). Attempts by the industry to respond to the ever growing fragmentation of target groups by creating smaller and smaller consumer segments and by introducing niche, micro and relational marketing techniques have so far shown limited success. Increased legal regulation for the promotion of certain products (e.g. tobacco and alcohol) and information overload due to the growing number of media channels in the attention economy have added to this. Also technological progress, such as the invention of new media channels or personalized digital video recorders with ad-skipping-facilities, contributes to this development.

A-priori-judgements for the social responsibility and ethics of communication based on a distinction between information and promotion or based on senders' identity, have become obsolete. Also the traditional distinction and separation of communication on the one hand and promotion on the other (as well as between advertising, marketing promotion and Public Relations) has become blurred, as strategic communication always includes promotional elements. In line with the previous distinction between "objective information" – pre-dominantly provided by public and non-governmental organisations on the one hand, and "commercial promotion", provided by private firms on the other, do not seem to be valid any longer, as also public and non-governmental organizations are communicating strategically and professionally in their own self-interest.

A recent study of new subtle marketing promotion in Denmark (Langer & Nielsen, 2002) identified three interconnected strategies for the renewal of professional communication practices in response to the development sketched out above. These are: 1) the application of new and non-traditional channels and formats in promotion activities; 2) the blurring of boundaries to other public discourses and social practices; and 3) the production of new promotional contents.

The application of new channels and formats includes the use of brand pushers and digital media channels (e.g. text and other messages on cell phones, the Internet), but also the use of media formats that had not been used for promotional purposes before, such as music, games, literature and teaching materials. It also entails a renewed attention to personal channels and WOM, as many studies have shown the importance of WOM in the formation of attitudes (Bone, 1995), in a purchase decision-making context (Bansal & Voyer, 2000) and in the reduction of risk associated with buying decisions (Murray, 1991; v. Wangenheim & Bayón, 2004). The blurring of boundaries between promotional commercial messages and other public discourses and social practices, such as journalism, public health information, entertainment or art, seeks to gain credibility from these discourses and produces *hybrid messages*, where promotional content is blended with other content (Balasubramanian, 1994). And by changing the content of promotional campaigns and applying a softer and less pushy approach, where promotional communication is rather seen as entertainment or education, professional communication practitioners seek to re-establish contact with consumers.

Stealth marketing reflects these interconnected strategies and alternative communication practices. The term is often used synonymously with other terms, such as embedded advertising, undercover, buzz, gonzo, guerrilla and viral marketing or product placements, hence creating confusion. In order to make it less fuzzy, I briefly will sort out the differences between these concepts: while stealth marketing and undercover marketing can be regarded

**114**

as synonymous terms, buzz and guerrilla marketing cannot. Stealth, buzz, gonzo and guerrilla marketing have in common that they signify unconventional ways of performing promotional activities on a low budget. But as defined by Levinson (1984), guerrilla marketing is not necessarily based on WOM, as it also refers to other media channels, such as t-shirts, the Yellow Pages, direct mail campaigns or ads in local community newschapters. Hence, guerrilla marketing refers to alternative low cost ways to do marketing specifically designed for small business. Neither is buzz marketing by definition also stealth marketing, although some buzz marketing can be. But buzz marketing refers basically just to the attempt to create highly intense and interactive WOM about a product or service (cf. Dye, 2000; Reichheld, 2003; Rosen, 2000). Finally, gonzo marketing as noted in Locke (2001) does not necessarily involve stealth marketing. Hence, neither guerrilla nor buzz and gonzo marketing are synonymous terms to stealth or undercover marketing.

Embedded advertising only refers to promotional messages blended with other mass media content and excludes all WOM techniques and other channels than the mass media. Viral marketing is defined as WOM by use of a digital platform (the Internet, e-mail, cellphones), but does not necessarily involve the application of covert means (cf. Datta, Chowdhury & Chakrabordy, 2005; Stanbouli, 2003; Subramani & Rajagopalan, 2003). Neither is a product placement in a movie or a TV-program stealth marketing if it is disclosed at the beginning and/or the end of the movie or TV program. D'Astous and Séguin (1999) suggested to distinguish between implicit, integrated explicit and non-integrated product placements, depending on whether information about the promotional sponsorship of a movie, a TV-program or similar is provided or not. Implicit product placement refers to that a product has a passive and contextual role in a program, such as when participants display the logo of a product or company. Integrated explicit product placement means that a product plays an active role in the program, such as when the product is shown or demonstrated. Non-integrated product placement refers to programs, where a product is explicitly presented without being integrated into the

115

content of the program, such as when the sponsor of a program is presented verbally or non-verbally in the program, e.g. in the movie credits/rolling title (cf. D'Astous & Séguin, 1999; Langer, 2005). Hence, non-integrated product placements are per definition not stealth marketing, whereas it depends on the specific context, i.e. whether an implicit or integrated explicit product placement is disclosed or not, whether we can talk about stealth marketing or not. What is important in the context of this study is that neither viral marketing nor product placement is stealth marketing by definition of the term. In addition, the terminological fuzziness also regards the different techniques applied in different cultures: For instance, in New Zealand public TV-channel TV One broadcasts promotional shows integrated in its breakfast-TV-show which are labeled "advertorials" despite of the fact that they are clearly announced and signaled in subtitles and by use of a different editorial host in a different studio. On the other hand, the editorial host is employed by the public broadcaster and the advertorial studio is designed in the same colors and the same interior architecture as the main site of the edited news show. In sum, the borderline between undercover and uncovered marketing is fluid, depending on the specific context.

Kaikati and Kaikati (2004, p. 6) define stealth marketing as "attempts to catch people at their most vulnerable by identifying the weak spot in their defensive shields ...anchored on the premise that WOM communication is the most effective form of promotion and that peer group recommendation is the ultimate marketing weapon". They list six stealth marketing techniques: viral marketing, the use of brand pushers, celebrity marketing, bait-and-tease marketing and embedded brands and logos in video games, in pop and rap music. Figure 3 provides a short definition of these types:

116

- **Viral marketing:** creating covert WOM via digital platform
- **Brand pushers:** hiring actors who approach people in real-life situations to slip them a covert commercial message
- **Celebrity marketing:** paying celebrities money to covertly promoting products
- **Bait-and-tease marketing:** getting people interested in something which is revealed later to be something quite different
- **Marketing in video games:** embedding brands and logos in electronic games
- **Marketing in pop and rap music:** embedding commercial messages in popular music

**Figure 3:** Kaikati and Kaikati's (2004) typology of stealth marketing

Although this typology displays some important types of stealth marketing, it is, however, not adequate. Other types of stealth marketing techniques include non-disclosed implicit or integrated explicit product placements in movies or TV programs, embedded brands or logos in TV news (fake news, video news releases (VNR's), advertorials) and other editorial media content, embedded brands or logos in fictional and non-fictional books, in art pieces (e.g. paintings) or even in political or religious messages.

The problem with the definition and typology of stealth marketing by Kaikati and Kaikati is that it does not include some important types of stealth marketing and reduces stealth marketing to covert WOM. While WOM indeed is the premise for some types of stealth marketing, such as the use of brand pushers, it is not the premise for other types (such as VNR's).

Hence, a sound definition of stealth marketing must be based on the latter part of what Kaikati and Kaikati (2004, p. 6) describe as its main objective: "The main objective is to get the right people talking (or just becoming aware of, RL) about the product or service *without it appearing to be company-sponsored*" (emphasis by RL). Based on this, the following definition of stealth marketing

117

is suggested: Stealth marketing is any promotional communication message by use of WOM or any other communication channel, which is designed and applied to disguise receivers about the senders' identity and/or to create obtrusiveness about the promotional purpose and character of the message in order to expose consumers to promotional messages below their threshold potential and their defensive shields.

This definition focuses on the main characteristic and main purpose of stealth marketing, namely to expose consumers to promotional messages by use of covert means. It does not reduce the purpose of stealth marketing to create WOM, embraces all potential channels that can be applied in stealth marketing and draws a distinctive line between covert and transparent communication. Figure 4 displays further examples of stealth marketing:

**Viral Marketing**
When 7Up/Dr. Pepper launched a new milk product, it hired and paid six teenagers to write promotional weblogs. Also McDonald applied fake-blogs in its marketing.

**Brand pushers**
When Sony Ericsson in 2002 launched its camera phone T68i, it hired actors in New York to pose as fake-tourists, who asked by-passers to take pictures of them.

Also Hennessy employed actors: when launching a new cognac brand, they hired 150 actors to go to targeted, trendsetting clubs and restaurants that didn't serve the brand on eight different national markets. These actors ordered loudly the drink or bought the drink for other guests. But brand pushers are not necessarily actors. Girls Intelligence Agency (GIA) claims to employ 40.000 covert tween influencers operating secretly (like the CIA).

**Celebrity marketing**
When Daimler-Chrysler introduced a re-designed Dodge Durano SUV in 2003, it tricked up five models for the personal use of sports celebrities. Actress Kathleen Turner appeared in 2002 on CNN to discuss her struggles with rheumatoid arthritis and failed to mention that producers of Enbrel, a drug that battles the condition, paid her to appear and to promote the brand.

118

**Payola**

Payola denotes the in most countries illegal practice of record companies paying money for the broadcast of records on music radio, if the song is presented as being part of the normal day's broadcast. New York State Attorney General has been prosecuting payola-related crimes in his jurisdiction. His office settled out of court with Sony BMG Music Entertainment and Warner Music Group in 2005, where both conglomerates agreed to pay $10 and $5 million respectively for distribution by Rockefeller Philanthropy Advisors to New York State non-profit organizations that will fund music education and appreciation programs throughout the state. Universal Music Group and EMI are currently under investigation.

**Product placements in video games (advertgames)**

Toyota paid Sony for their car to appear in the game "Grand Turismo". Dahl, Eagle & Fernandez, 2006) studied advertgames on 15 U.K. and multinational high profile advertisers from the food industry, including Cadbury, Kellogs, Ferrero, Milkyway, Nabisco, Nestlé, Kraft and Haribo, and concluded that the majority of these advertgames included pressures to purchase and not sufficiently separated content and advertising and applied viral marketing.

**Product placements in other channels**

In 2001 IBM was slapped with a fine, cleanup costs and attorney fees amounting to $ 120.000 after an ad agency spray-paints logos of a peace symbol, a heart and a penguin for IBM's "Peace, Love and Linux" campaign around the streets of San Francisco.

**Fake-witness in political marketing**

The daughter of the Kuwaiti ambassador to the U.S. appears in 1990 before a congressional caucus as an anonymous refugee, reporting that Iraqi invaders rip Kuwaiti babies from hospital incubators, thus contributing to the first Gulf war. PR-agency Hill & Knowlton hired her on behalf of the lobby group "Citizens for a free Kuwait" (see also Grunig, 1993).

**Figure 4:** Further stealth marketing examples

Whether a promotional message is stealth marketing or not is sometimes difficult to decide, as the following example of products mentioned in music illustrates: while it was revealed that

119

rapper Jay-Z was paid by Motorola for mentioning the brand in one of his songs, Adidas did not pay Run-DMC for the song "My adidas", who just and basically like the shoes. Neither did Nice Device receive payment for their song "Cool Corona" from the Mexican brewery. The examples illustrate that not all products mentioned in other content formats than traditional advertising also are stealth marketing messages, as mentioning a product can have other motivations than the purpose of (paid) promotion. However, many of the above examples raise serious concerns and substantial critiques that question the ethics and social responsibility of the companies involved. Leaving personal taste and opinion aside, how can we assess whether a particular communication campaign is ethically sound and socially responsible? The next section addresses this question for the case of stealth marketing communication practices.

### Stealth marketing: socially responsible and ethically sound?

Basic approaches to assess communication ethics are rooted in the works of philosophers of the age of enlightenment, such as Immanuel Kant (1724-1804), Jeremy Bentham (1748-1832), Thomas Hobbes (1588-1679), John Locke (1632-1704) and Jean-Jaques Rousseau (1712-1778), and can be seen as a reflective response to the social upheavals of the seventeenth and eighteenth century in Europe that included the decline of feudal authority and the rise of the modern capitalist nation state. Based on these philosophers' work, we can distinguish three basic approaches when addressing ethical basics, namely a deontological, a social contract and a utilitarian approach. These three approaches are summarised in the following table with regard to questions that can be asked to specific communication practices:

| | |
|---|---|
| **1.** | **Deontological approach:** |
| 1.1 | Does the communication practice violate any universal principle, rule or hypernorm, such as the right to know the truth? |

120

1.2 Does the communication practice violate any basic liberty, human and consumer right, such as the right to safety, to be informed, to choose and to be heard?
Does the communication practice violate any justice right, i.e. does it treat the consumer in a fair manner?

**2. Social contract approach:**
2.1 Is there any microsocial contract that is violated by the communication practice?
2.2 Who are the different stakeholders of the communication practice and how do these different stakeholders react on the communication practice?
2.3 How does the communication practice fit to the company's general policy in order to satisfy social demands and its' image and reputation?

**3. Utilitarian approach:**
3.1 What are the (potential) short and long term consequences and effects of the communication practice?
3.2 Who and how many persons are affected by the communication practice – and how?

**Figure 5:** Approaches to the ethical assessment of marketing communication practices

As recommended by Cohen (2005), the following sections assess stealth marketing ethics from these three perspectives.

*A deontological perspective on stealth marketing*
An assessment of the ethics of stealth marketing from a deontological perspective seems easy, as the very purpose of stealth marketing is to disclose the identity of the advertiser or the promotional character of the message as such, hence not telling the truth about the senders or messages identity and thus creating disguise and obtrusiveness. Moreover, stealth marketing violates basic consumer rights, such as the right to be informed and basic rights of justice, as stealth marketing a priori seeks to create inequality between the advertiser and stakeholders by avoiding informed consent.

121

A widely acknowledged deontological research model for communication ethics is Nebenzahl & Jaffe's (1998) communication ethics matrix. This two-dimensional model is used in order to determine the ethics of communication in terms of disguise and obtrusiveness. Disguise refers to the degree of source concealment, i.e. the extent to which the sponsor is identified and/or to which extent the sponsor is able to cloud the fact that the message is part of a promotional campaign. Obtrusiveness determines the degree to which the promotional message is secondary to more salient communication such as a casual conversation with a personal friend or a scene in a movie:

**Figure 6:** Advertising Ethics Matrix (Nebenzahl & Jaffe, 1998

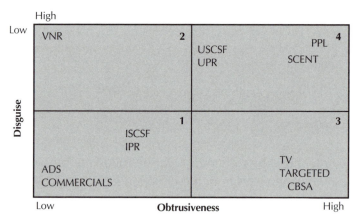

ISCSF: *Identified Short Commercially Sponsored Films*
IPR: *Identified Press Releases*
VNR: *Video News Releases*
CBSA: *Commercial Billboards in Sports Arenas*
UPR: *Unidentified Press Releases*
PPL: *Product Placement*

Communication within the quadrants 2 to 4 are of questionable ethics. Depending on the specific design, stealth marketing must be located in one of these quadrants, as it seeks to cover the sender and/or the promotional character of the message. Judging the ethics of stealth marketing based on this normative statement again seems easy: as the purpose of stealth marketing is precisely to cover the character of promotion and/or the company behind, it must obviously be unethical marketing communication.

Although the ethical assessment of stealth marketing from a deontological perspective appears to be a simple matter, a number of questions remain unanswered: First of all, it remains unclear whether the sheer attempt to cover the identity of the sender or the character of a promotional messages is unethical; or whether this attempt should be successful in order to assess a particular communication practice as unethical. Here, ethical judgements must distinguish between intentions and actual communication practices as the outcomes. Second, it remains open whether all stealth marketing techniques are equally unethical, or whether some stealth marketing techniques are more unethical than others. Third, one can ask whether the ethical assessment depends on whether the target market is a vulnerable consumer group, such as children. Fourth, it remains unclear, whether it it sufficient and ethically sound, if the identity of the sender is disclosed, but the promotional character of the message is not clear to stakeholders – and vice versa. Fifth, are there any ethical differences with regard to whether a promotional message is blended with editorial, entertainment, political, religious or other types of messages? These questions suggest a more nuanced assessment of stealth marketing, including an assessment from a social contract theory and a utilitarian perspective to marketing communication ethics.

*A social contract theory perspective on stealth marketing*
Individual consumers or particular groups can have their private or semi-private opinions about what they consider as ethical and social responsible communication. Private or semi-private opinions, attitudes and beliefs can, however, not be a sufficient guideline for general ethical judgements or political decisions about whether a social contract between marketers and society has been broken.

The International Code of Advertising Practice is one example for a social contract and self-regulatory code of conduct from the

123

International Chamber of Commerce (ICC). Other and similar ICC-codes address more specifically sales promotion, responsible food and beverage communications, sponsorships, direct marketing, environmental advertising, marketing and social research practice, and marketing and advertising using electronic media. Chapter 1 of the International Code of Advertising Practice states:

> "All advertising should be legal, decent, honest and truthful. Every advertisement should be prepared with a due sense of social responsibility and should conform to the principles of fair competition, as generally accepted in business.."

In addition, chapter 12 declares that advertising shall be clearly distinguishable from other media content and that it shall be easy to be identified and recognized as such:

> "Advertisements should be clearly distinguishable as such, whatever their form and whatever the medium used; when an advertisement appears in a medium which contains news or editorial matter, it should be so presented that it will be readily recognized as an advertisement." (ICC, 1997)

Other chapters in the International Code of Advertising Practice address the issues of honesty (chapter 3), social responsibility (chapter 4) or advertising targeted at children and young people (chapter 14). Based on this social contract, stealth marketing is clearly an unethical communication practice opposing the social responsibility of advertisers and marketers.

*A utilitarian perspective on stealth marketing*
Nebenzahl and Jaffe (1998, p. 811) emphasize that the previously presented deontological advertising ethics matrix only can predict the likelihood of whether a particular communication is more or less ethical. This likelihood needs further measurement by employing content analysis in order to evaluate a priori the extent of disguise and obtrusiveness of a particular communication technique as well as consumer research in order to estimate the pro-

124

portion of respondents, who do not believe that a particular message is sponsored by a commercial source. In line with this, the preamble of the International Code of Advertising Practice by the International Chamber of Commerce, ICC (1997) states: "Advertisements ...should be judged by their likely impact on the consumer, bearing in mind the medium used."

Hence, both Nebenzahl and Jaffe and the ICC suggest further investigations of the impact and effects of communication and recommend a combination of normative ideals with a utilitarian oriented empirical investigation of perceptions, consequences and results of particular communication techniques. Only content analysis can help to decide whether sponsors of a specific product placement seek to cover their sponsorship. Along with this, only empirical surveys among consumers can illuminate whether consumers actually are aware of sponsor names. Without a closer look at the outcomes of communication in terms of perceptions and effects, stealth marketing techniques as a whole can hardly be described as unethical or socially unacceptable from a utilitarian perspective.

Judging the ethics and social responsibility of stealth marketing from a utilitarian perspective appears, however, to be far more difficult. The most important problem is that we do not know very much about the consequences and effects of stealth marketing, as research addressing this topic is rare. Moreover, the few studies that do exist almost exclusively focus on product placements in television shows and movies and are inconclusive. Some suggest that stealth marketing is far from being a kind of "Wunderwaffe" that succeeds in seducing adult consumers' minds. Baerns (2003) reports a number of studies in Germany suggesting that product placements are less effective in terms of attention to promotional messages than traditional advertising formats. In a study on subliminal messages, DeFleur and Petranoff stated already in 1959: "It has been widely assumed that because people are not aware of subliminal messages, they are somehow 'helpless' against their suggestions. However, as a normal part of learning, audiences have developed 'mental callouses' against many forms of persuasion...There is perhaps just as much reason to assume that these protective habits would operate to *resist* subliminal persuasion as there is reason to assume that they would be ineffective against it." (DeFleur & Petranoff, 1959, p. 179) Hence, the authors emphasize that an assessment of the effects and consequences should not be based on outdated stimulus-response-models for communication.

In line with this, DeLorme and Reid (1999) investigated consumers' perceptions of product placements in movies and concluded that American movie audiences perceive and interpret product placements actively; and that in particular younger audience segments have a positive attitude towards product placements. These findings are supported by several other studies that report positive consumers' attitudes towards product placements, but also vary with regard to the product brand, media format and product placement type applied (cf. Gould, Gupta & Grabner-Kräuter, 2000; Gupta & Gould, 1997; Gupta, Balasubramanian & Klassen, 2000; Karrh, 1998; McKechnie & Zhou, 2003; Morton & Friedman, 2002; Nebenzahl & Secunda, 1993; Nelson, Keum & Yaros, 2004; Palazón & López, 2006; Russell, 2002; Tiwsakul & Hackley, 2005).

A nuanced utilitarian approach to the ethics of stealth marketing must acknowledge differences with regard to the particular strategies and techniques applied. Hence, blending promotional content with entertainment is probably less problematic in terms of effects and wider consequences than blending promotional content with editorial news or public information, as independent editorial news reporting and independent public authorities are of utter importance for the functioning of democracy and market economy. Targeting vulnerable consumer groups such as children in stealth marketing campaigns appears to be by far more dangerous and questionable than targeting media savvy and media literate adults, who base their consumption decisions on selective perception. Using stealth marketing in the promotion of dangerous products, such as tobacco, alcoholic beverages or pharmaceutical drugs is probably more ethically unsound due to the negative consequences than stealth promotion of clothing or cars.

Lantos (2001, p. 622) makes aware of the under-researched issue of consumer's responsibilities, e.g. that customers have an obligation to support socially responsible firms rather than socially irresponsible or socially indifferent businesses. Hence, "[s]ocial responsibility for marketing activities, then, is a collective responsibility, including outside partners and vendors such as suppliers of materials, parts, and services; wholesalers, retailers, and other distributors; advertising agencies and other marketing communication creators; marketing research firms and other information vendors; the media and other marketing communication carriers; government agencies; consumer protection champions; and even consumers themselves."

In conclusion, assessing the ethics of stealth marketing from a utilitarian perspective must consider the specific communication practice and its context, as well as all stakeholders and participants in the communication. There is a substantial need for more conclusive research results assessing the effects and consequences of stealth marketing applications. Such research is in industry's own interest, but so far industry has failed to engage in collaborative research with the academic community. As a result, many countries have chosen to impose greater restrictions on marketing communication based on a precautionary principle and "a judgment of probable influence" (Livingstone, 2005, p. 278), as recently introduced in Ireland on children's advertising (Eagle, 2006) or in Denmark as a general prohibition of stealth marketing in the new Danish Marketing Practice Act (Langer & Beckmann, 2006).

## Conclusion and implications

This chapter presented and defined stealth marketing as a new promotional tool that reflects three interconnected strategies for the renewal of professional marketing communication practices: 1) the application of new and non-traditional channels and formats in promotion activities; 2) the blurring of boundaries to other public discourses and social practices; and 3) the production of new promotion contents.

Based on a distinction between social responsibility and business ethics and on a short historical overview to ethical issues in marketing communication, the recent growth of stealth marketing has been critically discussed with regard to social responsibility and communication ethics. This assessment is based on a distinction between three approaches to marketing ethics: 1) a deontological perspective, 2) a social contract theory perspective, and 3) a utilitarian perspective. Communication practitioners can apply these three perspectives in an examination of their own practices in order to identify potential critiques from other stakeholders and in order to formulate counter arguments. For the case of stealth marketing, the application of these three perspectives revealed that the practice is definitely not socially responsible nor ethically sound from a deontological and a social contract theory perspective. It also showed that an assessment of stealth marketing from a utilitarian perspective is inconclusive due to the severe lack of reliable research results about effects and consequences of stealth marketing. As utilitarian ethics might be the only approach offering arguments in defence of stealth marketing practices, practitioners and the industry are called to engage in investigations of its effects and consequences for different stakeholders in particular contexts.

Implications for communication managers include that they could examine their communication practices based on the definition and typology of stealth marketing as well as based on the framework for such an assessment presented in this chapter. And maybe communication practitioners not just could, but should do so in order to protect their image and reputation.

Looking at the current state of affairs and as a closing thought, a precautionary principle must be applied by public policy makers and communication professionals as well as business regulators, when addressing questionable communication practices. After all, "[a]dvertising is a voluntary practice on the part of the advertiser, initialised by him and carefully designed to promote his interests. It is on the other hand only semi-voluntary from the consumer's point of view." (Attas, 1999, p. 58). Hence, a general and legal prohibition of stealth marketing appears to be appropriate and even mandatory, and should be combined with self-regulatory codes of conducts from the industry and media literacy education and training in order to protect consumers, especially children and young people, from negative impacts of persuasive communication and to enable them to make informed choices. Media literacy education programmes financed and supported by the industry are common in many countries, such as Canada, the U.K., New Zealand, Germany, The Netherlands and Belgium (cf. Eagle, 2006). However, in Denmark efforts so far have been limited to the legal prohibition of stealth marketing, leaving plenty of space for further initiatives pursued by public authorities and private business.

**Where do we go from here?**
Based on these reflections, communication practitioners could address the following questions when assessing whether a specific communication campaign or practice is ethically sound and socially responsible:

1. In what ways do you find stealth marketing ethical – and why?
2. In what ways do you find stealth marketing unethical – and why?
3. Are some stealth marketing techniques more ethical than others – and why?

## References

Ahmed, S. (2000): Stealth may the only future marketing has. *Marketing,* Nov.2, 32.

Attas, D. (1999): What's wrong with 'deceptive' advertising? *Journal of Business Ethics,* 21(1), 49-59.

Baerns, B. (2003): Separating advertising from programme content: The principle and its relevance in communication practice. *Journal of Communication Management,* 8 (1), 101-112.

Bansal, H.S. & Voyer, P.A. (2000): Word of mouth processes within a service purchase decision context. *Journal of Service Research,* 16(1), 74-94.

Balasubramanian, S.K. (1994): Beyond Advertising and Publicity: Hybrid Messages and Public Policy Issues. *Journal of Advertising,* 23(4), 29-46.

Bone, P.F. (1995): Word of mouth effects on short-term and long-term product judgements, *Journal of Business Research,* 32(3), 213-223.

Cohen, J. (2005): Appreciating, understanding and applying universal moral principles. *The Journal of Consumer Marketing,* 18(7), 578-594

Center for Media and Democracy (2006): *Stealth Advertising in the Entertainment Industry,* Report published on November 14, 2005, Madison (WI).

Dahl, S.; Eagle, L. & Fernandez, C.B. (2006): "Analyzing Advertgames: Active Dimensions or Actually Deception", in Podnar, K. and Jančič (eds.): *Contemporary issues in corporate and marketing communications: Towards a socially responsible future. Proceedings of the 11th International Conference on Corporate and Marketing Communications,* Ljubljana, April 21-22. Ljubljana: Fakulteta za družbene vede, pp. 118-189.

Datta, P.R.; Chowdhury, D.N. & Chakraborty, B.R. (2005): Viral marketing: new form of word-of-mouth through Internet. *The Business Review,* 3(2), 69-75

DeFleur, M. & Petranoff, R.M. (1959): A televised test of subliminal persuasion. *Public Opinion Quarterly,* 23(2), 168-180.

DeLorme, D.E. & Reid, L.N. (1999): Moviegoers' experiences and interpretations of brands in films revisited. *Journal of Advertising,* 28(2), 71-95.

Dye, R. (2000). The Buzz on Buzz, *Harvard Business Review,* November/December, 139-146.

D'Astous, A. & Séguin, N. (1999): Consumer reactions to product placement strategies in television sponsorship. *European Journal of Marketing,* 33(9/10), 896-910.

Eagle, L. (2006): Commercial Media Literacy: What does it do, to whom – and does it matter? in Podnar, K. and Jančič, Z. (eds.): Contemporary issues in corporate and marketing communications: Towards a socially responsible future. *Proceedings of the 11th International Conference on Corporate and Marketing Communications, Ljubljana, April 21-22, 2006.* Ljubljana: Fakulteta za družbene vede, pp. 324-330.

130

Folkes, V.S. & Kamins, M.A. (1999): Effects of Information about Firms' Ethical and Unethical Actions on Consumers' Attitudes. *Journal of Consumer Psychology*, 8(3): 243–259.

Gould, S.J.; Gupta, P.B. & Grabner-Kräuter, S. (2000): Product placements in movies: a cross-cultural analysis of Austrian, French and American consumers' attitudes toward this emerging, international promotional medium. *Journal of Advertising*, 29(4), 41-58.

Grunig, J.E. (1993): Public Relations and International Affairs: Effects, Ethics and Responsibility. *Journal of International Affairs*, 47(1), 137-162.

Gupta, P.B. & Gould, S.J. (1997): Consumers' perceptions of the ethics and acceptability of product placement in movies: Public policy issues and managerial implications. *Journal of Current Issues and Research in Advertising*, 19(1), 37-50.

Gupta, P.B., Balasubramanian, S.K. & Klassen, M.L. (2000): Viewers' evaluations of product placements in movies: product category and individual differences. *Journal of Current Issues and Research in Advertising*, 22(2), 41-52.

Huba, J. (2005): Exposing stealth marketing. Weblog published on January 11th 2005 at: *http://customerevangelists.typepad.com/blog/2005/01/exposing_stealt.html*

International Chamber of Commerce (1997): *International Code of Advertising Practice*. Accessed on April 20th 2006 from: http://www.iccwbo.org

Kaikati A.M. & Kaikati J.G. (2004), "Stealth marketing: how to reach consumers surreptitiously", *California Management Review* 46(4), 6-24.

Karrh, J.A. (1998): Brand placement: A review. *Journal of Current Issues and Research in Advertising*, 20(2), 31-48.

Langer, R. & Bruun Nielsen, A.D. (2002). *Skjult reklame – en undersøgelse af erfaringerne med denne reklameform, udviklingstendenser og reguleringsmulighederne*. Økonomi- og Erhvervsministeriet, Forbrugerstyrelsen, København.

Langer, R. (2003). New Subtle Advertising Formats: Characteristics, Causes and Consequences. In Hansen, F. and Bech Christensen, L. (Eds.), *Branding and Advertising* (pp. 232-265). Copenhagen: Copenhagen Business School Press.

Langer, R. (2005). Produktplaceringer som hybride budskaber. In Hansen, F., Bach Lauritsen, G. and Grønholdt, L. (red.), *Kommunikation, mediaplanlægning og reklamestyring*. København: Samfundslitteratur.

Langer, R. (2006a): When marketers push the envelope too far. *NZ Marketing Magazine*, May 2006.

Langer, R. & Beckmann, S.C. (2006): "Stealth Marketing – socially responsible and ethically sound communication?" in Podnar, K. and Jančič, Z. (eds.): Contemporary issues in corporate and marketing communications: Towards a socially responsible future. *Proceedings of the 11th International Conference on Corporate and Marketing Communications, Ljubljana, April 21-22, 2006*. Ljubljana: Fakulteta za družbene vede, pp. 11-15.

Lantos, G.P. (2001): The boundaries of strategic corporate social responsibility. *Journal of Consumer Marketing*, 18(7), 595-630.

Levinson, J.C. (1984): *Guerrilla Marketing: Secrets for making big profits from your small business*. Boston: Houghton Mifflin Company.

Livingstone, S. (2005): Assessing the research base for the policy debate over the effects of food advertising to children. *International Journal of Advertising*, 24(3), 273-296.

Locke, C. (2001): *Gonzo Marketing*, Reading (MA): Perseus Books.

McKechnie, S.A. & Zhou, J. (2003): Product placements in movies; a comparison of Chinese and American consumers' attitudes. *International Journal of Advertising*, 22, 349-374.

Morton, C.R. & Friedmann, M. (2002): I saw it in the movies: Exploring the link between product placement beliefs and reported usage behaviour. *Journal of Current Issues and Research in Advertising*, 24(2), 33-40.

Murray, K.B. (1991); A test of services marketing theory: consumer information acquisition activities, *Journal of Marketing*, 55, January, 10-25.

Nebenzahl, I.D. & Jaffe, E.D. (1998). Ethical Dimensions of Advertising Executions. *Journal of Business Ethics*, 17(7), 805-815.

Nebenzahl, I.D. & Secunda, E. (1993): Consumers' attitudes towards product placement in movies. *International Journal of Advertising*, 12(1), 1-11.

Nelson, M.R.; Keum, H. & Yaros, R.A. (2004): Advertainment or Advercreep? Game players' attitudes towards advertising and product placement in computer games. *Journal of Interactive Advertising*, 4(3), 1-30.

Palazon, J.T. & López, E.F. (2006): "Consumers' attitudes towards product placement in Spanish television sitcoms", in Podnar, K. and Jancic (eds.): Contemporary issues in corporate and marketing communications: Towards a socially responsible future. *Proceedings of the 11th International CMC-conference on Corporate and Marketing Communications, Ljubljana, April 21-22*. Ljubljana: Fakulteta za družbene vede, pp. 266-272.

Reichheld, F.F. (2003) The One Number You Need, *Harvard Business Review*, December, 46-54.

Rosen, Emanuel (2000): *The anatomy of buzz – how to create word of mouth marketing*. New York: Doubleday.

Russell, C.A. (2002): Investigating the effectiveness of product placement in television shows: The role of modality and plot connection congruence on brand memory and attitude, *Journal of Consumer Research*, 25, 357-362.

Stanbouli, K. (2003): Marketing viral et publicité. *Revue Française du Marketing*, May 2003; 192/193, 97-106.

Subramani, M.R. & Rajagopalan, B. (2003): Knowledge-sharing and influence in online social networks via viral marketing, *Communications of the ACM*, 46(12), 300-7.

132

Tiwsakul, R. & Hackley, C. (2005): Explicit, non-integrated product placement in British television programmes. *International Journal of Advertising*, 24(1), 95-111.

v. Wangenheim, F. & Bayón, T. (2004): The effect of word of mouth on service switching. Measurement and moderating variables. *European Journal of Marketing*, 38(9/10), 1173-1185.

Writers Guild of America (2005): *Are you SEELLING to ME?: Stealth Advertising in the Entertainment Industry*, White Chapter published on November 14, 2005, Los Angeles (CA) and New York (NY).

## Other sources:

*Press chapters*

- *Financial Times*, March 17, 2006, "Brand Communications: How Jamie Oliver is blurring the lines between advertising and entertainment"
- *The Independent*, January 14, 2005, "Naked truth about chef's baked beans on toast"
- *The National Business Rewiew*, February 17, 2006, "NZgirl's naked man ad hoax exposed"
- *The National Business Rewiew*, February 24, 2006, "Nzgirl comes clean on hoax campaign"
- *New Zealand Herald*, February 9, 2006, "They watched the sky and saw … nothing"

*Websites (all accessed on April 07, 2006)*

- Bait-and-tease campaigning New Zealand website nzgirls.com: *http://www.nzirl.co.nz*
- CBS's 60 minutes-show Undercover Marketing Uncovered: *http://www.cbs news.com/stories/2003/10/23/60minutes/main579657.shtml*
- Center for Media and Democracy (a consumer advocacy group keeping an eye on PR and advertising in corporate business): http://www.corpwatch. *org*, and which published the multimedia-report Fake TV News: Widespread and Undisclosed on April 06, 2006: http://www.prwatch.*org/ fakenews/release*
- Emanuel Rosen's Buzz Communication website: http://www.emanuel-rosen.com
- Jay Conrad Levinsson's Guerilla Marketing website: *http://www.gmarketing. com*
- The website of Ben McConnell and Jacki Huba, who published in 2003 the book Creating Customer Evangelists (Dearborn/Kaplan). The authors are business advisors and advisory board members of the Word of Mouth Association: *http://customerevangelists.com*
- Writers Guild of America: White Paper, cf. p. 107 Are you SEELLING to ME?: Stealth Advertising in the Entertainment Industry, published on November 14, 2005: *http://www.wga.org*

## Others:

- *Nzgirl does nothing, creates stir over BDO 'stunt'*, Press release from nzgirl. co.nz

# CHAPTER 6

# Stakeholder Communication Strategies[1]

*Mette Morsing & Majken Schultz*

*The acceptance – even embracing – of uncontrollability and inconsistency poses a significant challenge for the dialoguing organisation. Dialogue, by its nature (when it is genuine at least), takes time, is not efficient, cuts against hierarchical control, and does not assume a predetermined fixed understanding of how things (the world) are or what should be done.*

Andrew Crane & Sharon Livesey, 2003.

## Introduction

Messages about corporate ethical and socially responsible initiatives are likely to evoke strong and often positive reactions among stakeholders. Research has also pointed to the potential business benefits of the internal and external communication of corporate social responsibility (CSR) efforts (Maignan, Ferrel & Hult, 1999). However, while CSR is generally associated with positive corporate virtues (e.g. Johnson & Johnson, The Body Shop, Patagonia) and reflects an organization's status and activities with respect to its perceived societal obligations (Brown & Dacin, 1997), corporate CSR messages have also proven to attract critical attention (e.g. Starbuck, Shell, TDC). In fact, research shows that the more companies expose their ethical and social ambitions, the more likely they are to attract critical stakeholder attention (Vallentin, 2003; Ashforth & Gibbs, 1990). Other studies have triggered questions such as "if a company focuses too intently on communicating CSR associations, is it possible that consumers may believe that the company is trying to hide something?" (Brown & Dacin 1997, p. 81). Furthermore, stakeholder expectations regarding CSR are a moving target and must therefore be considered carefully on a continuous basis. While stakeholders previously directed negative attention primarily to particular industries (i.e. "sin stocks" of companies producing tobacco, alcohol, weapons, pornography, and so forth), CSR issues today have become more unpredictable and diverse, and involve, for example, child labour, GMOs (gene-modified organisms), hormones, union assembly rights or sweat shops, which in practice are concerns across many if not all industries. Furthermore, the number of CSR rankings and CSR surveillance institutions is increasing. Critical stakeholder attention is not restricted to a company's decisions and actions, but also to the decisions and actions of suppliers, consumers and politicians, which may spur criticism towards a company (e.g. Nike, Cheminova). In that sense, corporate CSR engagement today requires more sophisticated and ongoing stakeholder awareness and calls for more sophisticated CSR communication strategies than previously.

To increase our understanding of how managers can develop and maintain an ongoing awareness towards themselves and their environment, we argue, in line with others (Craig-Lees, 2001; Cramer, Jonker & van der Heiden, 2004), that the theory of sense-making is a fruitful approach to a better understanding of communication processes. Sense-making is inherently social (Weick, 1979), as we "make sense of things in organizations while in conversation with others, while reading communications from others, while exchanging ideas with others" (Nijhof & Jeurissen, 2006), implying that no manager or organisation make sense in splendid isolation (Craig-Lees, 2001). Yet the extent to which an individual – or an organisation – is able to integrate the sense-making of others will influence the individual's – or the organisation's – ability to strategically enact a productive relationship (Gioia et al., 1994). This implies that managers need to develop a sense of the organisation's internal and external environments (Thomas & McDaniel, 1990) and hereafter be willing to define a revised conception of the organisation. This process is what Gioia and Chittipeddi refer to as "interpretive work" (1991, p. 434) under the label "sense-making", i.e. trying to figure out what the others want and ascribe meaning to it. However, Gioia and Chittipeddi expand the notion of sense-making by introducing the concept of "sense-giving", putting a special focus on the managerial processes facilitating sense-making in organizations. According to Gioia and Chittipeddi, sense-making is followed by action in terms of articulating an abstract vision that is then disseminated and championed by corporate management to stakeholders in a process labelled "sense-giving", i.e. attempts to influence the way another party understands or makes sense. In contrast to Gioia and Chittipeddi, who have an internal focus on sense-giving and sense-making processes among managers and employees, we add an external focus as we suggest that by involving external stakeholders in corporate CSR efforts, managers and employees will also engage in the sense-giving and sense-making processes. Building on Gioia and Chittipeddi's terminology, we suggest that not only managers but also external stakeholders may more strongly support and contribute to corporate CSR efforts if they

137

engage in progressive iterations of sense-making and sense-giving processes, as this enhances awareness of mutual expectations.

Hence, this chapter outlines stakeholder theory with a focus on communication and, secondly, links stakeholder relations to the three CSR communication strategies proposed here: informing, responding and involving. Finally, the implications for managerial practice are discussed for those companies that want to communicate that they are ethical and socially responsible organisations. The chapter concludes by suggesting that communicating CSR introduces a new – and often overlooked – complexity to the relationship between sender and receiver of corporate CSR messages, which entails a managerial commitment to involving stakeholders in the ongoing sense-giving and sense-making processes.

### Stakeholder theory

While the stakeholder model was introduced to management theory many years ago by Freeman (1984), stakeholder management has developed into one of current management theory's most encompassing concepts (e.g. Donaldson & Preston, 1995; Mitchell, Agle & Wood, 1997; Stoney & Winstanley, 2001). Freeman's "stakeholder view of firm" (1984, p. 25) instrumentally defines a stakeholder as "any group or individual who can affect or is affected by the achievement of the firm's objectives" and he suggests that there is a need for "integrated approaches for dealing with multiple stakeholders on multiple issues" (1984, p. 26). While Freeman framed and demarcated stakeholders as elements of corporate strategic planning, he most importantly demonstrated the urgency of regarding stakeholders for the mission and purpose of the company, and in doing so, also suggested the positive financial implications of better relationships with stakeholders. Many other scholars have pursued exploration of the link between corporate social performance and financial performance, but the results are so far inconclusive (Margolis & Walsh, 2003).

In recent years stakeholder theory has emphasized the importance of engaging stakeholders in long-term value creation (Andriof et al., 2002). This is a process whose perspective focuses on developing a long-term mutual relationship rather than simply fo-

138

cusing on immediate profit. This does not imply that profit and economic survival are unimportant, but the process argument is that in order to profit and survive companies need to engage with a variety of stakeholders upon whom dependence is vital. The emphasis is moved from a focus on stakeholders being managed by companies to a focus on the interaction that companies have with their stakeholders based on a relational and process-oriented view (Andriof & Waddock, 2002, p. 19). This implies an increased interest in understanding how managers can manage not the stakeholders themselves, but relationships with stakeholders. As a result, this increases the scope of stakeholder relationships from public relations and marketing managers practicing their authority and communication skills to a strategic potential for all functional managers to relate to multiple stakeholders. Stakeholder relationships in this processual perspective are then a source of competitive advantage (Andriof & Waddock, 2002; Johnson-Cramer, Berman & Post, 2003; Post, Preston & Sachs, 2002) as those companies with strong relations to other organisations, institutions and partners are seen to be in a better position to develop relational rents through relation-specific assets, knowledge-sharing routines, complementary resource endowments and effective governance (Dyer & Singh, 1998).

The stakeholder relationship is assumed to consist of "interactive, mutually engaged and responsive relationships that establish the very context of doing modern business, and create the groundwork for transparency and accountability" (Andriof et al., 2002, p. 9). This brings the notion of participation, dialogue and involvement to the centre of stakeholder theory, with a clear inspiration (and aspiration) from democratic ideals. The implication is that while dialogue is the tool, agreement and consensus are most often regarded as the solution on which to base further decisions and action, and hence for the continuation of the collaboration. As argued by Johnson-Cramer, Berman & Post. "The essence of stakeholder dialogue is the co-creation of shared understanding by company and stakeholder." (2003, p. 149). Today, participation and dialogue have become a natural element of corporate self-presentations.

139

In the following, three CSR communication strategies are presented that cover the development from a classical monologue towards mutual and dialogue-based stakeholder relationships.

## Three CSR Communication strategies

Based on Grunig & Hunt's characterisation of models of public relations (1984), we unfold three types of stakeholder relations in terms of how companies strategically engage in CSR communication vis à vis their stakeholders, namely the "stakeholder information strategy", the "stakeholder response strategy" and the "stakeholder involvement strategy".

In 1984, public relations theory argued (Grunig & Hunt 1984, p. 22) that 50 % of all companies practiced one-way communication in terms of public information to their stakeholders, and only 35 % practiced two-way communication processes in terms of either two-asymmetric or two-way symmetric communication. This relates to the theory of sense-making in terms of public information building on processes of sense-giving, whereas two-way communication builds on processes of both sense-making *and* sense-giving. While some would agree that the prevalence of public information (sense-giving) is also a fairly accurate picture of corporate communication processes today, we suggest that there is an increasing need to develop sophisticated two-way communication processes (sense-making and sense-giving) when companies convey messages about CSR. While one-way information on corporate CSR initiatives is necessary, it is not enough for a company to build and maintain legitimacy.

The following is a presentation of the three CSR communication strategies: a one-way communication strategy, a two-way asymmetric communication strategy and a two-way symmetric communication strategy, each of which we relate to the processes of sense-giving and sense-making (Table 1).

**Table 1:** Three CSR communication strategies

| | The stakeholder information strategy | The stakeholder response strategy | The stakeholder involvement strategy |
|---|---|---|---|
| **Communication ideal:** (Grunig & Hunt, 1984) | Public information, one-way communication | Two-way asymmetric communication | Two-way symmetric communication |
| **Communication ideal: sense-making and sense-giving** | Sense-giving | Sense-making ⇩ Sense-giving | Sense-making ⇕ Sense-giving – in iterative progressive processes |
| **Stakeholders:** | Request more information on corporate CSR efforts | Must be reassured that the company is ethical and socially responsible | Co-construct corporate CSR efforts |
| **Stakeholder role:** | Stakeholder influence: support or oppose | Stakeholders respond to corporate actions | Stakeholders are involved, participate and suggest corporate actions |
| **Identification of CSR focus:** | Decided by top management | Decided by top management, Investigated in feedback via opinion polls, dialogue, networks and partnerships | Negotiated continuously in interaction with stakeholders |
| **Strategic communication task:** | Inform stakeholders about favourable corporate CSR decisions and actions | Demonstrate to stakeholders how the company integrates their concerns | Invite and establish frequent, systematic and pro-active dialogue with stakeholders, i.e. opinion makers, corporate critics, the media, etc. |
| **Corporate communication department's task** | Design appealing concept message | Identify relevant stakeholders | Build relationships |
| **Third party endorsement of CSR initiatives:** | Unnecessary | Integrated element of surveys, rankings and opinion polls | Stakeholders are themselves involved in corporate CSR messages |

141

## Stakeholder information strategy

In the "stakeholder information strategy", similar to Grunig and Hunt's public information model, communication is always one-way, from the organisation to its stakeholders. Communication is basically viewed as "telling, not listening" (Grunig & Hunt, 1984, p. 23), and therefore the one-way communication of the stakeholder information strategy has the purpose of disseminating information, not necessarily with a persuasive intent, but rather to inform the public as objectively as possible about the organisation. Companies adopting a stakeholder information model engage in active press relations programs and concurrently produce information and news for the media, as well as a variety of brochures, pamphlets, magazines, facts, numbers and figures to inform the general public. Governments, non-profit organisations and many businesses primarily use the public information model: The company "gives sense" to its audiences.

The stakeholder information model assumes that stakeholders are influential as they can either give support in terms of purchasing habits, showing loyalty and praising the company, or they can show opposition in terms of demonstrating or boycotting the company (Smith, 2003). Therefore, the company must inform stakeholders about its good intentions, decisions and actions to ensure positive stakeholder support. Quite a few companies engage in CSR initiatives because corporate managers believe it is morally "the right thing to do" (Paine, 2003), and this often sincere wish to improve social conditions in the local or global community support their stakeholder information strategy. Top management, confident the company is doing the right thing, believes the company just needs to inform the general public efficiently about what it is doing to build and maintain positive stakeholder support. One strategic task of stakeholder information strategies is to ensure that favourable corporate CSR decisions and actions are communicated effectively to the company's stakeholders. The task of the corporate communications department is to ensure that a coherent message is conveyed in an appealing way and that the focus is on the design of the concept message (van Riel, 1995), i.e. that the CSR message conveys, for

142

example, how the CSR initiatives demonstrate a generally shared concern, are linked to the core business and show organisational support (Scott & Lane, 2000). It is outside the realm of this strategy to consider that external stakeholders, i.e. third party stakeholders, should endorse corporate CSR initiatives. Trustworthy communication originates from the company itself.

### Stakeholder response strategy

The stakeholder response strategy is based on a "two-way asymmetric" communication model – as opposed to the two-way symmetric model of the stakeholder involvement strategy. In both models, communication flows to and from the public. But there is a conspicuous difference between the two models in that the two-way asymmetric assumes an imbalance from the effects of public relations in favour of the company, as the company does not change as a result of the public relations, rather the company attempts to change public attitudes and behaviour. Hence, the company needs to engage stakeholders by making the corporate decisions and actions relevant for them because the company needs the external endorsement from external stakeholders. The corporate communication department will typically conduct an opinion poll or a market survey to make sense of where the company has – hopefully – improved and can improve its CSR efforts. Communication is perceived as feedback in terms of finding out what the public will accept and tolerate. This is an evaluative mode of measuring whether a particular communication initiative has improved stakeholder understanding of the company – and vice versa. Corporate management will champion and "give sense" to its decisions according to the market survey results in which managers "make sense".

Although these communication processes are perceived as two-way methods in Grunig and Hunt's public relations models, we elaborate on their model as we stress that responding to stakeholders is still rather sender-oriented. The stakeholder response strategy is a predominantly one-sided approach, since the company has the sole intention of convincing its stakeholders of its attractiveness. We, therefore, highlight stakeholder responsive-

143

ness as a re-active strategy rather than a pro-active engagement in the communication processes. Stakeholders are perceived as being influential, but as passively responding to corporate initiatives. In a company's attempts to understand stakeholder concerns in a CSR perspective, it runs the risk of only hearing its own voice being reflected back; the company asks its stakeholders questions within a framework that invites predominantly the answers it wants to hear. What aspires to be a two-way-communication mechanism is really a one-way method of supporting and reinforcing corporate actions and identity. As the stakeholder response strategy is a frequently used communication model within CSR communication, and as many CSR initiatives assume stakeholder sensitivity, we find this latter point important, and will therefore return to it in the discussion.

**Stakeholder involvement strategy**
The stakeholder involvement strategy, in contrast, assumes a dialogue with its stakeholders. Persuasion may occur, but it comes from stakeholders as well as from the organisation itself, each trying to persuade the other to change. Ideally, the company as well as its stakeholders will change as a result of engaging in a symmetric communication model, i.e. progressive iterations of sensemaking and sense-giving processes. Because stakeholder involvement strategy takes the notion of the stakeholder relationship to an extreme, companies should not only influence but also seek being influenced by stakeholders, and therefore change when necessary.

Rather than imposing a particular CSR initiative on stakeholders, the stakeholder involvement strategy invites continuous negotiations with its stakeholders to explore their concerns vis à vis the company, while also accepting changes when they are necessary. By engaging in a dialogue with stakeholders, the company ideally ensures not only that it keeps abreast of its stakeholders' changing expectations, but also of its potential influence on those expectations, as well as letting those expectations influence and change the company itself.

144

The stakeholder involvement strategy is in harmony with the stakeholder information strategy in the assumption that stakeholders are influential in terms of their support of or opposition to the company, and concurs with the stakeholder response strategy in that stakeholder expectations should be investigated using survey methods. The involvement strategy, however, further assumes that while informing and surveying is necessary, it is not sufficient. Stakeholders need to be involved in order to develop and promote positive support as well as for the company to understand and concurrently adapt to their concerns, i.e. to develop its CSR initiatives. Therefore, the stakeholder involvement strategy suggests that companies engage frequently and systematically in a dialogue with their stakeholders in order to explore mutually beneficial action – assuming that both parties involved in the dialogue are willing to change. We shall later exemplify how such a dialogue may be employed in practice.

In organisational practice, the primary top managerial task in the stakeholder involvement strategy becomes one of ensuring that the organisation is capable of establishing a concurrent and systematic interaction with multiple stakeholders. The communication task becomes one of ensuring a two-way dialogue (Grunig & Hunt, 1984) in an almost Habermasian[2] sense, in which the primary aim is to bring about mutual understanding, rational agreement, or consent. Since no top management is capable of engaging in dialogue with multiple stakeholders nonstop, the organisational implication is an "integrated form" (Weaver, Trevino & Cochran, 1999) of stakeholder-thinking in which the corporate CSR program depends on its ability to integrate not only organisational members' CSR concerns, but also to integrate stakeholders' CSR concerns in a continuous dialogue. Corporate policies dictating what organisational units can and cannot do with respect to certain stakeholder groups are "sure to fail to establish successful transactions with the stakeholder, no matter how well intentioned the policy" (Freeman, 1984, p. 162), since they neither motivate nor integrate changing expectations.

While these three CSR communication strategies have been presented to underline the increased necessity for managers to in-

145

corporate learning and techniques to support more stakeholder involvement, there is only little evidence that two-way communication processes are the norm being practiced. In the following, we discuss this apparent corporate hesitation and the challenges of engaging in two-way communication processes.

## Discussion

In this section we draw on prior research on communication and the concepts of sense-giving and sense-making, as we discuss how corporate managers may improve their stakeholder relations as they communicate their CSR activities in terms of (1) pointing at CSR information as a double-edged sword, (2) non-financial reports as a means for subtle CSR communication, and (3) involving stakeholders in CSR communication as a pro-active endorsement.

### *CSR information – a double-edged sword*

In line with empirical studies on CSR communication (Lawrence, 2002; Lingard, 2006; Windsor, 2002) as well as older (Arnstein, 1969) and more recent (Smith, 2003) theoretical debate on stakeholders and stakeholder participation, we contend that corporate CSR initiatives are considered important by the general public. However, it is unclear how companies should communicate their CSR initiatives: in corporate advertising, corporate campaigns or in minimal releases such as annual reports and websites, or some other channel. On the one hand, companies are inclined to concentrate on developing efficient one-way communication, i.e. to "give sense" to stakeholders about corporate CSR efforts. According to Grunig & Hunt (1984), this is the most preferred way of engaging with stakeholders. On the other hand, corporate managers also seem to avoid communicating CSR efforts too conspicuously.

The hesitation to communicate CSR efforts in corporate campaigns is supported by Ashforth & Gibbs' discussion (1990) on the legitimacy risks for those companies that are perceived as over-accentuating their good deeds. Ashforth and Gibbs' analysis also suggests a preference for communicating CSR initiatives through

146

minimal releases as they argue that conspicuous attempts to increase legitimacy may in fact decrease legitimacy. Ashforth & Gibbs refer to this as the challenge of the "self promoter's paradox" (1990, p. 188) which suggests that companies that overemphasise their corporate legitimacy run the risk of achieving the opposite effect. They argue that conspicuous CSR communication often is associated with and stem from organisations that attempt to defend their corporate legitimacy or from companies that have experienced a legitimacy problem: "the more problematic the legitimacy, the greater the protestation of legitimacy" (Ashforth & Gibbs, 1990, p. 185). Too much "sense-giving" regarding CSR efforts may then be counter-productive. It is, therefore, argued that companies already perceived as legitimate constituents do not need to communicate their CSR efforts loudly. With reference to impression management, Ashforth and Gibbs suggest that individuals who believe that others are aware of their desirable qualities tend to be less self-aggrandizing than individuals who do not. If companies are not granted positive recognition from their stakeholders, they tend to find it necessary not only to exemplify desirable qualities, but also to promote them. Thus the promotion of desirable qualities such as CSR will tend to evoke scepticism if a company is stigmatized beforehand with a bad reputation or if a company is experiencing a legitimacy threat such as a corporate scandal. While Ashforth and Gibbs take this argument to one extreme by pointing at companies with a legitimacy problem, we extend their argument by suggesting that contemporary companies increasingly need to prepare for potential legitimacy problems.

As argued in the introduction, CSR is a moving target. Some years ago, CSR had narrower and more well-defined limits, whereas today any globally operating company may in principle be associated with the violation of for example human rights or animal rights, as companies increasingly are held responsible for their suppliers' or customers' actions. Any company may in fact encounter legitimacy problems at some point. On the one hand, informing about CSR initiatives may be a means of preparing to avoid such a legitimacy problem by informing stakeholders about

147

corporate CSR initiatives. On the other hand, CSR communication may in fact provoke a legitimacy problem if a company encounters a stakeholder concern about its legitimacy. Information on CSR initiatives may then retrospectively be perceived as a means of covering-up or accommodating for the legitimacy problem, which in turn reinforces stakeholder scepticism towards CSR initiatives and corporate legitimacy. Hence, a straightforward "stakeholder information strategy" turns out to have a double edge.

*A means towards subtle communication: non-financial reports*
Second, prior research has argued that implicit forms of communication such as organisational rituals and folklore are perceived to be more credible than explicit forms such as press releases and policy statements (Martin, 1992). This argument suggests that CSR communication will be perceived as more plausible if it is indirect and subtle, such as, for example, in the presentation of quantitative achievements and "objective data" in non-financial reports.

Yet, potential regional differences must be considered. Scholars have pointed to certain cross-cultural differences in the type of responsibilities that stakeholders assign to and appreciate to businesses (Maignan & Ferrell, 2003). Maignan and Ferrell's study shows that French and German businesses were not as concerned as US-based companies about communicating CSR activities on corporate websites (Maignan & Ralston, 2002). The explicit North American CSR approach (Matten & Moon, 2004) with its strong tradition for philanthropic giving and high expectations to corporate CSR efforts, seems to encourage stakeholders to welcome more conspicuous CSR communication than in the European context – including the Scandinavian one – with its traditions for more implicit and less conspicuous CSR approaches.

Nevertheless, while non-financial reports with "objective data" may be used as a type of "subtle CSR communication", they are still predominantly designed as a means to "give sense" to potentially critical stakeholders. They are produced to inform and convince public audiences about corporate legitimacy, and as such,

148

they are framed within a one-way communication perspective. In addition, they may be illusory as they may possibly lead managers to conclude that they control meanings and perceptions among stakeholders (Crane & Livesey, 2003).

Non-financial reports may seem an appropriate response and "sense-giving" tool for making stakeholders aware of corporate CSR efforts, but, as we would like to point out, they also raise the potential risk of organisational self-absorption. Organisational communication research has shown that one of the major risks for communication in practice is that corporate managers publish the information which they themselves find important, taking pride in what is presented, and therefore also believe it is what other stakeholders want to hear (Morgan, 1999; Christensen & Cheney, 2000) Prior research has pointed to the risk of self-fulfilling prophecies in market surveys and opinion polls (Christensen, 1997). In the case where managers are to communicate issues of social responsibility to stakeholders, managers may be tempted to reinforce information on issues they themselves identify with and take a pride in regardless of stakeholder concerns, because social responsibility often implies a personal moral designation for managers (Lozano, 1996; Pruzan, 1998). The risk is that in deciding what CSR issues to communicate and how to do it, managers become what Christensen & Cheney refer to as "self-seduced and self-absorbed" (2000), not realizing that other stakeholders may be uninterested in the information presented, and more importantly, that other stakeholders may not find it appropriate for companies to publish information on how good they are. To avoid this trap of self-absorbed CSR communication, close collaboration with stakeholders on the relevance of what CSR issues to emphasize and report on may possibly increase organisational awareness regarding stakeholder expectations. This dialogue contributes to the identification of potentially critical issues of importance for corporate legitimacy and a company's reputation.

One example illustrating our argument is demonstrated in the encouragement to involve stakeholders, which is increasingly used as an argument for giving awards for best non-financial reporting. For instance, the European Sustainability Reporting

149

Awards (ESRA) emphasises stakeholder relations as a separate criteria for the reports to demonstrate, "Stakeholder relationships (e.g.: basis for definition and selection of major stakeholders, approaches to stakeholder consultation, type of information generated by stakeholder consultations, use of stakeholder feedback)." (ESRA, 2005, p. 4). Our contention is that reporting on stakeholder involvement may be done with or without real stakeholder involvement, but that the latter form, actively involving stakeholders in sense-making and sense-giving processes on CSR issues, is a more promising path as opposed to emphasising "sense-giving" in engaging stakeholders by eloquent persuasion. In the following section, we further explore how to involve stakeholders pro-actively.

### Involving stakeholders in CSR communication: pro-active endorsement

We suggest that communicating messages that claim to represent a true image of corporate initiatives such as CSR will benefit from a pro-active third party endorsement, i.e. that external stakeholders express their support of corporate CSR initiatives. This implies that managers need to understand how to carefully enact the dynamic processes of sense-giving and sense-making in order to develop the endorsement in practice. Further, we suggest that this happens during the development of corporate CSR efforts, and for this purpose, some companies have already demonstrated how non-financial reporting holds a potentially promising tool for managing some of the complexity of CSR communication. Today, however, many non-financial reports are still expressions of a sophisticated yet conventional "stakeholder information strategy" or "stakeholder response strategy" (see for example, the SAS Group's Annual Report & Sustainability Report, KMD's Strategic Report 2004; and Novozymes' Annual Integrated Report 2004). While these corporate non-financial reports inform about stakeholder relations and demonstrate engagement in stakeholder concerns, it is most often done through a simple listing of the partners with whom the company interacts on an infrequent basis (see e.g. Danisco 2004, SAS 2004). Shell's "People, Planet and Profit" from 2003, and Brown & Williamson Tobacco's "Social and Environmental Report 2001/2" are other examples of companies demonstrating that they are aware of the importance of stakeholder dialogue. Brown and Williamson Tobacco writes, for example: "Here we outline some steps we have taken to help us to ensure we manage the dialogue and reporting process with the same level of commitment as any other aspect of the business" (2001/2: 38). In addition, BNFL states that "It is our aim to talk openly about issues that concern you, our stakeholders".

While these companies state how much they acknowledge the importance of stakeholder dialogue, stakeholders are not given a voice in those reports. We would like to point out the potential of developing a more pro-active commitment by external stakeholders, as we draw on Gioia and Chittipeddi's notion of sense-giving and sense-making. In the following examples, we show the involvement of external stakeholders in these processes, arguing that there are benefits from developing and maintaining stakeholder relationships by inviting external stakeholders to critically raise CSR concerns in public in collaboration with the company.

Novo Nordisk, a pharmaceutical company in the business of diabetes treatment, is among the most highly reputed companies in Denmark. Novo Nordisk's non-financial reporting is an inspiring and sophisticated example of how a company has managed to handle its CSR communication challenges in a manner that approaches the two-way symmetric model as outlined in the "stakeholder involvement strategy". In 2002, Novo Nordisk began involving stakeholders in the actual reporting. Critical and highly-involved stakeholders were given a voice in the report, as they were invited to comment and critique on issues which they perceived as being of particular concern in their relations with Novo Nordisk. For example, Søren Brix Christensen of "Doctors without Frontiers" was given a page under the heading, "How can we improve the access to diabetes treatment by selling our products at prices affordable in the developing countries, while we maintain a profitable business?" (Novo Nordisk Sustainability Report 2002, p. 27), to express that he strongly believes that the medical industry needs to take responsibility and sell medicine at cost price. In a similar set-up in 2003, Lars Georg Jensen, programme coordinator for global policy in the Danish chapter of the World Wide Fund for Nature, critically addressed the question of "How can we be focused on investing in the health of society and yet not compromise the need to invest in the global environment?" (Novo Nordisk Sustainability Report 2003, p. 47). A number of managers and employees were also given a voice in the non-financial reports, but giving loyal members a voice remains a more conventional and less risky communication mechanism than inviting critical external stakeholders to comment and critique on shared concerns within the frame of CSR. By inviting external stakeholders inside, so to speak, Novo Nordisk opens the possibility for new issues to emerge and become integrated, hence inviting a concurrent reconstruction of the CSR efforts as stakeholder concerns develop and change. Although the communication is of course controlled from Novo Nordisk's corporate headquarters, it nevertheless allows controversial dilemmas for Novo Nordisk's core business to surface.

Another example of the pro-active involvement of stakeholders is Vodafone's social report from 2004, which demonstrates how the company involves the capital market, the public, opinion makers and customers in identifying critical issues and actions by bringing these voices into the report. Rather than being communicated to, the critical stakeholders become co-responsible for the corporate CSR messages, as they locally articulate their shared concern vis á vis the company. Instead of imposing corporate norms for CSR initiatives on stakeholders, the invitation to participate and co-construct the corporate CSR message increases the likelihood that these stakeholders and those who identify with them will identify positively with the company.

The external endorsement of corporate CSR messages differentiates itself from other endorsement strategies in the sense that critical issues come to the surface. Rather than giving a completely positive and almost saintly impression of corporate CSR initiatives, which may evoke scepticism, Vodafone communicates that it acknowledges that the company has a way to go yet, but that it is trying to act more socially responsible by taking stakeholder concerns into consideration. Vodafone reports on controversial issues of great importance for its business, such as electromagnetism and health, responsible marketing, inappropriate content, junk mail, and so forth. In addition, Vodafone brings critical survey results as well. Similarly, Novo Nordisk brings issues such as obesity, the distribution of wealth, poverty and health and hormones in their report. Many of these issues are reported and commented on by external stakeholders.

By letting critical stakeholders have their own comments in the reports, Novo Nordisk and Vodafone indicate that they listen to stakeholders, and that they dare to bring forward stakeholders' concerns in their public annual report.

Concerns about the corporate motives behind such invitations to participation and public dialogue were raised already many years ago and it pointed at the inequalities of the partners and the power-play of the strategic dialogue. Based on studies of federal community programmes, Arnstein warned that "participation without redistribution of power is an empty and frustrating process for the powerless" (Arnstein, 1969, p. 216). He argues that participation can cover a broad range of graduations of participation, from manipulation to citizen control (in what he labels a "ladder of citizen control"), and that no matter what practical reality participation is enacted in, the underlying issue is the same: "Nobodies" attempting to become "somebodies" with enough power to make the target institutions responsive to their views, aspirations and needs. As an extension of Arnstein's ladder typology, it has also recently been argued that while dialogue can be beneficial for all constituents if they are genuinely motivated for dialogue, participation and dialogue can also be expensive, time-consuming and, in fact, lead to counterproductive activities that does not build trust, facilitate collaboration or enhance the value of the corporation. Similarly, Crane and Livesey question the assumption that more involvement and dialogue leads to more understanding. They argue that dialogue may lead to cynicism and distrust when it is "instrumentally and superficially employed" and not "genuinely adopted" (Crane & Livesey, 2003, p. 40).

153

While we can only agree with these concerns about the risks of the exploitation of stakeholders and other malfunctions connected to participation, dialogue and stakeholder involvement – and in fact, to the whole democratic project – we also question how one is to know *when* stakeholders are "genuinely motivated for dialogue" and *when* dialogue is "instrumentally and superficially employed" as opposed to "genuinely adopted". Most importantly, we argue that the way organisations give and make sense about themselves and their practices are not neutral activities, but constitutive actions that contribute to the continuous enactment of the organisational reality (Weick, 1979). From that perspective, the communicative strategies of stakeholder involvement and dialogue contributes to the enactment of such involvement, creating more awareness of the critical potential of business-stakeholder relations. It can be argued that the "stakeholder involvement strategy" is an ideal, and that neither Novo Nordisk nor Vodafone are examples of "genuine" two-way symmetric communication, and that no sustainability report can ever be an expression of real two-way symmetric communication. Yet, we contend that *striving* towards stakeholder involvement and an improved mutual understanding of stakeholder expectations towards business and vice versa, are crucial elements in its enactment. In this process, CSR communication is a forceful player for all partners.

**Conclusion**

Our chapter has built on the recent development of theories on stakeholder management and critically drawn on public relations theory in the development of three strategies for CSR communication in order to better conceptualize how managers inform, respond to and involve important stakeholders. In line with this development of stakeholder theories, it is our main contention that stakeholder involvement becomes increasingly more important for ensuring that a company stays in tune with changing stakeholder expectations. CSR is a moving target, making it increasingly necessary to adapt to and change according to shifting stakeholder expectations, but also to influence those expectations.

In particular, we focus on three areas of strategic importance for managers as they embark on CSR communication. First, the general assumption that managers need to improve their corporate "stakeholder information strategy" to keep the general public better informed about CSR initiatives to achieve legitimacy and good reputations is challenged. Such a communication strategy has a narrow focus on sense-giving and runs the risk of the "self-promoter's paradox". Second, we point at the increasing importance of subtle CSR communication such as annual reports and websites as a more appropriate and sensitive means of CSR communication rather than corporate advertising or corporate CSR campaigns. However, we suggest that such minimal releases would benefit from responding to, and even more extensively involving, stakeholders directly in a mutual construction of CSR communication. Although such a communication strategy is minimal in terms of number of channels and public exposure, it allows maximum flexibility and a strong focus on content. As a result, we suggest that communicating messages claiming to represent corporate CSR initiatives, would benefit from a third party endorsement, i.e. external stakeholders becoming involved and expressing their support – and concern – of corporate CSR initiatives in actual corporate CSR messages by taking an active part in both the sense-giving and the sense-making process.

### Where do we go from here?
While we have critically examined the "stakeholder information strategy" and the "stakeholder response strategy", we point out that these strategies should not be underestimated. Companies must "give sense" as well as "make sense". We suggest, however, that there is an increasing need for managers to be able to handle the simultaneous interdependency between these strategies and to engage in new and more complex relations with their stakeholders, and that this includes involving these stakeholders in actual corporate CSR communication. We propose that managers

and students of CSR communication in particular need to address the following issues:

- Which CSR communication strategy do you encounter most often from companies? Why?
- What do you see as the advantages and the risks of the stake-holder involvement strategy?
- Do external stakeholders want to be involved in corporate CSR communication? Why? Why not?

## References

Andriof, J. & Waddock, S., (2002). "Unfolding stakeholder engagement". In: Andriof, J., Waddock, S., Husted, B. & Rahman, S.S., (eds.) *"Unfolding stakeholder Thinking. Theory, Responsibility and Engagement"*. Sheffield: Greenleaf Publishing, 19-42

Andriof, J., S. Waddock., Husted, B. & Rahman, S.S. (eds.). (2002). *Unfolding Stakeholder Thinking. Theory, Responsibility and Engagement*. Sheffield: Greenleaf Publishing

Arnstein, S.R. (1969). "A ladder of citizen participation". *Journal of the American Institute of Planners* 35, 216-224.

Ashforth, B.E. & Gibbs, B.W. (1990). 'The double-edge of organizational legitimation'. *Organization Science* 1:2, 177-194

Brown, T. J., & Dacin, P.A. (1997). "The company and the product: Corporate associations and consumer product responses". *Journal of Marketing*, 61(1), 68-84.

Christensen, L.T. & Cheney, G. (2000). "Self-absorption and Self-seduction in the Corporate Identity Game". In Hatch, M.J., Schultz, M. & Larsen, M.H. (eds.), *The Expressive Organization*: 256-270. Oxford: Oxford University Press

Christensen, L.T. (1997). "Marketing as auto-communication". *Consumption, Markets and Culture*. 1:3, 197-227

Craig-Lees, M. (2001). "Sense making: Trojan horse? Pandora's box?. *Psychology & Marketing*, 18:5, 513-526

Crane, A. & Livesey, L. (2003). "Are you talking to me? Stakeholder communication and the risks and rewards of dialogue". In Andriof, J., Waddock, S. Husted, B. & Rahman, S.S. (eds.). *"Unfolding Stakeholder Thinking. Relationships, Communication,* Reporting *and Performance"*: 14-38. Sheffield: Greenleaf Publishing

Cramer, J., J. Jonker & van der Heijden, A. (2004). "Making sense of corporate social responsibility", *Journal of Business Ethics*, 55: 215-222

Donaldson, T. & Preston, L.E. (1995). "The stakeholder theory of the corporation: Concepts, evidence and implications". *Academy of Management Review*, 29: January, 65-91.

Dyer, J.H. & Singh, H. (1998). "The relational view: Cooperative strategy and sources of inter-organizational competitive advantage". *Strategic* Management *Journal*, 23:4, 660-679

ESRA, European Sustainability Reporting Awards (2003). Report of the Judges. For more info contact Flemming Tost (ft@hlrevision.dk)

Freeman, R.E. (1984). *"Strategic* Management. *A Stakeholder Approach"*. Marshfield, MA: Pitman.

Gioia, D.A. & Chittipeddi, K. (1991). "Sensemaking and sensegiving in strategic change initiation". *Strategic Management Journal*, vol. 12:6, 433-448.

Gioia, D.A., Thomas, J.B., Clark, S.M. & Chittipeddi, K. (1994). "Symbolism and strategic change in academia: the dynamics of sensemaking and influence". *Organization Science*, vol. 5:3, 363-383.

Grunig, J.E. & Hunt, T. (1984). "Managing Public Relations. Fort Worth: Harcourt Brace Jovanovich College Publishers.

Johnson-Cramer, M.E., Berman, S.L. & Post, J.E. (2003), "Re-examining the concept of "stakeholder management". In: In: Andriof, J., Waddock, S., Husted, B. & Rahman, S.S. (eds.) *"Unfolding Stakeholder Thinking. Relationships, Communication, Reporting and* Performance*"*: 145-161. Sheffield: Greenleaf Publishing

Lawrence, A.T. (2002). "The drivers of stakeholder engagement: reflections on the case of Royal Dutch/Shell". In: Andriof, J., Waddock, S. Husted, B. & S.S. Rahman (eds.). *"Unfolding Stakeholder Thinking. Theory, Responsibility and Engagement"*: 185-2000. Sheffield: Greenleaf Publishing

Lingard, T. (2006). "Creating a corporate responsibility culture. The approach of Unilever UK". In: Kakabadse, A. and M. Morsing (eds.) *"Corporate Social Responsibility. Reconciling Aspiration with Application"*, 86-104. London: Palgrave Macmillan

Lozano, J. M., (1996). "Ethics and management: a controversial issue". *Journal of Business Ethics*, 15, 227-236

Maignan, I. & Ferrell, O.C. (2003). "Nature of corporate responsibilities. Perspectives from American, French, and German consumers". *Journal of Business Research*, 56, 55-67

Maignan, I., Ferrell, O.C. & Hult, G.T.M. (1999). "Corporate citizenship: Cultural antecendets and business benefits". *Journal of the Academy of Marketing Science*, 27:4, 455-469

Maignan, I. & Ralston, D. (2002). "Corporate social responsibility in Europe and the US: Insights from businesses' self-presentations". *Journal of International Business Studies*, 33, 497-514.

Margolis, J.D. & Walsh, J.P. (2003). "Misery *loves companies:Rethinking social initiatives by business"*. Administrative Science Quarterly, vol. 48, no. z, 268-305.

Martin, J. (1992). "Cultures in Organizations. Three Perspectives". New York: Oxford University Press.

Matten, D. & Moon, J. (2004). "A conceptual framework for understanding CSR". In Habisch, A., Jonker, J. Wegner, M. & Schmidpeter, R. (eds.) *Corporate Social Responsibility Across Europe*: 335-356. Berlin: Springer Verlag

Mitchell, R.K., Agle, B. & Wood, D. (1997). "Toward a stakeholder identification and salience: Defining the principle of who and what really counts". *Academy of Management Review*, 22:4, 853-886

Morgan, A. (1999). *Eating the Big Fish.* How *"Challenger Brands" can Compete Against Brand Leaders.* New York: John Wiley & Sons Inc.

158

Nijhof, A., Fisscher, O. & Honders, H. (2006). "Sustaining competences for corporate social responsibility: a sensemaking perspective". *Working Chapter,* Enschede: University of Twente

Novo Nordisk's Sustainability Report. (2002). *"Sustainability Report"*

Novo Nordisk Sustainability Report. (2003). *"What Does Being There Mean to You?"*

Paine, L. S. (2003). *Value Shift. Why Companies Must Merge Social and Financial Imperatives to Achieve Superior Performance.* MacGraw-Hill: New York

Post, J.E., Preston, L.E. & Sachs, S. (2002). *Redefining the Corporation, Stakeholder Management and Organizational Wealth.* Stanford University Press: Stanford

Pruzan, P. (1998). "From control to values-based management and accountability". *Journal of Business Ethics,* vol. 17

Scott, S.G. & Lane, V. R. (2000). "A stakeholder approach to organizational identity". *Academy of Management Review.* 25:1, 43-62

Smith, N. C. (2003). "Corporate social responsibility: whether or how? *California Management Review,* 45:4, 52-73

Stoney, C. & Winstanley, D. (2001). "Stakeholding: confusion or utopia? Mapping the conceptual terrain". *Journal of Management Studies.* 38:5, 603-626

Thomas, J.B. & McDaniel, R.R. (1990). "Interpreting strategic issues: Effects of strategy and top management team information processing structure. *Academy of Management Journal,* 33, 286-306

Van Riel, C.B.M. (1995). *Principles of Corporate Communication.* London: Prentice Hall.

Vallentin, S. (2003). *Pensionsinvesteringer,* etik *og offentlighed – en systemteoretisk analyse af offentlig meningsdannelse.* København: Samfundslitteratur

Weaver, G.R., Trevino, L.K. & Cochran, P.L. (1999). 'Integrated and Decoupled Corporate Social Performance: Management Commitments, External Pressures, and Corporate Ethics Practices'. *Academy of* Management *Journal,* 42:5, 539-552.

Weick, K. (1979). *"The Social Psychology of Organizing".* Reading, MA: Addison-Wesley

Windsor, D. (2002). "Stakeholder responsibilities: lessons for managers". In Andriof, J., S. Waddock, B. Husted and S.S. Rahman (eds.). *"Unfolding Stakeholder Thinking. Theory, Responsibility and Engagement"*: 137-154. Sheffield: Greenleaf Publishing.

## Notes

1. This chapter is a based on: "CSR Communication: Information, Response and Involvement Strategies", Business Ethics: A European Review (BEER), vol. 4, 2006. We would like to thank Blackwell Publishing as well as Chris Cowton,

editor of BEER and professor André Nijhof, special issue editor for granting us permission to publish a shortened version of the chapter for this book.

2. Sociologist Jürgen Habermas developed the idea of discourse ethics in which all stakeholders must engage and be heard in an equal and power-free dialogue in order to promote democracy. In a well-known quote he states that, "At any given moment we orient ourselves by this idea that we endeavor to ensure that (1) all voices in any way relevant get a hearing, (2) the best argument available to us given our present state of knowledge are brougtht to bear, and (3) only the unforced force of a better argument determines the 'yes' and 'no' responses of the participants." (Jürgen Habermas, Justification and Application, 1993:163)

# Communicating with Stakeholders about CSR

# CHAPTER 7

# Consumers' perceptions of and responses to CSR: So little is known so far

*Suzanne C. Beckmann*

*How selfish soever man may be supposed,*
*there are evidently some principles in his nature,*
*which interests him in the fortune of others, and render*
*their happiness necessary to him, though he derives*
*nothing from it except the pleasure of seeing it.*

Adam Smith, The Theory of Moral Sentiments, 1759

### Consumers as stakeholders

Why do consumers perform altruistic acts such as financial contributions to charitable organizations, paying more for environmentally responsible products or even donating organs? One explanation is the human desire to experience a "warm glow" (Andreoni, 1990), which contradicts the traditional economists' view of people as selfish utility maximizers. But do consumers also experience a "warm glow" vis-à-vis companies that perform altruistic acts and reward them, thus leading to enhanced corporate reputation, brand image and customer loyalty?

One of the central arguments in favour of corporate commitment to and engagement in social responsibilities is providing a "yes"-answer to this question. It is embedded in the general stakeholder argument: a socially responsible company is supposed to address the concerns and satisfy the demands of its main stakeholders (e.g., Donaldson & Preston, 1995; Jones, 1995; Maignan, Ferrell & Hult, 1999; Waddock, 2000) – those actors who can, directly or indirectly, affect, or be affected by, corporate activities such as customers, suppliers, employees, shareholders, the media, investors, regulators, and interest organisations (cf., Freeman, 1984).

Consumers are definitely one of the key stakeholders of companies in the marketing exchange process (Folkes & Kamins, 1999; Hunt & Vitell, 1992). However, research addressing the relationships between CSR activities and consumers-as-stakeholders' perceptions, attitudes and behaviours is so far quite underresearched. Moreover – as will be seen below – the few studies investigating consumers and marketing management in this context are concerned with a wide and not necessarily coherent range of issues. Additionally, studies explicitly investigating consumers' responses to the communication of CSR are scarce, while some research more implicitly addresses consumer responses or non-responses often conceptualized as brand evaluations or purchase intentions.

Consequently, this chapter addresses the central question of what we know so far as to when, why and how consumers respond to which CSR activities? This assessment will then be used

164

to identify crucial research issues that are of specific relevance for organisations willing to engage in CSR activities and interested in communicating their engagement to one or more of their main stakeholders. A brief introduction to the history of CSR-related thinking in consumer and marketing management research provides the background necessary to understand the currents status of affairs.

**Old wine in new bottles?**
Traditionally, and put very simply, marketing managers have conceptualised marketing performance in terms of sales, profit, and/or market share goals in relation to a particular product or service within a particular time period, taking a shareholder perspective. However, a stakeholder perspective is increasingly gaining ground, and companies have been put under growing pressure to exhibit good corporate citizenship in each country in which they operate (Pinkston & Carroll, 1994), both in marketing and general managerial terms. Public discourse indicates that companies today are more than ever supposed to fulfil their economic, legal, ethical, and discretionary obligations not only vis-à-vis their shareholders but increasingly also towards employees, customers, other stakeholders, and the community at large (Sen & Bhattacharya, 2001). Corporate social responsibility (CSR) has thus become a popular concept with practitioners as well as academics (Brown & Dacin, 1997; Handelman & Arnold, 1999; Osterhus, 1997) and it is strongly advocated that CSR activities should be regarded as the entry ticket to doing business in the $21^{st}$ century (e.g., Altman, 1998).

However, this suggestion is by no means new. Both the management and marketing literature have discussed social responsibility for many decades, dating back to at least the 1930s in the USA (e.g., Berle & Means, 1932). Especially the 1960s and 1970s witnessed a strong interest that re-surfaced in regular intervals until to date. For instance, Austin (1965) argued that business leadership had to appraise the social effects of its strategic policy decisions and technological advances, not least to prevent too much governmental interference through regulations. Along similar

165

lines, Grether suggested in 1969 that social involvement of private business was necessary and should occur through the open competitive market system, thus meeting the requirements of both social performance and competitive market performance: "Inevitably, large, diversified national and multinational corporations interlinked so broadly and deeply at so many levels carry very heavy social responsibilities" (p. 41). In (West) Germany, the discussion of companies' social responsibility can be traced back to the 1970s, for instance with Ulrich's concept of the firm as quasi-public institution (1977), and resulted in "External Social Reporting" (Brockhoff, 1979; Dierkes, 1974) long before "Ethical auditing" was introduced in Denmark. And the US Council on Economic Priorities published in 1986 what they called in the subtitle "A provocative guide to the companies behind the products you buy every day" (Lydenberg et al., 1986).

Similar interest and concerns were raised in the marketing literature. For instance, Lazer (1969) called for a much broader understanding of the marketing concept that sees marketing responsibilities extending beyond the profit realm and as "an institution of social control instrumental in reorienting a culture from a producer's to a consumer's culture" (p. 3) – a perspective that later found resonance in the concept of market orientation (Jaworski & Kohli, 1993; Kohli & Jaworski, 1990). Similarly, Lavidge (1970) claimed that marketing not only had become broader in function and scope, but was increasingly confronted with requests to redress irresponsibilities. He also underlined the dynamics of requirements: "... history suggests that standards will be raised. Some practices which today are generally considered acceptable will gradually be viewed as unethical, then immoral, and will eventually be made illegal" (p. 25) – a statement that certainly holds true if one looks at the past three decades since.

Another strand of the marketing literature was concerned with social marketing, i.e., the applicability of marketing concepts to the advancement of social causes (e.g., Kelley, 1971; Kotler & Zaltman, 1971). Along similar lines, cause-related marketing became a popular topic, defined as the "the process of formulating and implementing marketing activities that are characterized by

166

an offer from the firm to contribute a specified amount to a designated cause when customers engage in revenue-providing exchanges that satisfy organizational and individual objectives (Varadarajan & Menon, 1988, p. 60; see also Cornwell & Smith, 2001; Lafferty & Goldsmith, 2005; Strahilevitz, 1999). The 1980s and 1990s then saw a more managerial approach to marketing, social responsibility and business ethics (e.g., Drumwright, 1994; Robin & Reidenbach, 1987; for a meta-analysis of the marketing and consumer research literature with focus on environmental issues see Kilbourne & Beckmann (1998).

The marketing literature mainly uses the same understanding of the rationale of CSR as do other disciplines: a socially responsible company is supposed to address the concerns and satisfy the demands of its main stakeholders (e.g., Donaldson & Preston, 1995; Jones, 1995; Maignan, Ferrell & Hult, 1999; Waddock, 2000) – those actors who can, directly or indirectly, affect, or be affected by, corporate activities such as customers, suppliers, employees, shareholders, the media, investors, regulators, and interest organisations. However, what elements actually constitute CSR is less agreed upon, stretching from Carroll's (1998) "four faces of corporate citizenship" embracing economic, legal, ethical and philanthropic components to Lantos (2001, 2002) who argues for rejecting altruistic (philanthropic) CSR, but including ethical and strategic objectives of CSR.

## Mapping the field

Again, a brief historical overview assists in understanding the roots of the consumer perspective on CSR. Similar to the management and marketing literature, consumer behaviour studies – in the Anglo-Saxon literature – can be traced back to the 1970s, most of them referring to Berkowitz's & Lutterman's (1968) profiling of the "traditional socially responsible personality." Typical for the marketing interest at that time, most studies focused on first demographic, later also sociographic and psychographic criteria in order to pinpoint viable consumer segments for socially responsible marketing efforts (Anderson & Cunningham, 1972; Brooker, 1976; Kinnear & Taylor, 1973; Kinnear, Taylor & Ah-

167

med, 1974; Mayer, 1976; Webster, 1975; Scherhorn & Grunert, 1988). Results of these studies were frequently inconclusive and sometimes contradictory. The "green" segment research stream nonetheless precipitated, at least for a short period, a flurry of green products, green ads, and interest in energy conservation, waste handling and recycling. Another major stream of research, beginning in the early 1980s, investigated the antecedents of socially responsible behaviours such as recycling or buying of "green" products, sometimes with the objective to develop communication campaigns to support such purchase decision and disposal behaviour. Again, results were inconclusive in developing the link between environmental attitudes and environmentally responsible behaviour (Balderjahn, 1988; Beckmann, 2005a, 2005b). This stream also introduced other concepts such as knowledge measurements, motivation, peer influence, cost-benefit analysis, and financial incentives as variables to the study designs (see both Kilbourne & Beckmann, 1998, and Ölander & Thøgersen, 1995 for reviews).

In general, many consumer behaviour studies are grounded in the cognitive information-processing paradigm and assess – more or less explicitly – the antecedents, correlates and consequences of various stages in the consumer decision-making process: need recognition -> information search -> evaluation of alternatives -> purchase -> post-purchase activities and evaluation of experiences with the product or service. These stages can be interpreted as follows in the context of CSR:

- Need recognition refers to consumers' awareness of and interest in companies' CSR activities as an additional and non-functional product attribute that is derived from, for instance, environmental attitudes or beliefs that purchase decisions have political implications. In other words, "needs" are here understood as reflecting the desire to express symbolic values beyond utilitarian values.
- Both information search, actively and passively, and the evaluation of alternatives are influenced by attitudes and beliefs concerning product, brand and/or company. This means

168

that consumers may actively look for information on the type and extent of CSR activities of companies to facilitate the fulfilment of symbolic values. It may also mean that brands with which consumers have a strong relationship are preferred to other brands regardless of the level of the brand owner's CSR commitment. Attitudes and beliefs, in turn, are clearly influenced by personal, non-commercial and commercial sources of information.

- Purchase is most often measured as purchase intentions, in this case concerning products and services from companies engaging in CSR activities.
- Experiences with purchased products and services are insofar relevant, as negative experiences for instance concerning quality expectations might counterbalance attitudes and hence decrease consumer loyalty even for CSR active companies.

Very few studies in the consumer/CSR context, however, address this sequence explicitly. In most cases, one or two stages and a selection of their corresponding concepts are investigated – both by qualitative and quantitative methods. It is also important to point out that the stages can be iteratively linked and that some of the concepts are not necessarily related in a clear-cut cause-effect sequence. The table below therefore reflects this somewhat muddy state of affairs (and thereby the complexity of the antecedents of human decision-making) in that the four main stages are only implicitly represented.

Some other limitations do also apply: In many of the studies referred to, only certain aspects of CSR activities are addressed, thus providing a limited picture of consumer responses to CSR. Rarely, the whole spectrum of activities is addressed which could either indicate that most companies do not engage in the full range of CSR or they are only known for a limited set of CSR activities – or, from a methodological perspective, that study design becomes too complicated to deliver valid and reliable results if the full range were to be investigated.

Another important caution concerns the fact that most studies reviewed here have been conducted in the USA, which for cultural, political and historical reasons limits the generalizability of their findings to a European or even Scandinavian setting (cf. Beckmann, Morsing & Reisch in this book on explicit versus implicit CSR, following the framework by Matten & Moon, 2004).

### What we know and what we don't know

A broad range of academic journals – published in English – within marketing, consumer research and communication studies was examined to find studies that investigated consumer responses to CSR.[1] The main findings of these studies are compiled in Table 1, aiming at following the above model of decision-making stages.

**Table 1:** Main findings concerning consumers and CSR

| Main findings | Source |
|---|---|
| Consumers are aware of and interested in CSR and say that CSR is a purchase criterion | Creyer & Ross, 1997<br>Handelman & Arnold, 1999<br>Lewis, 2003 |
| CSR increases positive attitudes towards the company and/or the brand | Brown & Dacin, 1997<br>Lichtenstein, Drumwright & Braig, 2004<br>Murray & Vogel, 1997 |
| CSR functions as "insurance policy" in crisis situations: the importance of pro-active CSR commitment | Dawar & Pillutla, 2000<br>Dean, 2004<br>Klein & Dawar, 2004<br>Ricks, 2005<br>Werther & Chandler, 2005 |
| Consumers assess the fit between CSR initiatives and the company's reputation and past behaviour, and use the timing of initiatives as informational cue | Becker-Olsen, Cudmore & Hill, 2006<br>Dean, 2004<br>Ricks, 2005 |
| CSR activities have positive spill-over effects to strategic alliances (sponsorships, co-branding, not-for profit) | Cornwell & Smith, 2001<br>Lafferty & Goldsmith, 2005<br>Ross, Patterson & Stutts, 1992 |

| | |
|---|---|
| Consumers' attitudes are more affected by un-ethical behaviour than by pro-CSR behaviour | Elliott & Freeman, 2001<br>Folkes & Kamins, 1999 |
| Lack of knowledge, awareness and/or concern – and very little knowledge about which companies are CSR committed or not | Auger et al., 2003<br>Belk, Devinney & Eckhardt, 2005<br>Boulstridge & Carrigan, 2000<br>Carrigan & Attalla, 2001 |
| Consumers' support of the CSR domain chosen by the company matters | Lichtenstein, Drumwright & Braig, 2004<br>Sen & Bhattacharya, 2001 |
| Trade-off effects in favour of traditional decision criteria ("Old habits die hard") | Andreau et al., 2004, 2005<br>Beckmann, Christensen & Christensen, 2001<br>Boulstridge & Carrigan, 2000<br>Carrigan & Attalla, 2001<br>Mohr, Webb & Harris, 2001 |
| Product category and/or price play a role | Elliott & Freeman, 2001<br>Mohr & Webb, 2005<br>Strahilevitz, 1999<br>Strahilevitz & Myers, 1998 |
| Little willingness to pay more: the effect of personal cost-benefit analyses | Creyer & Ross, 1997<br>Osterhus, 1997 |
| Skepticism and cynicism concerning corporate CSR (communication) | Mohr, Webb & Harris, 2001<br>Sen & Bhattacharya, 2001<br>Swaen & Vanhamme, 2004 |
| Consumers distinguish between personal and social consequences of ethical/unethical company behaviour | Baron, 1999<br>Pitts, Wong & Whalen, 1991 |
| Pro CSR consumers do exist, but profiling them is difficult | Auger et al., 2003<br>Hustad & Pessemier, 1973<br>Mohr, Webb & Harris, 2001<br>Roberts, 1995, 1996 |
| National and cultural differences do exist | Andreu et al., 2004, 2005<br>Maignan & Ferrell, 2003 |

Grouping these results into the four stages, they can be summarized as follows:

171

- "Need recognition" (awareness, knowledge and interest): The majority of consumers confess to interest in CSR issues, but there is considerable heterogeneity among consumers in terms of awareness and knowledge of companies' CSR activities. The majority of consumers seem not to be aware that by and large many companies engage in at least some kind of CSR activities. And other consumers are skeptical or even cynical about companies' CSR communication.

- Information search and evaluation of alternatives/attitudes and beliefs: In general, consumers have a favourable attitude towards companies that engage in CSR. Several aspects however complicate the picture – overall company reputation, the fit between company and cause, personal connection to the cause that is represented by the company's CSR activity, distinction between proactive and reactive CSR initiatives, product quality and price. And it goes for almost all instances that the relationship between expressed attitudes and active consumer choice is weak.

- Purchase (intentions): Most consumers are unwilling to compromise on core attributes such as price and quality. However, a pro-active stance towards CSR functions as an "insurance policy" in, for instance, product-harm crises. Similarly, consumers appear to be more resilient to negative information about a CSR committed company and stay loyal when there is an occasional lapse on its part. Additionally, consumers are obviously more sensitive to unethical than to responsible behaviour, i.e. "doing bad" hurts more than "doing good" helps.

- Post-purchase experiences: Since the majority of consumers, as stated above, trade off CSR features for "traditional" attributes, a negative experience with product or service quality will in most cases backfire and thus prevent re-purchase despite CSR activities.

All these findings are complicated by the fact that there are individual, social and national differences that cut across the stages and concepts associated with them. And unfortunately they do not relate in a simple, straightforward manner to, for instance,

172

demographics such as gender and age or one's socioeconomic position in society. Nor can they be predicted conclusively from situational factors such as the product, price or purchase environment. Moreover, individual differences also may involve selectively ethical interests: the same consumer choosing a brand because it is environmentally responsible produced may be unaware of or disinterested in issues such as fair worker treatment and racial discrimination.

Surprisingly little is known so far about consumers' reactions to CSR communication as such. Some of the results of mainly qualitative studies indicate that many consumers appreciate the discrete way and reject bragging about achievements – a finding that is somewhat contradictory to the request of needing more information. Another important issue seems to be the source of CSR information, where company-independent sources appear to be the preferred ones (e.g., Swaen & Vanhamme, 2004; the importance of source credibility in marketing communications in general was recently analysed by Eisend, 2006). Media then should play an important role – however, a recent survey among Danish students revealed that interest has fallen by 13 % in January 2006 compared to October 2003 (Beckmann, 2004; Børsen 2006), despite the fact that CSR during this time period has featured prominently in the press and in teaching (see also the chapter by Kjær in this book).

One of the few consistent results that emerged in several studies though indicate that an important predictor of ethical consumer behaviour is past behaviour relating to social causes – in other words an anti-nuclear energy activist in the late 1970's becomes an organic produce consumer in the 1980s and a CSR rewarding customer in the 1990s. Consumer attitudes are then one possible foundation on which to construct a segmentation that may inform marketing and strategic CSR communication.

On the basis of their focus groups with UK consumers, Carrigan & Attalla (2001) suggest a matrix that provides exactly this foundation. An adapted version is shown in Figure 1.

**Figure 1:** Consumer awareness and response matrix

CSR awareness

| | High | Low |
|---|---|---|
| **High** | caring and ethical | confused and uncertain |
| **Low** | cynical and disinterested | oblivious |

CSR response

"Caring and ethical" consumers are those who seek out information on CSR and act according to their attitudes. They are the most likely to respond to strategic CSR communication. Engaging the "confused and uncertain" in a dialogue is probably rather difficult, as they are interested but remain bewildered by the lack of guidance and contradictory information about CSR. The "cynical and disinterested" are also hard to address, since they are not convinced that companies are truly socially responsible and, moreover, value other attributes such as price, quality and convenience as least as high than CSR. Finally the "oblivious" are mainly a lost case since they are unaware of CSR as such. However, a change in life circumstances may trigger interest, for instance new mothers who have been previously unaware of Nestlé's activities in relation to baby food may then seek out other brands and companies.

This matrix corresponds to some degree to findings from the US where Mohr, Webb & Harris (2001) explored how much consumers really care about a company's level of social responsibility. On the basis of 44 semi-structured interviews they grouped consumers into four categories following Andreasen's (1995) model of stages in behaviour change: precontemplation, contemplation, action, and maintenance. While precontemplators (34 %

of the sample) are not considering CSR in purchase decisions (and a few of them are even opposed to CSR), contemplators (26 %) are thinking about it or have done so in the past, but CSR is still not an important criterion. The action-oriented (18 %) have decided to base at least some of their buying on CSR considerations, and maintainers (22 %) use the CSR criterion in much of their purchasing. Precontemplators are similar to the "cynical and disinterested" and "oblivious" consumers of Carrigan and Attalla, contemplators resemble the "confused and uncertain" and action-oriented and maintainers look quite like the "caring and ethical".

**The methodology factor**
There is, however, another important issue that affects conclusions and recommendations on how to communicate CSR. All the research studies listed in Table 1 were scrutinized for the methodology applied to data collection and analyses. Three different generic approaches were identified: questionnaires in survey studies often analysed by simple frequency and correlation analyses, experimental designs leading to more advanced multivariate analyses, and qualitative research using text and content analysis. The overall finding – regardless of respondent type, concepts studied or cultural factors – reveals a strong and consistent effect of methodology:

- Opinion poll and attitude type surveys render high levels of consumer interest in CSR and usually positive effects on product/brand/company evaluations and purchase intentions
- Experimental and quasi-experimental designs lead to either inconclusive or more complex results
- Qualitative research (focus groups, in depth interviews) mainly reveals disinterest, lack of knowledge and skepticism

The cynical conclusion is therefore that the preferred outcome should determine the data collection method: if the board of directors shall be convinced of the necessity of a CSR policy then present opinion poll results, if to decide which CSR activity fits which target group combine surveys and experimental design,

175

and if to refute attempts to introduce CSR activities choose focus groups.

The constructive approach is, of course, to carefully choose the most appropriate method(s) for answering satisfactorily a given research question. Along similar lines, Bhattacharya & Sen (2004, p. 22) state: "...underscores the need for better measurement models of CSR that capture and estimate clearly the effects of a company's CSR actions on its stakeholders, including its consumers."

**Conclusion**

Reviewing the past decade of research into consumers, marketing and CSR, it can safely be stated that the effects of CSR initiatives are anything but straightforward and depend on a number of factors that are intertwined in a complex manner: consumers interest in some CSR and disinterest in other CSR activities (which in turn is grounded in values held by citizen-consumers), information and knowledge level, consumer-company congruence, relevance of other product/brand attributes, evaluations of trade-offs between CA (corporate associations) and CSR, and perceived credibility of information source. Furthermore, there are national and/ or cultural differences that suggest a strong influence of the economic, technological, political and social context within which any assessment of the (communication) effects of CSR activities on consumers' responses need to be analysed.

So the answer to the introductory question of whether consumers experience a "warm glow" vis-à-vis CSR committed companies is: yes, quite a few consumers feel positively, and yes, they will reward these companies, though much more in an intangible – enhanced corporate reputation and brand image – than a tangible manner that is directly reflected in the bottom-line. CSR's influence on consumers' behaviour is much more complex and tentative that its effects on their attitudes and beliefs. Moreover, consumers are more sensitive to negative CSR information than to positive CSR information, thus increasing the risk of boycott in events of perceived social irresponsibility (Beckmann & Langer, 2003).

176

**Where do we go from here?**
Based on the above, the contribution that marketing (communication) management can make in the context of consumers and CSR is then suggested to be embedded in three sets of questions – and without claiming comprehensiveness:

Who are they?
- What do we know about our target group?
- What are their interests (CSR domain)?
- What is the context of their potential ethical purchase behaviour?
- Who are other influential stakeholders (e.g., media)?
- Which consumer segments are more likely to trade-off CSR for other product/service attributes?

What and how should be communicated?
- Which ethical issues are top-of-mind for a given target group?
- How are CSR issues ranked in importance by a given target group?
- Under which conditions does CSR communication have a positive, negative or neutral effect?
- Which media channels should be chosen once the above is known?

How well aligned are company performance, communication performance and CSR performance?
- Is the fit between company offering and chosen CSR cause logical, trustworthy and convincing?
- Is there a past negative history that can colour the perception of the present alignment or attempts for alignment?

Hence, there is still a lot left we need to know about strategic CSR communication and consumers!

## References

Altman, B. W. (1998). Transformed corporate community relations: A management tool for achieving corporate citizenship. *Business and Society Review*, 102/103, 43-51.

Anderson, T. W. & Cunningham, W. H. (1972). The socially conscious consumer. *Journal of Marketing*, 36(3), 23-31.

Andreasen, A. R. (1995). *Marketing Social Change – Changing Behaviour to Promote Health, Social Development and the Environment*. San Francisco, CA: Jossey-Bass.

Andreoni, J. (1990). Impure altruism and donations to the public good – A theory of warm glow giving. *Economic Journal*, 100(401), 464-477.

Andreu, L., Beckmann, S. C., Bigné, E., Chumpitaz, R. & Swaen, V. (2004). Corporate Social Responsibility in the eye of the beholder: The case of European business students. In: *Proceedings of the 33rd European Marketing Academy (EMAC) Conference*. Murcia: University of Murcia.

Andreu, L., Beckmann, S. C., Bigné, E., Chumpitaz, R. & Swaen, V. (2005). An international comparison of CSR perceptions. In: DeMoranville, C. W. (Ed.), *Proceedings of the 12th World Marketing Congress – Marketing in an interconnected World: Opportunities and challenges*, Academy of Marketing Science, Münster.

Auger, P., Burke, P., Devinney, T. M. & Louviere, J. J. (2003). What will consumers pay for social features? *Journal of Business Ethics*, 42, 281-304.

Austin. H. W. (1965). Who has the responsibility for social change – business or government? *Harvard Business Review*, July-August, 45-52.

Balderjahn, I. (1988). Personality variables and environmental attitudes as predictors of ecologically responsible consumption patterns. *Journal of Business Research*, 17, 51-56.

Baron, J. (1999). Consumer attitudes about personal and political action. *Journal of Consumer Psychology*, 8(3), 261-275.

Becker-Olsen, K. L., Cudmore, B. A., & Hill, R. P. (2006). The impact of perceived corporate social responsibility on consumer behaviour. *Journal of Business Research*, 59, 46-53.

Beckmann, S. C. (2004). Corporate Social Responsibility – Danish business students' perspective. In: *Proceedings of the 33rd European Marketing Academy (EMAC) Conference*. Murcia: University of Murcia.

Beckmann, S. C. (2005a). In the eye of the beholder: Danish consumer-citizens and sustainability. In: Grunert, K. G. & Thøgersen, J. (Eds.), *Consumers, policy and the environment*, pp. 265-300. New York, NY: Springer.

Beckmann, S. C. (2005b). Information, consumer perceptions, and regulations: The case of organic salmon. In: Krarup, S. (Ed.), *Environment, information and Consumer behaviour*, pp. 197-215. Cheltenham, UK: Edward Elgar.

Beckmann, S. C. & Langer, R. (2003). Consumer-citizen boycotts: Facilitators, motives and conditions. In: *Proceedings of the 32nd European Marketing Academy (EMAC) Conference*. Glasgow: University of Strathclyde.

Beckmann, S. C., Christensen, A. S. & Christensen, A. G. (2001). "Myths of nature" and environmentally responsible behaviours: An exploratory study. In: *Proceedings of the 30th European Marketing Academy Conference*, Bergen: Norwegian School of Management.

Belk, R. W., Devinney, T. & Eckhardt, G. (2005). Consumer ethics across cultures. *Consumption, Markets and Culture*, 8(3), 275-289.

Berkowitz, L. & Lutterman, K. G. (1968). The traditional socially responsible personality. *Public Opinion Quarterly*, 32, 169-182.

Berle, A. A. & Means, G. C. 1944 (1932). *The modern corporation and private property*. NY: Macmillan.

Bhattacharya, C. B. & Sen, S. (2004). Doing better at doing good: When, why, and how consumers respond to corporate social initiatives. *California Management Review*, 47(1), 9-24.

Boulstridge, E., & Carrigan, M. (2000). Do consumers really care about corporate responsibility? Highlighting the attitude-behaviour gap. *Journal of Communication Management*, 4(4), 355-368.

Brockhoff, K. (1979). A note on external social reporting by German companies: A survey of 1973 company reports. *Accounting, Organization and Society*, 4, 77-85.

Brooker, G. (1976). The self-actualizing socially conscious consumer. *Journal of Consumer Research*, 3, 107-112.

Brown, T. J., & Dacin, P. A. (1997). The company and the product: Corporate associations and consumer product responses. *Journal of Marketing*, 61 (1), 68-84.

Børsen, 24.02.2006, p. 15: "Dalende interesse for etiske virksomheder".

Carrigan, M. & Attalla, A. (2001). The myth of the ethical consumer – do ethics matter in purchase behaviour? *Journal of Consumer Marketing*, 18(7), 560-577.

Carroll, A. B. (1998). The four faces of corporate citizenship. *Business and Society Review*, 100/10, 1-7.

Cornwell, T. B. & Smith, R. K. (2001). The communications importance of consumer meaning in cause-linked events: findings from a US events for benefiting breast cancer research. *Journal of Marketing Communications*, 7, 213-229.

Creyer, E. H., & Ross, W. T. (1997). The influence of firm behavior on purchase intention: Do consumers really care about business ethics? *Journal of Consumer Marketing*, 14 (6), 421-432.

Dawar, N. & Pillutla, M. (2000). Impact of product-harm crisis on brand equity: The moderating role of consumer expectations. *Journal of Marketing Research*, 37(May), 215-226.

179

Dean, D. H. (2004). Consumer reaction to negative publicity. *Journal of Business Communication*, 41(2), 192-211.

Dierkes, M. (1974). *Die Sozialbilanz: Ein gesellschaftsbezogenes Informations- und Rechnungssystem.* Frankfurt am Main.

Donaldson, T., & Preston, L. E. (1995). The stakeholder theory of the corporation: Concepts, evidence, and implications. *Academy of Management Review,* 20(1), 65-91.

Drumwright, M. E. (1994). Socially responsible organizational buying: Environmental concern as a noneconomic buying criterion. *Journal of Marketing,* 58, July, 1-19.

Dutton, J. M., Dukerich, J. M. & Harquail, C. V. (1994). Organizational images and member identification. *Administrative Science Quarterly,* 39(2), 239-63.

Elliott, K. A. & Freeman, R. B. (2001). *White hats or Don Quixotes? Human rights vigilantes in the global economy.* Cambridge, MA: National Bureau of Economic Research.

Eisend, m. (2006). Source credibility in marketing communications. *Marketing: Journal of Research and Management,* 2 (1), 43-60.

Folkes, V. S. & Kamins, M. A. (1999). Effects of information about firms – ethical and unethical actions on consumer attitudes. *Journal of Consumer Psychology,* 8(3), 243-59.

Freeman, R. E. (1984). Strategic Management: A Stakeholder Approach. *Academy of Management Review,* 24, 233–236.

Grether, E. T. (1969). Business Responsibility toward the Market. *California Management Review,* 12(1), 33-42.

Handelman, J. M., & Arnold, S. J. (1999). The role of marketing actions with a social dimension: Appeals to the institutional environment. *Journal of Marketing,* 63(July), 33-48.

Hunt, S. D. & Vitell, S. J. (1992). The general theory of marketing ethics: a retrospective and revision. In: Smith, N. C. and Quelch, J. A. (Eds.), *Ethics and Marketing,* pp. 775-784. Homewood, IL: Irwin.

Hustad, T. P. & Pessemier, E. A. (1973). Will the real consumer activist please stand up: An examination of consumer's opinions about marketing practices. *Journal of Marketing Research,* 10(August), 319-24.

Jaworski, J. & Kohli, A. K. (1993). Market orientation: Antecedents and consequences. *Journal of Marketing,* 57(3), 53-70.

Jones, T. M. (1995). Instrumental stakeholder theory: A synthesis of ethics and economic. *Academy of Management Review,* 20(2), 404-437.

Kelley, H. H. (1971). *Attribution in Social Interaction.* New York: General Learning Press.

Kinnear, T. C. & Taylor, J. R. (1973). The effect of ecological concern on brand perceptions. *Journal of Marketing Research,* 10, 191-197.

Kinnear, T. C., Taylor, J. R. & Ahmed, S. A. (1974). Ecologically concerned consumers: Who are they? Journal of Marketing, 38, 20-24.

180

Kilbourne, W. E. & Beckmann, S. C. (1998). Review and critical assessment of research on marketing and the environment. *Journal of Marketing Management,* 14(6), 513-532.

Kohli, A. K. & Jaworski, J. (1990). Market orientation: The construct, research propositions, and managerial implications. *Journal of Marketing,* 54 (April), 1-18.

Klein, J., & Dawar, N. (2004). Corporate social responsibility and consumers' attributions and brand evaluations in a product-harm crisis. *International Journal of Research in Marketing,* 21(3), 203-217.

Kotler, P. & Zaltman, G. (1971). Social Marketing: An approach to planned social change. *Journal of Marketing,* 35(July), 3-12.

Lafferty, B. A. & Goldsmith, R. E. (2005). Cause-brand alliances: does the cause help the brand or does the brand help the cause. *Journal of Business Research,* 5, 423-429.

Lantos, G. P. (2001). The boundaries of strategic corporate social responsibility. *Journal of Consumer Marketing,* 18(3), 205-230.

Lantos, G. P. (2002). The ethicality of altruistic corporate social responsibility. *Journal of Consumer Marketing,* 19(7), 595-630.

Lavidge, R. J. (1970). The growing responsibilities of marketing. *Journal of Marketing,* 34(Jan), 25-28.

Lazer, W. (1969). Marketing's changing social relationships. *Journal of Marketing,* 33(Jan), 3-9.

Lewis, S. (2003). Reputation and corporate responsibility. *Journal of Communication Management,* 7(4), 356-364.

Lichtenstein, D. R., Drumwright, M. E. & Braig, B. M. (2004). The effect of corporate social responsibility on customer donations to corporate-supported nonprofits. *Journal of marketing,* 68(4), 16-32.

Lydenberg, S. D., Marlin, Alice T., Strub, S. O. & the Council on Economic Priorities (1986). *Rating America's corporate conscience.* Reading, MA: Addison-Wesley.

Maignan, I. & Ferrell, O. C. (2003). Nature of corporate responsibilities: Perspectives from American, French, and German consumers. *Journal of Business Research,* 56(1), 55-67.

Maignan, I., Ferrell, O. C. & Hult, G. T. M. (1999). Corporate Citizenship: Cultural antecedents and business benefits. *Journal of the Academy of Marketing Science,* 27(4), 455-69.

Matten, D. & Moon, J. (2004). A conceptual framework for understanding CSR. In: Habisch, A., Jonker, J., Wegner, M. and Schmidpeter, R. (Eds.), *Corporate Social Responsibility Across Europe,* p. 335-356.

Mayer, R. N. (1976). The socially conscious consumer – another look at the data. *Journal of Consumer Research,* 3(2), 113-115.

181

Mohr, L. A. & Webb, D. J. (2005). The effects of Corporate Social responsibility and price on consumer responses. *The Journal of Consumer Affairs*, 39(1), 121-147.

Mohr, L. A., Webb, D. J. & Harris, K. E. (2001). Do consumers expect companies to be socially responsible? The impact of corporate social responsibility on buying behavior. *The Journal of Consumer Affairs*, 35(1), 45-72.

Murray, K. B., & Vogel, C. M. (1997). Using a hierarchy-of-effects approach to gauge the effectiveness of corporate social responsibility to generate goodwill toward the firm: Financial versus non financial impacts. *Journal of Business Research*, 38, 141-159.

Ölander, F. & Thøgersen, J. (1995). Understanding of consumer behaviour as a prerequisite for environmental protection. *Journal of Consumer Policy*, 18(3), 345-385.

Osterhus, T. L. (1997). Pro-Social Consumer Influence Strategies: When and How Do They Work? *Journal of Marketing*, 61(4), 16-29.

Pinkston, T. S., & Carroll, A. B. (1994). Corporate citizenship perspectives and foreign direct investment in the US. *Journal of Business Ethics*, 13 (2), 157-169.

Pitts, R. E., Wong, J. K. & Whalen, D. J. (1991). Consumers' evaluative structures in two ethical situations: A means-end approach. *Journal of Business Research*, 22, 119-130.

Ricks Jr., J. M. (2005). An assessment of strategic corporate philanthropy on perceptions of brand equity variables. *Journal of Consumer Marketing*, 22(3), 121-134.

Roberts, J. A. (1995). Profiling levels of socially responsible consumer behaviour: A cluster analytic approach and its implications for marketing. *Journal of Marketing Theory and Practice*, Fall, 97-117.

Roberts, J. A. (1996). Will the real socially responsible consumer please step forward? *Business Horizons*, 39(1), 79-83.

Robin, D. P. & Reidenbach, E. R. (1987). Social responsibility, ethics, and marketing strategy: Closing the gap between concept and application. *Journal of Marketing*, 51(1), 44-58.

Ross, J. K., Patterson, L. T. & Stutts, M. A. (1992). Consumer perceptions of organizations that use cause-related marketing. *Journal of the Academy of Marketing Science*, 20(1), 93-97.

Scherhorn, G. & Grunert, S. C. (1988). Using the causality orientations concept in consumer behaviour research. In: P. Vanden Abeele (Ed.), Psychology in micro & macro economics. *Proceedings of the 13th Annual Colloquium of the International Association for Research in Economic Psychology, Vol. 2.* Leuven: Katholieke Universiteit Leuven.

Sen, S., & Bhattacharya, C. B. (2001). Does doing good always lead to doing better? Consumer reactions to corporate social responsibility. *Journal of Marketing Research*, 38, 225-243.

182

Strahilevitz, M. (1999). The effects of product type and donation magnitude on willingness to pay more for a charity-linked brand. *Journal of Consumer Psychology*, 8(3), 215-241.

Strahilewitz, M. & Myers, J. G. (1998). Donations to charity as purchase incentives: How well they work may depend on what you are trying to sell. *Journal of Consumer Research*, 24(4), 434-446.

Swaen, V. & Vanhamme, J. (2004). When "what you say" matters less than "where you say it": Influence of corporate social responsibility arguments and source of information on consumers' reactions and attitudes toward the company. In: *Proceedings of the 33rd European Marketing Academy (EMAC) Conference.* Murcia: University of Murcia.

Ulrich, P. (1977). *Die Grossunternehmung als quasi-öffentliche Institution: Eine politische Theorie der Unternehmung.* Stuttgart.

Varadarajan, P. R. & Menon, A. (1988). Cause-related marketing: A coalignment of marketing strategy and corporate philanthropy. *Journal of Marketing*, 52(July), 58-74.

Waddock, S. (2000). Integrity and mindfulness: Foundations of corporate citizenship. In: M. McIntosh and A. Warhurst (eds.), *2000 Annual Warwick Corporate Citizenship Conference,* 10-11 July: University of Warwick: the UK.

Webster, F. E. (1975). Determining the characteristics of the socially conscious consumer. *Journal of Consumer Research*, 2(3), 188-196.

Werther, W. B. Jr. & Chandler, D. (2005). Strategic corporate social responsibility as global brand insurance. *Business Horizons*, 48, 317-324.

## Notes

1. These journals included (in random order) Journal of Consumer Policy, Journal of Consumer Research, Journel of Consumer Affairs, Journal of Public Policy & Marketing, Journal of Marketing, Business & Society, Journal of Business Ethics, Journal of Communication, Journal of Communication Management, Journal of Marketing Communications, Journal of Consumer Marketing, Journal of the Academy of Marketing Science.

183

# CHAPTER 8

# Communicating CSR to consumers: An empirical study

*Lucia A. Reisch*

*Consumers and their representative organisations have therefore an important role to play in the evolution of CSR. If CSR is therefore to continue to serve its purpose, strong lines of communication between enterprises and consumers need to be created.*

Commission of the European Communities, COM (2002) 347 final.
Communication from the Commission concerning Corporate Social Responsibility:
A business contribution to sustainable development. Brussels, 2.7.2002.

## CSR and consumers in Denmark

The issue of communicating Corporate Social Responsibility (CSR) to consumers is rather low on the public and corporate agenda in Denmark. Compared to other European countries such as the UK, the Netherlands, and Germany, there have been only a few initiatives to break down the rather complex topic of CSR in order to make it more communicable to consumers (Reisch, 2006). For instance, in 2001, the Danish National Consumer Agency had introduced the transparency initiative "Etikbasen" or "CSR scorecard", a database where CSR information could easily be retrieved by consumers. However, the project could not create the critical mass of neither demand for the data by consumers nor of supply of information by corporations, and was hence closed down after only a few years. Today, the topic appears every now and then in media campaigns, such as the recent cross-media campaign of fair trade "Max Havelaar products" that was run in cooperation with Danish retail chains. It is also covered in the widely read consumer magazine *Tænk* issued by the Danish consumer organisation *Forbrugerrådet*. The magazine regularly publishes background reports and "ethics tests" of companies selling, e.g., bananas, mobile phones, toys, and chocolate. However, in spite of its professional design and comparatively large readership – each issue is distributed to about 40,000 Danish households and institutions – the magazine reaches mostly the "usual suspects", namely the critical consumers and the active information seekers.

This situation is somewhat surprising, since the concept of "stakeholder thinking" has become one of the cornerstones of industrial democracy in Scandinavia (Nasi, 1995). Consumers and consumer advocate groups as important stakeholders could be expected to play a more vital part in promoting CSR policies (Dyhr, 2003). In recent academic research, Scandinavian consumers have indeed been characterized as frontrunners regarding "political consumerism" (Tobiasen, 2004) – at least when judged on the base of a low threshold definition of the term "political consumer". A representative Danish study (Goul Andersen & Tobiasen, 2001) found for the year 2000 that 21 % of all adult

Danes had boycotted products within the past twelve months, 45 % had deliberately chosen certain products for political, ethical, or environmental reasons, and most had done both. The tendency to boycott and to choose "ethical" products is explained by the high prevalence of postmaterialist attitudes, a specific political culture, a high quality of life, and the presence of political consumerist labelling schemes, amongst other factors (Micheletti & Stolle, 2004).

Regarding interest in CSR issues, three types of Danish consumers have been described (Dyhr, 2003): the "holier-than-thou" (1 %), the conscious consumers (9 %), and the majority (90 %) that usually does not express political views via their consumption. Hence, there should be a notable demand for CSR consumer information at least from the 10 % interested consumers. While in spite of the public attention cycle to sustainability issues, Danish consumer-citizens have long been socialized to consume environmentally and (to a lesser degree) socially responsible, there are some factors that currently undermine their interest in sustainability issues, namely: the unprecedented rapid product innovation; the long-term trend towards individualization and emancipation from social class categories; and the increase of stress and time pressure. The average Dane spends less than ten minutes a day on his/her daily shopping and has hence no time for many considerations or to read a lot of product information. In addition, the average Dane is not knowledgeable enough to evaluate the highly complex CSR issues (Dyhr, 2003).

While acknowledging these factors as important barriers, the lack of interest might also be a "chicken-and-egg-problem": It can be assumed that if CSR would be more visible on the public agenda and would be covered more intensely in the mass media, then consumers would be more interested in it and would eventually actively look for more information. Yet, Danish companies have been very reluctant to enter strategic CSR communication and a tradition of "walk but don't talk" is pervading (see Morsing & Schultz in this book). A recent study estimates that 75 % of Danish small and medium sized companies are engaged in CSR issues, but that only 33 % communicate their policies and en-

187

gagement, and very few communicate their CSR activities towards consumers (TNS Gallup, 2005).

Yet, there are signs of change: New large governmental programmes, in cooperation with the EU, to promote CSR and its communication to stakeholders have recently been introduced by the Danish government. Also, Danish industry is slowly getting more interested and involved in strategic CSR communication, spurred by the needs of a globalized market and global standards. Moreover, as opposed to the mid 1990s when most CSR initiatives focused on social aspects of employment and integration of minority issues, a picture of "strategic ambiguity" as regards CSR contents (Morsing & Langer, 2006) has emerged: Today, CSR in Denmark also includes aspects of human rights, the environment, and the Third World – which might be of interest for a broader group of consumers. Last but not least, Denmark hosts some of the world's top CSR performers, Novo Nordisk. This may positively influence market standards, since Danish employers are competing with the "frontrunners" for human resources and reputation.

It is against this backcloth, that this chapter presents research on CSR consumer communication. The key proposition is that the "how" of consumer communication is an underestimated (and under-researched) factor of success, and that corporations should be more daring in their attempts to reach the important consumer-stakeholders. More specifically, it is proposed that – if carefully employed – CSR communication can successfully involve emotional and entertaining mass mediated communication elements, and is not necessarily confined to fact-oriented, emotionally "neutral" communication styles. In other words: We argue that CSR consumer communication is not "just for the brains",[1] but should also reach consumers' hearts to be effective.

Following up this basic assumption, the chapter first reports on research on communicating messages on sustainable consumption intended to induce behavioural change. Here, CSR messages are viewed as a specific type of sustainable consumption messages. Then, the design and intermediate results of a research project on the communication of sustainable consumption and pro-

188

duction which is currently carried out in Germany, are reported. The potentials and pitfalls of the case of "Project Balance's" multi-channel emotion-based communication strategy are discussed, and managerial implications are drawn.

## Mapping the concept of "CSR consumer communication"

CSR communication is part of the broader discussion on "sustainability communication" (Reisch, 2005). Basically, two meanings of the concept have to be distinguished:

Firstly, there is the meaning of acceptance of *responsibility through communication* which reflects a company's goal for a dialogue based two-way concept of responsibility and transparency as sketched above. Examples are efforts to engage in stakeholder outreach (e.g., in dialogue forums); a voluntary full declaration of ingredients which goes beyond legal obligations; or a general transparency policy regarding business conduct as propagated by the British "Business in the Community" initiative.

Secondly, there is *communication on CSR*. The instruments comprise the whole arsenal of marketing and corporate communication such as: product-based sustainability communication, labelling, cross media advertising, point of sale marketing, sponsoring and PR, campaigns, as well as sustainability reporting. CSR messages are also diffused in strategic alliances with non-commercial partners, mostly NGOs, via modern marketing tools such as cause-related-marketing, public-private-partnerships in campaigning, event-marketing, multimedia-marketing, and Internet based transparency initiatives. Furthermore, non-commercial senders communicate CSR issues to consumers via tools such as CSR testing[2] and publication of "saints & sinners" lists.[3]

It is obvious that CSR *through* communication will support the credibility of communication *on* CSR, and that the latter is prone to be deemed as "window dressing" if there is just a shadow of a doubt on the company's willingness to listen to and respond to stakeholders. Also, a basically responsive company will be better prepared to react early and adequately in case of "scandals". Hence, the two strategies are mutually reinforcing – but can also be mutually destructive if one of them fails.

189

If CSR communication primarily targets consumers, we speak of *consumer oriented CSR communication*. For the purpose of this chapter, it is useful to further specify the concept (based on Schrader, Halbes & Hansen, 2005):

- In matters of *content*, it refers to the corporate behaviour (i.e., production processes, supply chains, transformative marketing) and/or to social, ethical, and ecological aspects of specific products or services (i.e., process quality); it does not, however, cover traditional product quality issues and does not focus on economic aspects.
- As regards the *sender*, it can be produced and transmit by the company itself (or its agencies), by independent institutions and experts (e.g., NGOs, consumer councils, product testing institutions), the media, government, science, or other sources; the perceived credibility of the sender is a decisive determinant for attention to and relevance of the information (Eisend, 2006).
- In reference to *format*, it can have the form of one-way information ("push") or of a two-way dialogue and exchange ("pull") between corporation and consumers as well as other stakeholder groups; it can be presented in either strictly content-oriented or emotionalized forms, depending on the target group (target group orientation) and the aim of the communication process (e.g., raise attention, convince stakeholders, retrieve knowledge from consumers).
- In respect of *goals*, it aims at enabling consumers to make consumption decisions that are in line with their personal values regarding ethical, social, and/or environmental aspects of corporate behaviour; it also aims at sensitizing and educating consumers and at heightening their awareness for CSR issues; finally, it wants to provide an opportunity for the corporation to exchange views with consumers in multiple forms and herewith stay close to the market.

## Behavioural science research on sustainable consumption

For more than two decades, behavioural consumer research has been investigating individual and institutional limitations preventing sustainable consumption behaviour ("barriers") as well as enabling factors for the performance of more sustainable lifestyles ("drivers"). Before the 1990s, this research was conducted under the label of "environmental" and "prosocial" behaviour (see e.g., Reisch & Røpke, 2004). For the development of efficient intervention strategies, knowledge about the underlying psychological variables is indispensable, and has been analyzed both as a function of stable dispositions as well as of environment-specific cognitions and emotions. While the explanatory power of generalized personality traits and broad beliefs (e.g., control beliefs, altruism, and generalized social responsibility) on various sustainable attitudes and behaviours has proven to be low and inconsistent (Kaiser et al., 2001), environment-specific cognitions exert powerful and stable effects on sustainable behaviour (Montada & Kals, 2000). In sum, it has been shown that moral reasoning is a powerful motivational base for overcoming interest-shifts, social traps, lock-ins, and high-cost perceptions. Hence, intervention programmes have at least two entry points: They can aim at creating risk awareness (via providing information and knowledge) and/or providing immediate behaviour solutions in order to increase the perceived behavioural control (i.e., showing concrete, low cost behavioural alternatives).

Yet, this is only half of the story. For a long time, sustainability behaviour research has neglected the powerful and stable impact of various categories of emotions. This omission can most probably be explained by the prevalence of rational choice-based action theories such as Ajzen and Fishbein's (1980) Theory of Reasoned Action, the Theory of Planned Behaviour (Ajzen, 1991), or Bagozzi & Warshaw's (1990) Theory of Trying. Their basic assumption is summarized in the formula of the restricted, resourceful, expecting, evaluating, maximizing man (Coleman & Fararo, 1992). Obviously, emotions do not fit and are not considered in these theories.[4] However, studies on the emotional foundations of sustainable (usually only environmental) behaviour have shown

191

that the moral cognitive perspective of the underlying motives for sustainable behaviour is supplemented by moral emotions. Another emotional source is represented by emotional affinity or simply love of nature. Whereas moral emotions are traced back to moral cognitions, feelings of love toward nature are based on nature experiences, which should ideally be made with significant others. In contrast, ecological fear and the experience of ecological burdens are less important (Kals & Meas, 2002).

**Marketing research on CSR and consumers**

From a marketing perspective, research on the impact of CSR information on consumers has brought mixed results (see Beckmann in this book). On the one hand, benefits from CSR have been documented in its link to consumers' positive product and brand evaluations, brand choice, and brand recommendations (Brown & Dacin, 1997; Drumwright, 1994; Sen & Bhattacharya, 2001) and purchase intent (Mohr & Webb, 2005). There is empirical evidence that CSR affects consumers' routine purchasing decisions as well as the evaluation of new products. This holds in particular true for consumers that hold strong beliefs on CSR. A recent field study by Sen, Bhattacharya & Korschun (2006) showed that (the few) individuals who were aware of the respective CSR initiative had more positive company-related associations, displayed greater organizational identification with the company, indicated a greater intent to purchase products, seek employment, and invest in the company than respondents who were unaware of the initiative. The authors conclude that CSR activity has the potential to increase not only CSR associations, attitudes, and identification but also the intent of stakeholders to commit personal resources (e.g., money, labour) to the benefit of the company.

Another benefit of CSR is that it can offer a crucial advantage to managers by providing a means of insuring financial performance against negative events (Peloza, 2006). It has been shown that a credible CSR consumer communication can be some sort of insurance policy against the negative impact of untoward events such as ethical scandals (Creyer & Ross, 1997) and product-harm crises (Klein & Dawar, 2004). For many consumers, a "CSR halo" seems to exert an enduring influence on company attributions which in turn have a domino effect on brand evaluations and purchase intentions.

On the other hand, empirical evidence is by far not clear-cut. CSR is only one (and on average not even important) criteria in consumers' purchasing decisions, synergy effects are not automatically created, brand value has even proved to decrease when combined with CSR issues, consumers' interest is at the most lukewarm, the topic is highly complex and full of contradictions and trade-offs (which means that information costs are high), CSR and classical product quality do not seem to go hand in hand, and finally, there is a general scepticism and cynicism as regards corporations as communicators of political issues in general (Maignan & Ferrell, 2003; Mohr, Webb & Harris, 2001; Swaen & Vanhamme, 2004).

**Explorative research on consumer oriented CSR communication**
Research on CSR communication is still scarce. CSR communication has been conceptualized as a moderating factor of socially responsible corporate behaviour with the functions of presenting CSR images, asserting stakeholder identification, and stimulating stakeholder interactions (Maignan & Ferrell, 2004). An explorative interview study of 13 large German banks and chemical companies (Glombitza, 2005) found that the stated goals of corporate CSR communication are quite ambitious. Most frequently, the interviewed managers mentioned both communicative and economic goals, namely: image building; societal acceptance; better risk management; the development of new business areas; repositioning and profiling of the brand; demarcation towards competitors; motivation of employees; sustainable growth; increase of corporate/shareholder value; better rating by rating agencies; competitive edge in recruitment of high potentials. In another recent Germany study, nearly all of the 32 interviewed experts – representing corporations, consumer policy, and sustainability science – regard CSR as a business case (Schrader, Halbes & Hansen, 2005). In addition to the above mentioned

benefits, interviewees mentioned an improved customer loyalty, better investor relations, and the creation of a "good-will-buffer" for times of crisis as benefits.

As has been pointed out by NGOs (Frankental, 2001), an indicator of the real value that companies attach to CSR is where they locate this function within the organizational structure – whether it is an adjunct of PR, or embedded across the organization horizontally and vertically. The above mentioned study found that the organization of CSR communication is indeed very different, ranging from distinct Sustainability Committees, Sustainability Councils, and CSR Committees to ad hoc CSR management teams (Glombitza, 2005). Based on these findings and on the communication strategy employed, the author distinguishes three "CSR communication types": the *leaders* who proactively promote CSR development in the industry; the *duteous* that conform to industry standards, and the *laggards*, who only adhere to CSR if absolutely necessary. While such a typology might be a useful heuristic for strategic activism, categorizing becomes problematic when companies mix their CSR communication targeting different consumer segments.[5]

In the German studies (Glombitza, 2005; Schrader, Halbes & Hansen, 2005), many interviewees pointed at the fact that a serious CSR strategy cannot be confined to well-tuned and sophisticated communication. Such a "CSR light" approach runs risk to be perceived as a PR-gimmick and can hence backlash on the company's image. Rather, a CSR strategy comprises the systematic integration of CSR issues in the whole management process. Only if CSR becomes an integral part of corporate behaviour, so the prevailing attitude, can it usefully be employed to promote Corporate Identity via Corporate Communication (see Morsing & Schultz in this book). On a strategic level, the success of CSR communication is seen to depend on a consistent internal and external communication strategy. On an operative level, different instruments for effective consumer oriented CSR communication have been discussed by both practitioners and researchers. Transparent constructive-critical *Business-to-Stakeholder communication,* which has long been used for Issues Management in

194

various forms, is cited for its potential to discuss strategic communication issues. *CSR stakeholder reports*, while being the most
popular instrument, bear the disadvantages of one-way "push"
communication. In fact, end consumers don't read such reports.
Therefore, the 2005 Global Stakeholder Report on CSR recom-
mends: "Don't try to reach private consumers with your CSR report. They will neither read nor value it. To reach consumers use
different communication tools" (Pleon Kothes Klewes, 2005, p.
26). Traditional *media relations / public relations* always need a
high news value that triggers emotions – something CSR issues
usually cannot provide (Steinert & Klein, 2002). *Community relations* are an important instrument in particular for companies with
a high local impact. In the UK, for instance, the company association "Business in the community" (www.bitc.org.uk) aims at improving the relations between corporations and community.
Cause *related marketing (CRM)* is marketing with social and ecological benefits that try to capture the trend towards political consumption. CRM offers a high potential for emotionalized communication, and, according to the website of the business initiative
CSR Europe, CRM "as part of Corporate Social Responsibility is
good, profit making, business sense". Finally, *employee communication* can improve the identity-match between employee and
companies, herewith increasing motivation and hence efficiency.

*Communication to induce behaviour change – a conceptual basis*
Prior research on the communication of health messages has
shown that positive emotional appeal serves to move a target audience from non-interest and non-knowledge to a stage of contemplation of behavioural change (Monahan, 1995). While fear
appeals were more counterproductive than effective – provoking
defence mechanisms and preventing attention (Hale & Dillard,
1995) – the communication of positive emotions has proved to be
much more conducive to behavioural change.

Following Andreasen (1995), approaches to induce behavioural change in consumers can be grouped into five alternatives:

195

1. the *education approach* with its focus on educating people, but bears the risk of boomerang effects;
2. the *persuasion approach* used in social advertising with a focus on arguments and motivational "hot buttons"; however, persuasion bears the risk of being perceived as a pushy "selling approach";
3. the *behavioural modification approach* that stresses the principles of learning theory of learning and rewards; although successful, the approach is very costly and can hence be only applied to individuals or small groups;
4. the *social influence approach* that uses campaigns directed at influencing community norms and collective behaviour; while being promising, the approach is limited to situations in which social issues and norms are well understood and accepted, the pressures to conform are extremely strong, and the behaviour to be influenced is socially important and visible (e.g., in smoking campaigns); the more educated and emancipated the individual consumer, the less likely that group norms would have a major role to play;
5. the *social marketing approach* that comprises features of the above in a comprehensive and integrated manner; it places customer behaviour at the centre, uses the "Four P's" as intervention, relies on market research, and carefully segments target markets.

For the promotion of CSR issues, social marketing seems to be the most promising approach. It shares most of the characteristics unique to the field, namely: invisible benefits and consequences while costs are real; benefits to (geographically and temporally remote) third parties; intangibles that are difficult to portray; the need for long term engagement due to large amounts of complex information; the need to change basic values; and the need to get outside opinion leaders on board.

In consumer behaviour research, high-involvement behaviours are conceptualized as being developed through definable stages. To date, several of such stage models have been proposed (e.g., McGuire, 1976; Maibach & Cotton, 1995). For the purpose of CSR communication research, the *Transtheoretical Model of Be-*

*haviour Change* (Prochaska & DiClemente, 1984) is a valuable theoretical base. According to the model, consumers proceed through the following five stages: *precontemplation* (i.e., consumers do not think of the behaviour as being appropriate for them; this can be due to ignorance, to presumed irrelevance, or to principles); *contemplation* (i.e., consumers think about and evaluate recommended behaviours); *preparation* (i.e., consumers have decided to act and prepare, e.g., search for brands and stores); *action* (i.e., consumers are doing the behaviour the first time or first several times); and *confirmation* (i.e., consumers are committed to the behaviour and have no desire or intention to return to the earlier behaviour). The model has undergone considerable field testing – including CSR research (Mohr, Webb & Harris, 2001) – and has been validated as useful. According to this research, it is possible to separate target consumers into these five groups and to employ the appropriate intervention strategy in order to fulfil the respective marketing task, namely: create awareness and interest; change values; motivate behavioural change; create action; and maintain change (Andreasen, 1995). The aim is to move consumers to the next stage, not to bring everyone to "confirmation stage". This will more likely be reached with tailored messages and tailored media use.

**The case of "Project Balance": Design and research goals**
"Project Balance" is set up as both, a public "trendsetting initiative" with the aim to enforce sustainability communication in the German general public and media, as well as an academic research project that accompanies this initiative and evaluates its outcomes. The goals of Project Balance are twofold: firstly, to fuel communication and public discourse on sustainable consumption and production with a cross media approach (i.e., TV, Internet, print, and podcast) based on emotionalized messages; and secondly, through accompanying research, to gain deeper insight into how such communication processes empirically work and what their factors of success and failure are. Conceptually, the project is designed as a transdisciplinary practice project with several academic and practice partners from academia, the media, and media

197

research. In order to receive permanent feedback from other stakeholders, it is consulted by a board of advisors composed of academic experts from environmental psychology, sustainable development, green marketing, ethics, communications research, as well as of practitioners from NGOs, consumer organizations, the German Council of Sustainable Development, the leading German media research institution "Grimme Institut" among others. The project approach is iterative research, i.e., research is seen as a continuous process, not as a one-way activity with a neat beginning and end. It resembles an upward spiral of exploration, planning, structuring, pretesting, implementing, monitoring, and replanning.[6] In its dual approach, the project is an example of "action research". The project is sponsored by the German Ministry of Research and Education and runs for three years (2004-2007).

The basic hypothesis of Project Balance is that the use of emotionalized and entertaining communication messages can be a successful tool in promoting attention to, interest in, positive attitudes towards, knowledge of, and finally, positive behavioural intentions / willingness criteria regarding sustainable consumption and production issues of the "broad masses". This hypothesis is based on empirical evidence in environmental campaigns (Lichtl, 1999) as well as on respective results of social marketing research sketched above (Andreasen, 1995, 2001).

The project follows a two-step approach: Firstly, viewers' attention, interest, and sympathy via "limbic" social marketing tools (i.e., triggering positive emotions) are gained; secondly, convincing cognitive messages are transmitted that inform and confirm prior attitudes towards behaviour change (Reisch, 2005). It is hypothesized that an "ecotainment" (Lichtl, 1999; Kreeb, 2001) approach, i.e., the use of a social marketing concept based on positive emotions and entertaining features, is more effective than the hitherto predominant fact-oriented style of consumer information. Prior research has shown that the latter reaches – at best – the "usual suspects", i.e., the more educated und principally interested consumers.

A major barrier for communication efforts is the information overload in today's attention economy. It is estimated that not more than 5 % of actively sent corporate communication directed to consumers is received (Kroeber-Riel, 2003). The metaphor of the "atomization of the media" might give one explanation why consumers show less interest in classic corporate one-way "push-communication". Media research points at viewers' ad avoidance strategies such as zapping or cutting out/fast forwarding commercials via digital video recorders. Hence, an alternative lies in using two-way "pull-media" such as the Internet, where recipients select their own contents and have a dialogue option to exchange views and voice their opinions (IBM Global Business Services, 2006). Project Balance aims at developing and testing a cross-media strategy of push and pull-media, with a TV clip as a teaser that redirects viewers to become users, readers, and ideally, "doers".

**Project Balance in practice**
The project focuses on the very beginning of the multi-stage consumption processes, namely the generation of attention to and possibly attitude formation through communication. The more ambitious goals of reaching later stages in the consumption process with more specific information, service tools for consumers, and deeper background information should be provided via other media outlets such as print ("Welt der Wunder" print magazine), websites (*www.weltderwunder.de*; with rubric "balance"), and podcasts (*www.balance-podcast.de*). In order to increase target group exposure, the messages have to be placed in media channels the target audience, i.e., people that are not or hardly interested in sustainability issues, normally uses. Hence, before the projected took off, channels were carefully selected regarding reach, frequency, impact, and cost.[7] During the project, cross media spin-offs – a website, a print magazine, and a podcast show – have been developed. Currently, Internet TV is explored.

The primary channel for the sustainability messages is the TV show "Welt der Wunder" ("World of Wonders"), aired on the private television program RTL II. The reasons for the choice of programme and channel can be summarized as follows:

199

1. From commercial audience research, it is known that both "Welt der Wunder" and RTL II's core audience is less educated and less interested in environmental and social issues than the average German. During the project, this was verified by our own research based on GfK's viewer profiles. Hence, RTL II and "Welt der Wunder" viewers represent our target group quite well.

2. We were able to get a gratuitous access to detailed audience research data which is collected by German *Gesellschaft für Konsumforschung* (GfK) in Nuremberg. The access to these data enables to track viewers' switch on-switch off behaviour for every second of programme and advertisements.

3. Research on the effectiveness of health communication has shown that more effective campaigns use multiple media, use repetition of a single message either in the form of retransmission of the original message or in slight variations of the basic theme, and that they use the news media as a means of increasing their visibility (Backer, Rogers & Sopory, 1992). The TV Show "Welt der Wunder" is currently the most popular science programme in German TV with about four million viewers per show. The show is aired weekly during prime time (Sundays at 7 p.m.) and repeated twice during the week on a news channel (n-tv).

4. The TV show host is a well known celebrity and "brand" himself in Germany. Hence, it was expected that he enjoys high credibility, and audiences will particularly attend to messages delivered and presented by him. It turned out that this is an important asset, since it helps to drag viewers onto the website and the rubric "balance".

5. The editorial staff, scriptwriters, and the producer are open and interested enough to embrace the project group's continuous "sustainability coaching" efforts. In practice, this is highly important since the freedom of the press forbids any external intrusion in the making of a programme. The content and working of the TV clips is fully in the responsibility of the journalists.

## Accompanying research design of Project Balance

The accompanying research of Project Balance is split up into three research modules carried out by the three research teams: media research, consumer research, and marketing research. There is a close interaction between those teams, in particular between media and consumer research. Figure 1 sketches the project modules and their main research methods.

**Figure 1:** Overview of Project Balance
Source: Project Balance (2006), Internal Interim Report

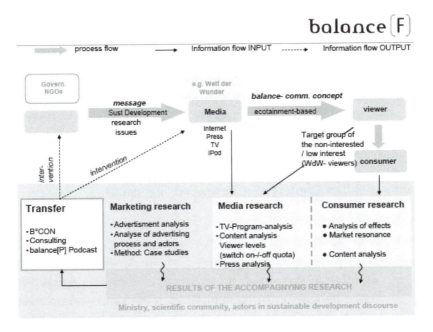

Consumer research basically carries out reception analysis and content analysis. Both direct measures (e.g., questionnaires, video taping) and proxy measures (e.g., switch on-switch off data) are used. Data are retrieved mainly from focus group discussion, expert group discussions, individual interviews, case studies with companies (e.g., on their CSR strategy), market response analysis, and computer assisted qualitative data analysis (CAQDA; performed with ATLAS.ti) of the aired TV clips. Moreover, viewers are profiled via GfK data and the employment of standardized instruments measuring their propensity to environmental and socially conscious consumption. The criteria of analysis are: comprehensibility of the message, attractiveness (measured by polarity profiles and direct questions), emotional appeal (before and after design), acceptability, and relevance (with the proxy measure of remembrance of contents and emotions).

Special attention is given to the measurement of emotions. While there has been a significant increase of research in affective processes in consumer behaviour research (overview in Richins, 1997), information about the nature of emotions and their measurement is still scarce. In the consumer research module of Project Balance, the measurement of emotions is performed with the German version (Krohne et al., 1996) of the US instrument PANAS (Positive and Negative Affect Schedule by Watson & Clark (1988) and individual interviews with "consensual validation" (Mangold, 2001).

**Intermediate results**

In order to evaluate the initial results, we follow again Andreason's (1995) description of stage-appropriate marketing tasks:

1. *Create awareness and interest*: In the case of Project Balance, most of the target group members are in the stage of precontemplation. Hence, it is important to show new behavioural possibilities, to show their relevance, to communicate that the proposed behaviour is not antithetical to the values of, or even a trend in the consumers' reference groups[8] (e.g., presenting a celebrity who is consuming fair trade coffee; showcasing stylish "Lifestyles of Health and Sustainability" – LOHAS), and that it will improve audience members' own lives (e.g., presenting benefits and positive consequences in a positive enjoyable frame that creates positive emotions and attitudes). The appropriate tools are the provision of positive emotional stimuli and education on behavioural alternatives. Viewer surveys conducted on the Project Balance website after the clips were

202

aired showed that the "sustainability" clips were perceived at least as interesting and attractive as the other clips in the show that did not feature sustainability issues. Moreover, most of the clips were able to create positive emotions. Those clips with negative emotions and a fear appeal were less liked and less well remembered.

2. *Change values*: Some members of the target group are in the contemplation stage, where they consider and evaluate proposed behaviours. For those viewers, it is important to showcase the benefits and to reduce perceived costs of behavioural alternatives. In Project Balance, the TV clip showcasing the thriftily use of compact detergent, focuses on the individual benefits (i.e., money saving, less environmental harm, health aspects) of "washing right". There is also "demarketing" in the sense that the individual and environmental cost of the behavioural alternative – conventional filler boosted washing powder – is emphasized. On an emotional level, compact detergent is presented as the modern high tech alternative, the washing powder with fillers as outdated, dull, and even ridiculous.

3. *Motivate*: For those consumers who have reached stage three – preparation – it is important to provide easily accessible information and "service" guidance in order to reduce transaction cost to a minimum. Consumers at this stage are ready for a more extended information search. Here, a three to eight minutes TV clip reaches its limits as information carrier. A solution is to guide viewers explicitly via the show host to the website (www.weltderwunder.de) where additional material (e.g., on the European "wash right" campaign, a voluntary initiative by the large washing detergent producers) and service tools (e.g., a service module that computed the optimal amount of detergent when the user entered her zip code) are provided. As log file analysis showed, many viewers are indeed directed straight to the website and make use of its offers: Some of them opt for re-viewing the sustainability clips of the latest shows, and actively search for more information in the rubric "balance". Many look at the print magazine and the podcast show, which are both advertised on the website; finally, some have participated in balance quizzes (that serve the project as a measure of

knowledge creation), filled in questionnaires on the perception of the clips (to be used by the research project), chat with other community members, the producer, or the scientists. From a conceptual view, TV viewers become Internet users, and the one-way passive information has been supplemented by an active and selective information search process with the option of two-way communication (Chats).

4. / 5. *Create action and maintain change*: Securing repeat behaviour and reinforcing desired behaviour are hence the final tasks of behaviour modification. Sustainability communication can be helpful in presenting successful examples and of reducing perceived barriers to action. Research on sustainable consumer behaviour has pointed at the necessity of high quality (i.e., fast, precise, independent) feed back that can provide the necessary rewards. Without going into detail, communities (virtual or real) can play an important role in feed-backing, rewarding, and punishing. However, as outlined above, Project Balance does not comprise systematic follow-ups, monitoring, and measuring of behaviour change or its maintenance itself, but limits its research to behavioural intentions.

**Discussion and management implications**

The chapter described one possible alternative to communicate CSR issues to a broad, largely uninterested audience. However, regarding both practice and research, there are still a number of pot-holes along the way which have to be kept in mind when a company decides to engage in CSR communication: Not all consumers are interested in CSR issues, and within the group of the interested, it is not yet easy for them to distinguish those firms that merit patronage from all others. The cost of motivating the non-interested consumers might be prohibitively high, and hence, resources could eventually be better allocated to support the "sustainability case". Then, it is questionable whether and in how far consumers will alter consumption choices to reward good CSR behaviour. And finally, it is not clear that firms can detect these changes and link them to the corporation's CSR activities. However, to show that there is a business case for mass mediated CSR communication and that it is a worthwhile investment for consumer activists and policymakers, all these links should be in place.

While the research presented in this chapter has been carried out in Germany, the focus of the present book is on Danish companies and Danish audiences. The intercultural dimension of the concept of CSR has been picked up by a number of recent studies (Echo Research, 2001). Depending on the type of market economy, the tradition, reliability, and breadth of the social security systems, as well as on cultural factors, the interest in and response to CSR is quite different in Europe, the US, and Asia. While in many European countries "social responsibility" is still closely associated with the system of social market economy and hence primarily directed towards the state (this holds particularly true for the Scandinavian countries), in the US, CSR is associated with active measures and programmes of corporations and with a long tradition of philanthropic activities. Hence, it would be interesting to test whether a mass mediated CSR communication approach such as the one presented in this chapter would be a worthwhile endeavour in Denmark. Prior research (Morsing & Thyssen, 2003) casts doubt on that, showing that the Danish public is quite suspicious about strong CSR communication efforts, especially if they are not transported in the appropriate channels. As noted above, the Danes find that companies should rather "walk but not talk", i.e., downplay rather than conspicuously showcase their CSR efforts. The preferred communication channels seem to be the less bold ones such as annual reports and corporate web-sites, rather than advertising and public relations.

### Where do we go from here?
The research overview and discussion of the ongoing Project Balance in this chapter thus lead to the following questions for reflection:

- Should the company target consumers at all as a separate target group?
- If yes, how can they be reached best? Are emotionalized campaigns an option? Do they fit in the strategic marketing and

communication approach of the firm? Where are the specific risks and benefits of such a strategy?

- Strategic partnering: Who are potential – most importantly: credible – partners in such communication efforts?

## References

Ajzen, I. (1991). The theory of planned behaviour. Some unresolved issues. *Organizational Behavior and Human Decision Processes*, 50, 179-211.

Ajzen, I. & Fishbein, M. (1980). *Understanding attitudes and predicting social behaviour.* Englewood Cliffs, NJ: Prentice Hall.

Andreasen, A. R. (1995). *Marketing social change: Changing behavior to promote health, social development, and the environment.* San Francisco, CA: Jossey-Bass.

Andreasen, A. R. (2001). *Ethics in social marketing.* Washington, DC: Georgetown University Press.

Backer, T. E., Rogers, E. M. & Sopory, P. (1992*). Designing health communication campaigns: What works?* Newbury Park, CA: Sage.

Bagozzi, R. P. & Warshaw, P. (1990). Trying to consume. *Journal of Consumer research,* 17, 127-140.

Beardan, W. O. & Etzel, M. J. (1982). Reference group influences on product and brand purchase decisions. *Journal of Consumer Research,* 9, 181-186.

Brown, T. J. & Dacin, P. A. (1997). The company and the product: Corporate associations and consumer product responses. *Journal of Marketing,* 61(1), 68-84.

Coleman, J. S. & Fararo, T. J. (1992) (Eds.). *Rational choice theory: Advocacy and critique.* Newbury Park: Sage.

Creyer, E. H. & Ross, W. T. (1997). The influence of firm behavior on purchase intention: Do consumers really care about business ethics? *Journal of Consumer Marketing,* 14(6), 421-432.

Drumwright, M. E. (1994). Socially responsible organizational buying: Environmental concern as a noneconomic buying criterion. *Journal of Marketing,* 58(3), 1-19.

Dyhr, V. (2003). CSR as a competitive factor in a consumer perspective. In: Morsing, M. & Thyssen, C. (eds.), *Corporate Values and Responsibility – the Case of Denmark, pp.* 281-287. Copenhagen: Samfundslitteratur.

Echo Research (2001). Giving it back 2: Corporate Social Responsibility in the global market. *An Integrated Report on Corporate Social Responsibility in Global Markets 2001-2 prepared by Echo Research, Surrey, UK.*

Echo Research (2003). CSR 3: Corporate Social Responsibility and the financial community – friends or foes? *Report prepared by Echo Research, Surrey, UK.*

Eisend, M. (2006). Source credibility in marketing communication: A meta-analysis. Marketing: *Journal of Research and Management.* 2(1), 43-60.

Frankental, P. (2001). Corporate social responsibility – a PR invention? Corporate Communications: *An International Journal,* 6(1), 18-23.

Glombitza, A. (2005). *Corporate Social Responsibility in der Unternehmenskommunikation.* Berlin/Munich: poli-c-books.

Goul Andersen, J. & Tobiasen, M. (2001*). Politisk forbrug og politiske forbrugere. Globalisiering og politik i hverdagslivet.* Århus: Magtudredninden.

207

Hale, J. L. & Dillard, J. P. (1995). Fear appeals in health promotion campaigns: Too much, too little, or just right? In: E. W. Maibach & R. L. Parrott (Eds.). *Designing health messages*, pp. 65-80. Newbury Park, CA: Sage.

IBM Global Business Services (2006). *Konvergenz oder Divergenz? Erwartungen und Präferenzen der Konsumenten an die Telekommunikations- und Medienangebote von morgen.* Stuttgart: IBM Deutschland GmbH.

Kaiser, F.G., Fuhrer, U., Weber, O., Ofner, T. & Bühler-Ilieva, E. (2001). Responsibility and ecological bahviour. A meta-analysis of the strength and the extent of a causal link. In: A. E. Auhagen & H.-W. Bierhoff (Eds.). Responsibility. *The many faces of a social phenomenon*, pp. 109-126. London: Routledge.

Kals, E. & Maes, J. (2002). Sustainable development and emotions. In: P. Schmuck & W. Schultz (Eds.). *Psychology of sustainable development*, pp. 97-122. Norwell, MA: Kluwer Academic Publishers.

Klein, J. & Dawar, N. (2004). Corporate social responsibility and consumers' attributions and brand evaluations in a product-harm crisis. *International Journal of Research in Marketing*, 21(3), 203-217.

Kreeb, M. (2001). Ecotainment. In: W. F. Schulz et al. (Eds.).: *Lexikon Nachhaltiges Wirtschaften (Lehr- und Handbücher zur ökologischen Unternehmensführung und Umweltökonomie)*, pp. 73-75. Munich: Oldenbourg.

Kroeber-Riel, W. (2003). *Konsumentenverhalten. 8th ed.* Munich: Vahlen.

Krohne, H. W., Egloff, B., Kohlmann, C.-W. & Tausch, A. (1996). Untersuchungen mit einer deutschen Version der „Positive and Negative Affect Schedule" (PANAS). *Diagnostica*, 42(2), 139-156.

Lichtl, M. (1999). Ecotainment: *Der neue Weg im Umweltmarketing.* Vienna / Frankfurt: Wirtschaftsverlag.

Maibach, E. W. & Cotton, D. (1995). Moving people to behaviour change: A stages social cognitive approach to message design. In: E. W. Maibach & R. L. Parott (Eds.). *Designing health messages*, pp. 41-64. Newbury Park, CA: Sage.

Maignan, I. & Ferrell, O. C. (2003). Nature of corporate responsibilities: Perspectives from American, French, and German consumers. *Journal of Business Research*, 56(1), 55-67.

Mangold, R. (2001). Digital Emotionen – wo bleiben die Gefühle bei medialen Informationsangeboten? In: *Hallische Medienarbeiten aus der Medien- und Kommunikationswissenschaft der Martin-Luther-Universität Halle-Wittenberg*, Vol. 6, No. 4.

McGuire, W. J. (1976). Some internal psychological factors influencing consumer choice. *Journal of Consumer Research*, 2, 302-319.

Micheletti, M. & Stolle, D. (2004). Swedish political consumers: Who they are and why they use the market as an arena for politics. In: M. Boström, A. Føllesdal, M. Klintman, M. Micheletti, & M. Sørensen (Eds.). Political consumerism: Its motivations, power, and conditions in the Nordic countries and elsewhere. *Proceedings from the 2nd International Seminar on Political Consumerism*, Oslo, August 26-29, 2004, pp. 145-164.

Mohr, L. A. & Webb, D. J. (2005). The effects of corporate social responsibility and price on consumer responses. *The Journal of Consumer Affairs*, 39(1), 121-147.

Mohr, L. A., Webb, D.J. & Harris, K. E. (2001). Do consumers expect companies to be socially responsible? The impact of Corporate Social Responsibility on buying behavior. *Journal of Consumer Affairs*, 35, 45-72.

Monahan, J. L. (1995). Thinking positively: Using positive affect when designing health messages. In: E. Maibach & R.L. Parott (Eds.). *Designing health messages*, pp. 81-113. Thousand Oaks, CA: Sage.

Montada, L. & Kals, E. (2000). Political implications of environmental psychology. *International Journal of Psychology*, 35(2), 168-176.

Morsing, M. (2003). Conspicuous responsibility: Communicating responsibiilty – to whom? In: Morsing, M. & Thyssen, C. (Eds.). *Corporate Values and Responsibility – the Case of Denmark*, pp. 145-154. Copenhagen: Samfundslitteratur.

Morsing. M. & Langer, R. (2006). CSR-communication in the business press: Advantages of strategic ambiguity. *Chapter presented at the 11th International Conference on Corporate and Marketing Communications*, Ljubljana, April 21$^{st}$-22 2006.

Morsing, M. & Thyssen, C. (2003) (Eds.). *Corporate values and responsibility – the Case of Denmark*. Copenhagen: Samfundslitteratur.

Nasi, J. (1995). *Understanding stakeholder thinking*. Helsinki: LSR-Julkaisut Oy.

Peloza, J. (2006). Using Corporate Social Responsibility as insurance for financial performance. *California Management Review*, 48(2), Special Issue on Strategies for Corporate Social Responsibility, 52-72.

Pleon Kothes Klewes (2005). *Accounting for good: the Global Stakeholder Report 2005 – the second world-wide survey on stakeholder attitudes to CSR reporting*. Amsterdam / Bonn: Pleon Kothes Klewes.

Prochaska, J. O. & DiClemente, C. C. (1984). *The transtheoretical approach: Crossing the traditional boundaries of therapy*. Homewood, IL: Dow Jones-Irwin.

Reisch, L. A. (2005). Kommunikation des Nachhaltigen Konsums: Forschung und Praxis. In: G. Michelsen & J. Godemann (Eds.). *Handbuch Nachhaltigkeitskommunikation, Grundlagen und Praxis*, pp. 461-470. Munich: Ökom.

Reisch, L. A. (2006). Consumer-oriented offers of CSR information in selected EU-countries – Denmark. *Expert Report prepared for imug, Hannover, on behalf of the German Federal Ministry of Food, Agriculture, and Consumer Protection (BMELV)*. Copenhagen: Copenhagen Business School, Dept. of Intercultural Communication and Management (IKL) (in print).

Reisch, L. A. & Røpke, I. (2004) (Eds.). *The ecological economics of consumption*. Cheltenham: Edward Elgar.

Richins, M. L. (1997). Measuring emotions in the consumption experience. Journal of Consumer Research, 24(September), 127-146.

Schoenheit, I. & Wirthgen, A. (2006). *Wirkungen von vergleichenden Untersuchungen zur Corporate Social Responsibility bei Verbrauchern – am Beispiel der Stiftung Warentest. Imug Arbeitspapier Nr. 16/2006*. Hannover: imug.

Schrader, U., Halbes, S. & Hansen, U. (2005). Konsumentenorientierte Kommunikation über Corporate Social Responsibility (CSR). *Erkenntnisse aus Experteninterviews in Deutschland. Imug Arbeitspapier Nr. 54/2005*. Hannover: imug.

Sen, S. & Bhattacharya, C. B. (2001). Does doing good always lead to doing better? Consumer reactions to corporate social responsibility. *Journal of Marketing Research*, 38(2), 225-243.

Sen, S., Bhattacharya, C. B. & Korschun, D. (2006). The role of corporate social responsibility on strengthening multiple stakeholder relationships: A field experiment. *Journal of the Academy of Marketing Science,* 34(2), 158-166.

Steinert, A. & Klein, A. (2002). Corporate social responsibility (CSR). Eine Herausforderung an die Unternehmenskommunikation. In: G. Bentele, M. Piwinger, & G. Schönborn (Eds.). *Kommunikationsmanagement,* pp. 1-26. Neuwied: Luchterhand.

Swaen, V. & Vanhamme, J. (2004). When "what you say" matters less than "where you say it": Influence of corporate social responsibility arguments and source of information on consumers' reactions and attitudes toward the company. In: *Proceedings of the 33rd European Marketing Academy (EMAC) Conference*. Murcia: University of Murcia.

TNS Gallup (2005). *Mapping of CSR activities among small and medium-sized enterprises*. People & Profit Phase 2. Report funded by The Danish National Labour Market Authority (Arbejdsmarkedstyrelsen) / Danish Commerce and Companies Agency (Erhvervs- og Selskabsstyrelsen) and the European Communities (The European Social Fund).

Tobiasen, M. (2004). Political consumerism in Denmark. In: M. Boström, A. Føllesdal, M. Klintman, M. Micheletti & M. Sørensen (Eds.). Political consumerism: its motivations, power, and conditions in the Nordic countries and elsewhere. *Proceedings from the 2nd International Seminar on Political Consumerism,* Oslo, August 26-29, 2004, pp. 113-144.

Watson, D. & Clark, L. A. (1988). Development and validation of brief measures of positive and negative affect: The PANAS Scales. *Journal of Personality and Social Psychology,* 54(6), 1063-1070.

## Notes

1. This is what Danish TDC's marketing and sponsorship director said when arguing for the positive effect that the company's CSR has on consumer perception (as cited in Morsing, 2003, p. 148).

210

2. Between 2004 and 2005, the highly respected independent German product testing institute "Stiftung Warentest" (*www.stiftung-warentest.de*) has performed and published several "CSR tests" of corporations as a pilot study. The tests were based on a set of 39 core criteria and 15-25 product specific criteria. The results were published in the same issue as the product tests of the respective companies (for an evaluation see: Schoenheit & Wirthgen, 2006).

3. For instance, the "Perception Index" published by the British Echo Research Group, listing "Saints and Sinners" and tracking their rise and fall (Echo Research, 2003).

4. Lately, CSR research has explicitly called for future research to examine how consumer emotions might affect or be affected by CSR perceptions (Klein & Dawar, 2004).

5. For instance, the German frozen food producer FRoSTA markets a premium brand (FRoSTA) with the USP of a purity requirement with the full declaration of all contents and the promise of no preservatives, no colourings, no flavour enhancer, no preservatives, and organic quality. The communication of the "Reinheitsgebot" is performed via highly emotionalized commercials and a respective seal on the packaging. At the same time, FRoSTA markets a conventional product line with medium quality as a trade brand with only obligatory declaration of contents.

6. For a detailed overview of concept, partners, and research design see the Interim Reports of the project (available from the author) and the project website *www.balance-f.de.*

7. For a detailed comparison of strengths and weaknesses of alternative media for nonprofits see: Andreason, 1995, p. 212, Table 6.3.

8. Reference groups can be membership groups, aspiration groups, and negative reference groups (e.g., Bearden & Etzel, 1982).

211

# CHAPTER 9

# The Uncertainties of Strategic CSR communication: Business-NGO Relations

*Susse Georg*

*Mindfulness preserves the capability to see the significant meaning of weak signals and to give strong responses to weak signals. This counterintuitive act holds the key to managing the unexpected.*

K. W. Weick & K. M. Stucliffe (2001:4) Managing the Unexpected

## Introduction

The widely publicized Brent Spar incident in 1995 is almost iconic of what business does *not* want to happen, which is to figure prominently in the mass media in ways that are beyond corporate control. Greenpeace an environmental NGO, accomplished what many had thought would be impossible – they succeed in pressuring Royal Dutch/Shell to reverse one of their subsidiaries', Shell UK, decision to dump the defunct oil rig Brent Spar in the North Sea; despite the fact that Shell UK had sound technical and environmental grounds for an off shore disposal of the rig and that they had the UK government's approval of their plans. There was one thing that they did not have, however, and that was the publics accept of their plan. Greenpeace's campaign, which included extensive, well planned and dramatic media coverage of activists chaining themselves to the rig at open sea (Backer, 2005), widespread consumer boycotts of Shell in a number of European countries, and the fire-bombing of two German petrol stations, caused so much political and economic havoc that Royal Dutch/Shell stood down from dumping Brent Spar (Grolin, 1998; Tsoukas, 1999).

Heralded as a modern day version of David and Goliath (Tsoukas, 1999), Greenpeace's victory over Shell is but one example of NGO-activism. There are numerous other examples of NGO campaigns, e.g. the Free Burma Coalition, Friends of the Earth, Global Exchange, which have also targeted specific companies and/or brands. However, what sets the Brent Spar controversy apart from other examples is that it so clearly demonstrated how effective and convincing non-governmental organizations can be in staging media coverage, effecting public backlash and, consequently, in shaping corporate behaviour. The controversy was an 'eye-opener' for business – it showed how quickly the seemingly weak signals of NGO critique could be made public and strong, and how devastating this could be. By not attending to these signals in time, Royal Dutch/Shell suffered not only substantial operational costs but also quite a bit of reputational damage as extensive media coverage undermined corporate legitimacy and tainted Shell's image (Tsoukas, 1999).

214

The issue of ensuring corporate legitimacy has much attention in the years that have passed since the Brent Spar incident, particularly in light of the growing importance attributed to corporate reputation (Fombrun, 1996). As a consequence, there is a renewed and intensified interest in attending to one's most important stakeholders and to managing them (Clarkson, 1995; Donaldson & Preston, 1995; Freeman, 1984), and strategic communication is generally considered to be an important means to this end. There are, however, a few things that can make this a challenging task: One, identifying which stakeholders are the most important to communicate with is in itself a tricky task. After all, Shell did not know how important Greenpeace and the public would be in the Brent Spar incident until *after* the damage was done. Second, the fact that stakeholder concerns change and vary further complicates the task. The Brent Spar incident was primarily a controversy about one relatively well-defined issue – mitigating the environmental consequences of dumping an oil rig. Even though this and many other environmental concerns are far from trivial, they were relatively well defined compared to, for instance, corporate social responsibility. Usually cast as a matter of protecting human rights, ensuring social justice, providing decent working conditions, prohibiting child labour, etc., CSR has numerous facets and is subject to so many interpretations that not only are the ways in which companies are expected 'to do good' increasing, but there is also a great deal of uncertainty as to what 'good' entails. This uncertainty makes developing a communications strategy for what to say to whom somewhat daunting.

This chapter addresses the challenges of corporate attempts at managing one particular type of stakeholder; a stakeholder that is often cast as a critic of corporate social responsibility – non-governmental organizations. The chapter focuses on the different ways in which NGOs and companies can communicate and interact, and on what implications different communication strategies can have for companies' ability to attend to changes in their surroundings. There are, presumably, as many proponents for communicating with NGOs on environmental and CSR-related issues as there are opponents: There are many businesses who

215

claim that strategic communication with NGOs is a good thing because it can reduce reputational risks and allow for differentiation, both of which can give the company a competitive edge. Whereas others, in keeping with the often-cited Milton Friedman's quote that 'the business of business is business', maintain that strategic communication with NGOs is likely to be a waste of corporate resources (see also the chapter by Guthey et al.). For NGOs, engaging with corporations may serve as a means for changing corporate behaviour or, on a more pessimistic note, lead to co-optation. Viewed from this perspective, strategic communication with NGOs is tantamount to window-dressing, 'green-wash', and empty rhetoric.

Rather than continuing in this vein of either-or, this chapter develops a more pragmatic approach to understanding corporate strategic communication with NGOs, and argues that it can affect both corporations and NGOs in ways that can help both types of organizations become more mindful of changes in their surroundings and, hopefully, become better at 'managing the unexpected' (Weick & Sutcliffe, 2001). In doing so, this chapter draws upon different strands of organizational literature to highlight the different modes of strategic communication companies can use when addressing NGOs and NGO critique. The chapter focuses on four issues:

- Why are NGOs interesting?
- What does strategic communication with NGOs entail?
- What can strategic communication with NGOs 'do' to the company?
- What are the managerial implications?

It is an exploratory analysis, drawing on examples from existing studies to demonstrate the potentials and pitfalls of this particular vein of strategic CSR communication. The chapter begins by identifying and characterizing NGOs and then moves on to give and discuss examples of the two main modes of corporate communication – one-way and two-way communication. The chapter

216

concludes with some of the challenges of strategic CSR communication with NGOs.

## NGOs – organizing the future

Unlike many other organizations, NGOs are often defined by
what they are *not*: they are non-governmental, non-business and
not for profit organizations. They are, however, often considered
as prototypical for social activism (Davis et al., 2005). Although
social activism, once primarily associated with religious groups,
has a long history, NGO-activism has a relatively short history
dating back to the 1960s and 1970s. Many of the more well-
known NGOs were founded at this time, e.g. the World Wildlife
Foundation (1961), Amnesty International (1961), Friends of the
Earth (1968), Greenpeace (1971) and Human Rights Watch
(1978). Since then, the number of NGOs has proliferated and
NGO membership has soared in most countries, e.g. high and
middle income countries have witnessed close to a fifty percent
increase in membership growth in 1990-2000, whereas the low
income countries have only experienced a twenty percent growth
(SustainAbility, The Global Compact & United Nations Environmental Programme, 2003, p. 8). And according to SustainAbility
et al. (2003), NGO membership may be supplanting that of trade
unions and parties as the desired form of political engagement.
These developments are primarily attributed to governmental
changes in the emergent and transition economies that allow for
the proliferation of NGOs; the rolling back of government in the
developed economies, thus, enticing groups to take action and to
target business rather than government; and the development of
new communication technologies that allows news to travel fast
SustainAbility et al. (2003, p. 8).

NGOs come in many shapes and sizes: ranging from small
'grass root' organizations, engaged in highly localized issues, to
large, professionally managed organizations that operate on a
global scale. It appears that the number of NGOs operating internationally has increased over the years: according to the Year-
book of International Associations, the number of NGOs operating internationally has increased with almost 90 % from 183 or-

217

ganizations in 1973 to 959 in 2000 (Smith, 2005, p. 232-233). Historically organized around single issues such as either human rights *or* environmental concerns, there has been a marked growth in the 1990ies in the number of organizations with a multi-issue focus, e.g. focusing on human rights, development *and* environment. With a broadening of their scope and an increasing in members, NGOs have access to more economic resources thus increasing their economic significance. NGOs are, as SustainAbility et al. (2003, p. 11), "valued at over 1 trillion USD a year, and employing 19 million paid employees", and if one were to consider NGOs as a sector it would, according to SustainAbility SustainAbility et al., rank as the world's eighth-largest economy. Some NGOs are because of the money involved becoming businesses in their own right. On top of their traditional concerns, they are becoming increasingly concerned with membership issues and branding.

Regardless of differences in size and structure, NGOs have several features in common. For one, they generally receive a lot of attention, particularly from the media, and their potential for bringing about change is much celebrated. Second, they are highly value-driven. They operate either in support of or in opposition to particular issues, which involves either protecting or challenging existing rights and entitlement structures. They are typically dedicated to issues involving alleviating harm, improving the quality of life, promoting development, and to issues that they feel government and business have not addressed correctly, if at all. They have, in other words, an implicit or explicit interest in creating a better future. Fuelled by visions of what should/ should not be or by visions of what could be – they seek to mobilize others around their ideas and goals in attempts at organizing the future. Another distinguishing feature is that NGOs are generally considered to be more trustworthy than both business and government. They stand apart from both, which puts them in the position of being a 'third party'. Moreover, they are usually assumed to be motivated by greater concerns than profits and/or power. Numerous opinion polls have documented that NGOs are not subject to as much public suspicion as government and, par-

218

ticularly, business. Indeed, it appears that it is only when NGOs team up with business – in partnerships – that their credibility is put on the line; the critique being that they will end up as 'lap dogs' rather than watch dogs (Argenti, 2004).

NGOs have a variety of tactics at their disposal, e.g., appealing to companies to change behaviour, and if that does not work, then organizing demonstrations or consumer boycotts against them and/or activating others – notably local governments or other key actors in the companies' value chain – to take action against the companies. Other tactics include evoking lawsuits and/or activating the media to render corporate behaviour more visible to a broader public as Greenpeace did in the case of Brent Spar. Less adversarial tactics include developing more collaborative relationships with business to achieve results that those involved feel are unattainable through other means. Some NGOs have chosen to specialize in one particular form of interaction. Others engage in all of these tactics, since they are not mutually exclusive, e.g. campaigns can lead to stakeholder dialogues or even partnerships as the involved organizations gain experience working together. There are, however, differences in how 'anti business', 'anti growth', or collaborative NGOs are branded or perceived to be, e.g. the World Wildlife Foundation (WWF) is generally considered to be more collaborative than, for instance, Greenpeace, Free Burma, and Attac!, all of which have developed much more confrontational approaches. These differences in tactics reflect differences in how the NGOs feel they best can achieve their goals.

### Why engage with NGOs?

What, then, from a business perspective, makes NGOs interesting organizations to communicate and collaborate with? There are four common and inter-related answers to this question: One, NGOs can – as the Brent Spar incident demonstrated – be extremely influential in not only setting the agenda for what is broadly considered as 'good corporate behaviour', but also in 'publicizing' whether or not companies live up to these codes of conduct. Their ability to focus on single issues, gain attention and enrol others in their cause, their watchdog' status and the high level of credibility associated with their 'outsider' perspective provides them with an autonomous authority in the public debates as to whether or not corporations are 'doing as good as they say'. With the development of the internet and other communication technologies, it is possible for even relatively small NGOs to reach large audiences. NGOs can, therefore, be quite influential in either providing companies with – or preventing them from getting – a 'licence to operate' (Elkington, 1997). Second, and closely linked to the above, is the claim that engaging with NGOs forces companies to be more open and accountable, and that this makes company operations more transparent. This is considered as essential for enhancing public trust. Third, NGOs are not only influential in swaying external stakeholders such as the media, consumers and policy makers, they are also important mediators of company communication to internal stakeholders, i.e., NGOs can act as vehicles for internal communication that can help build and sustain employee loyalty as well as recruit new employees. A fourth reason for engaging with NGOs is that they can offer another perspective on company performance and they can give business some indication of the socio-political and economic challenges to come – NGOs can provide business with insights as to how others view them and their actions as well as with different interpretations of what 'good corporate behaviour' is likely to entail now and in the future.

Whether or not it is possible to realize these benefits depends on the company motive for engaging with NGOs as well as the NGO's motives and tactics. Needless to say, both company and NGO motives/tactics vary greatly. As far as companies go, it appears that some engage with NGOs in an attempt to pre-empt NGO critique and others to accommodate it, and then there are still others that try to silence the critique by either ignoring it or by attempting to discredit the NGO-position. Although some may explain these differences in terms of altruism and the personal priorities of key company decision makers, the most prevalent explanation is that NGOs represents a threat or a risk, to which companies must in some way respond. This is usually hinged on arguments as

220

to how costly engaging with NGOs is likely to be in terms of operating and investment costs, how important avoiding/accommodating NGO critique is for protecting the corporate brand or reputation and how influential NGOs can be securing or undermining competitive advantage (Spar & La Mure, 2003).

However, for companies seeking to develop a strategic approach to their CSR communication, there are numerous ways of engaging with NGOs; each with their potential and pitfalls (see also the chapter by Morsing and Schultz).

## Two strategies for engaging with NGOs

Business has a host of communicative strategies at their disposal. For the sake of simplicity, these strategies can be roughly characterized as either one-way or two-way communication (Grunig & Hunt, 1984; cited in Cheney & Christensen (2000). The former usually entails the *transmission of information* from the company to its stakeholders or publics (internal as well as external ones), and it is based on the assumption that they have 'an information deficit' (Michael, 2002); i.e. they have no, little or the wrong understanding of company performance, and it is assumed that this can be corrected by providing them with more information regarding corporate values, practices, and the like.

The other communication strategy entails that both parties are actively involved in conversations with one another. Conversing is based on repeated *interaction* and patterned through turn-taking. Conversing calls for the participants to respond to each other, and the conversational processes work to provide each participant with insights about 'the other's' viewpoints and actions, while simultaneously providing each participant with the opportunity to reflect on their own interpretations and understandings. The conversational processes work to organize the participants' experiences and insights so that they not only learn about 'the other' but also about themselves; unless, of course, they withdraw from the conversation (Stacey, 2003, pp. 347-350). In contrast to the first-mentioned communicative strategy, the second strategy allows for developing a mutual understanding of the situation (or concern) at hand. Neither strategy is, however, guaranteed to be a success.

*One-way communication – comprehending NGO concerns*
When it comes to assessing what strategies companies are pursuing with regard to corporate CSR communication, an obvious place to look is at the increasing number of CSR-reports or sustainability-reports (see also the chapter by Nielsen and Thomsen). Judging from these reports, it appears as if the dominant communicative strategy is that of informing NGOs (and other stakeholders). The reports provide often lengthy descriptions of what companies are doing to become more environmentally and socially responsible and they signal the importance of CSR as a corporate concern. The flow of information is, however, decidedly one-way – the readers are passive recipients of the information. Viewed in this light, CSR-reporting (and other forms of one-way communicative strategies such as TV-spots, press releases and press briefings/meetings) can be considered as just another means of issue management where company disclosures are intended to shape or influence the *opinions* of NGOs and other stakeholders (Cheney & Christensen, 2000, pp. 237-239).

One of the informative strategy's drawbacks is that one can not be sure that the reports, TV-spots, etc., will be received the way in which they were intended. Companies have very little, if any, control over the ways in which their communication is received, i.e. if it is considered convincing and credible. What may be convincing to some stakeholders may not be so for others. It is, therefore, not surprising that many companies reporting on their CSR activities also have web-sites with facilities that allow stakeholders to 'tell them' their opinions. Royal Dutch Shell, for instance, added this facility to their web-site after the Brent Spar incident as part of their efforts to manage (and improve) their corporate reputation (Fombrun & Rindova, 2000). These features work as feed-back mechanisms that allow companies to identify and monitor their stakeholders' opinions without engaging directly with them. This can help companies 'read' their audiences and help them to *comprehend* why their actions are not always well

222

received. Armed with these insights companies are likely to be better equipped to refine and develop their communication materials and reporting practices. Although facilities such as these enable companies to get a better feel for their stakeholders' concerns by reversing the information flow – by allowing people to 'have their say' – it can hardly be considered as a dialogue or two-way communication. Moreover, in light of how highly mediated these information exchanges are, it is likely that the information will be subject to more divergent interpretations than if companies and NGOs were to engage more directly with one another and actively exchange views on the issues at hand.

*Two-way communication – apprehending NGO concerns*
Many of the companies reporting on CSR are, however, often also cited for more actively engaging with NGOs, indicating that companies need not and are not merely pursuing one communicative strategy. Companies are engaging in more interactive communicative practices that include round-tables, targeted stakeholder *dialogues* on specific issues (e.g. human and animal welfare/rights); working with NGOs in public consultation exercises regarding plant location and operation; and working with NGOs in community development projects, particularly in the developing countries.

Clearly, companies and NGOs differ with respect to motives, information, money and access to other resources, which precludes them from being 'on equal footing' in these interactive communicative practices. Judged in terms of access to resources and their proprietary knowledge, companies are more likely to be deemed as having 'the upper hand' in most dialogue processes, but whether or not this is an issue depends on how the dialogue processes proceed, i.e. on how business and NGO interact. If, for instance, the dialogue processes become too one-sided for the NGOs liking, then they have the option of withdrawing and reverting to more adversarial tactics. This may, in turn, change the table as to who has the upper hand. Companies can, of course, withdraw from the dialogue processes as well, but this may well be at a risk – they may have more to loose in terms of credibility

223

than the NGOs given that their credibility is generally higher than that of business.

There are, however, instances in which business and NGOs interaction has moved beyond engaging in dialogues, and where strategic communication has evolved into some form of *partnership*, in which NGO and business collaborate to, for instance, develop products that live up to both NGO and business criteria. Although there are no clear criteria as to the difference between dialogues and partnerships, it appears that one important feature is the duration of the business-NGO relationship. Among the most widely show-cased examples are the Environmental Defense Fund's work with McDonald's in the early 1990ies to develop an alternative to McDonalds foam packaging for their burgers and Greenpeace's involvement with DKK Scharfenstein (a former East-German company) to market a CFC-free refrigerator, Greenfreeze, that later was appropriated by the major manufacturers to become a global technology (see Livesey, 1993; Georg & Irwin, 2002). These are, in a sense, examples of 'user-driven innovation', in which the NGOs are acting on the behalf of potential, environmentally concerned 'end users'. The success of these partnerships is hinged on the fact that both NGOs and business felt that there were clear benefits to be gained from partnering, that the scope of their collaboration was relatively well-defined, and the processes evolved so that neither business nor the NGOs lost sight of their respective goals, i.e. developing products that were less environmentally polluting and marketable (Livesey, 1993; Georg & Irwin, 2002). Rather than emphasizing curtailing 'the bad', these initiatives focused on developing something for the 'common good' and, as such, offered both the NGOs and business an opportunity for increased positive visibility.

Another widely celebrated example of NGO-business cooperation is 'The Nordic Partnership' (NP) that was established by The World Wide Fund for Nature in the Scandinavian countries, the Danish media center 'Mandag Morgen', and seventeen key Scandinavian corporations in 2001. This partnership was dedicated to identifying and publicizing methods to ensure the development of sustainable business.

224

The key drivers for companies to become partners were the potentials for: risk management and innovation, attracting and retaining customers, and for being able to retain and attract employees (The Nordic Partnership, 2002, pp. 14-20). As for the NGO, WWF, their participation was hinged on the belief that "..The] private sector [is] increasingly important...New momentum is needed – new relations between NGOs, business and governments could be part of the answer..[in] establishing long term strategies for environmental and social responsibility". Moreover, NP provided WWF with the chance of realizing their mission of "getting influential actors around the same table to discuss the real issues and of working directly with them to demonstrate the (economic) viability of sustainable business". It was their hope that endeavours such as these could help to 'level the playing field', but more importantly it provide WWF with the possibility of introducing a new dynamism into the sustainability debate (Carstensen, 2003).

The NP's activities included conducting and publishing a number of surveys and studies[1] as well as hosting meetings, conferences and workshops on how companies can become more environmentally and socially responsible. Many of the partner companies were already 'known for the good', i.e. broadly acknowledge as environmentally proactive companies, and the NP provided them with a venue for demonstrating this to their stakeholders in yet another way – it allowed them to 'stand out' as more responsible than other (non-partner) companies. The NPs initiatives allowed the partners to tell themselves, other partners and non-partners about their actions to promote sustainable business, i.e. it as a place where they could 'talk the(ir) walk'. Presumably this also provided them (and other businesses) with insights so that they could improve their practices, and become better at 'walking the(ir) talk'. However, by 2004 the NP came to somewhat of an impasse with regard to how to continue their collaborative efforts (The Nordic Partnership, 2005). Unable to attract the necessary government funding that would allow the NP to evolve into something new – an independent, non-profit *association* that included government – they decided to dissolve the

225

partnership in 2005, because without sufficient external funding to match the commitment and resources of the initiators, it would not be possible to ensure the 'new' association's financial independence (Brinch-Pedersen, 2006).

Although the ways in which partnerships function will invariably vary, the above-mentioned examples indicate that, if both business and NGO have well-defined goals and they are interested in working towards a common goal, then it is possible that both organizations will have opportunities for learning about 'the other's' position and perhaps even developing activities/technologies that both consider to be mutually beneficial. Obviously, this need not always be the case: communication strategies based on interactively engaging with NGOs need not necessarily evolve into a learning situation and lead to consensus development or conflict resolution. They do, however, offer the *possibility* of doing so. Given the likely conflict of interests that most NGOs and business have, it is equally likely that 'start up' costs of the more interactive communication strategies are going to be high on both sides and involve a number of risks, e.g. companies being accused of buying into NGO reputation (legitimacy) and of co-opting them while the NGOs run the risk of being labelled lapdogs rather than watch dogs. Whether and to which extent this is the case is, however, situational – it depends on the parties involved, the issues, the stakes, their interaction and their other stakeholders view them. Broad sweeping claims as to the win-win situation of NGO-dialogues and/or partnerships or claims to the contrary, i.e. that they are zero-sum situations where one party (most likely the NGOs) are likely to loose, have a tendency to overlook the processes whereby these situations are created. And there is a tendency to treat the organizations involved as monolithic entities with unequivocal goals. Such simplifications gloss over the dynamics of business-NGO interaction and the managerial tensions that this involves.

By engaging with NGOs in the way that business has done in the above-mentioned examples, business is in a position to not only comprehend but also *apprehend* future challenges. Apprehension involves anticipating things to come and the act of seizing, taking hold (Michael, 2002, p. 367). Business is likely to be better equipped for this, if they engage more directly and actively with NGOs than if they maintain 'arms length' information strategies and media campaigns. More interactive communication strategies can provide business with access to the often highly specialized and extended networks of expertise that many NGOs have, thus, providing business with insights that might not otherwise have been accessible and which may be valuable input for reducing future risks and managing their reputation. On a similar note, NGOs may get access to 'insider knowledge' as to how companies operate that can be useful in later campaigns or initiatives. And both can draw upon the positive appeal carried by the notion of collaboration. However, in apprehending the future, issue management takes on a new dimension. Rather than just getting better at identifying and shaping the issues, companies can engage in issue creation.

### The apprehension of NGO concerns – some tensions

There is, however, an inherent tension in the apprehension of NGO concerns through partnerships: a tension that arises not, as commonly assumed, because of conflicts of interests, but because they have a tendency to 'disappear'. Although the repeated interaction that partnerships entail allows for learning and developing a deeper understanding of each other's organizational priorities, etc., there is a risk that this can go 'too far' or that it can be seen as going too far, particularly if insights about 'the other' are internalized in such a manner as give way to changing (company and NGO) priorities. In such instances, there is a danger that the partners' independence and integrity will be jeopardized. This is, perhaps, more likely to be a greater issue for the NGOs, since their credibility rests upon being an outsider, a third party, untainted by commercial interests. However, if the NGO looses credibility, then this might well jeopardize the business position, if the partnership looses credibility.

Unlike the informative strategy, which allows companies to comprehend NGO and public critique, and the interactive strategy of stakeholder dialogues that allows companies to not only

227

comprehend but also apprehend what is to come, partnerships hold the possibility of allowing the parties involved to "prehend" development (Michael, 2002, p. 368). Prehension, like apprehension is an act of taking hold or grasping, but differs in the sense that it is a less conscious. Prehension connotes messages that travel from one actor to another and the partial (re)constitution of the actors involved (Michael, 2002, p. 368). Prehension is an operation in which one entity 'grasps' another entity and makes that entity an object of its experience. It is not so much about relations as it is about relating and the transitions that take place in the course of doing so. The notion of prehension highlights the co-construction of the interacting organizations. Extended to the realm of corporate communication, this captures the tension in the ways in which some NGO-business partnerships work. Although the more collaborative approaches are likely to be more effectual in learning about and from NGOs than the less interactive forms of strategic communication, there is a danger that this can lead to a mutual constitution of the company and NGO that is at 'odds' with other stakeholders' beliefs and interests. Following from this, it appears that partners do need to keep each other a bit at arms length in order to maintain their organizational identity and integrity. They need to not only acknowledge but also maintain their different interests and competences so as to better maintain their separate roles in order to better identities and achieve their common goals.

### On the art of being mindful

Returning now to the Brent Spar incident, one could say that the scientific reports and the UK government's accept of Shell UK's plans of dumping the platform buffered them from the public concern to such an extent that they did not recognize let alone attend to the weak signals of public critique before it was too late. The communication strategy Shell developed after the incident allows them to inform their various stakeholders about corporate performance as well as monitor and perhaps their stakeholders, various and changing demands. It appears to have been an important step in making Shell more mindful of their sur-

228

roundings; particularly given that one of the key tenets of mindfulness is to focus on one's mistakes. Mindfulness entails more, though.

According to Weick and Sutcliffe (2001, p. 42), mindfulness entails "the combination of ongoing scrutiny of existing expectations, continuous refinement and differentiation of expectations based on newer experiences, willingness and capability to invent new expectations that make sense of unprecedented events, a more nuanced appreciation of context and ways to deal with it, and identification of new dimensions of context that improve foresight and current functioning." In keeping with this definition, it appears that the more interactive communication strategies are likely to provide those involved with more opportunities for refining and developing their expectations and for developing a greater sensitivity to their context than the more information-based communication strategies, thus, making the companies better equipped to give strong responses to weak signals.

This is not to say that the more interactive forms of corporate communication – stakeholder dialogues and partnerships – are the panacea for managing unexpected stakeholder reactions, because there is the danger that one or the other prehends the situation making it 'too much of a good thing' and undermining the credibility of these endeavours. The more interactive forms of corporate communication can, nevertheless, help companies apprehend changes in their surroundings by, on the one hand, keeping corporate confidence at bay as companies engage with their critics and by, on the other hand, simultaneously providing companies with useful insights into how things might be done differently. Avoiding the complacency that often accompanies (too much) corporate confidence is an important dimension of being mindful, because complacency can dull the way in which companies see things or even creates blind spots (as Shell was in the Brent Spar incident). Working with one's critics can help update companies on changing societal expectations that companies may not otherwise be able to 'pick up' when using communication strategies based on a one-way flow of information.

229

Being 'known for the good' when it comes to corporate social responsibility is, therefore, likely to entail more than providing stakeholder with all the necessary information, because the validity of this information can always be challenged. The tricky question is, then, how much more? The answer, in brief, is that it all depends on the companies and the NGOs involved, on their respective goals, opportunity structures (costs and benefits), preferences, and the ways they interact.

**Where do we go from here?**
NGO activism is relatively recent phenomenon that appears increasingly to have a stronger business focus, but the ways in which business is responding to this vary. This chapter has highlighted how strategic CSR communication allows for companies to become more mindful of unexpected changes in their surroundings. The chapter offers three perspectives:

- Informative communication strategies that allow companies to improve their understanding or comprehension of NGO concerns
- Interactive communication strategies involving, for instance, various forms of stakeholder dialogues that help companies comprehend and apprehend changes in their surroundings, thus, extending issue management to also entail issue creation
- Interactive communication strategies involving quite close collaboration in developing and expanding business activities that better allow companies to apprehend changing expectations but run the risk of prehending the situation or being unwittingly seized by 'the other' and becoming so close that organizational integrity is jeopardized.

The managerial challenge then is striking a balance between these corporate communication strategies and knowing which strategies to use with different NGOs. There is, however, no blueprint for success in these endeavours. It depends on the parties involved, their openness and responsiveness, and their interaction – it is in other words a matter of experimentation and experience. And it is a matter of asking the following questions:

- Which NGOs are current stakeholders and which might become stakeholders?
- Which strategies are to be used with which NGOs?
- Which communication strategy is the most appropriate, suitable and feasible for a given organisation at a given point of time?

## References

Argenti, P. A. (2004). Collaborating with Activists: How Starbuck Works With NGOs. *California Management Review*. Vol. 47 No. 1:91-116.

Backer, L. (2005). The mediated business of talk and pictures. In L. Füssel (ed.) *Corporate Environmental Governance*. Studentlitteratur. 205-243.

Brinch-Pedersen, M. (2006). Managing Director of the Nordic Partnership 2001-2005. Personal correspondence.

Carstensen, K. (2003). The NGO Case for Business Engagement, talk at Nordic Partnership Forum, November 3rd 2003, accessed at www.wwf.dk

Cheney, G. & Christensen, L. T. (2000). Organizational Identity: Linakges between Internal and External Communication. In Jablin, F. & L. Putnam. *The Handbook of Organizational communication – Advances in Theory, Research, and Methods*. Sage Publications: Thousand Oaks, Ca. p. 231-269.

Clarkson, M. (1995). A Stakeholder Framework for Analysing and Evaluating Corporate Social Performance. *Academy of Management Review* 20(2):92-117.

Davis, G. F., McAdam, D., Scott, W. R. & Zald, M. N. (2005). *Social Movements and Organization Theory*. Cambridge University Press: New York.

Donaldson, T. & Preston, L. E. (1995). The Stakeholder Theory of the Corporation: Concepts, Evidence and Implications. *Academy of Management Review* 20(1):65-91.

Elkington, J. (1997). Cannibals with Forks: *The triple bottom line of the 21st century business*. Capstone: Oxford.

Fombrun, C. (1996). *Reputation: Realizing the valued from the corporate image*. Harvard Business School Press: Boston.

Fombrun, C. J. & Rindova, V. P. (2000). The Roiad to Transparency: Reputation Management at Royal Dutch/Shell. In Schulz, M., M. J. Hatch & M. H. Larsen (eds.): *The Expressive Organization – Linking Identity, Reputation, and the Corporate Brand*. Oxford University Press: Oxford. P. 77-98.

Freeman, E. R. (1984). Strategic Management: A Stakeholder Approach. Pitman Publishing.

Georg, S. & Irwin, A. (2002). Re-interpreting Local-Global Partnerships. In de Bruijn, T. & Tukker, A. (eds.) *Partnership and Leadership – Building Alliances for a Sustainable Future*. Kluwer Academic Publishers.

Grolin, J. (1998). Corporate Legitimacy in Risk Society: *The Case of Brent Spar. Business Strategy and the Environment*. Vol. 7 No. 4:213-222.

Livesey, S. M. (1993). McDonald's and the Environment. *Harvard Business School Case No. 9-391-108*. Harvard Business School Press: Boston.

Michael, M. (2002). Comprehension, Apprehension, Prehension: *Heterogeneity and the Public Understanding of Science*. Science, Technology, & Human Values, Vol. 27 No. 3, Summer 2002: 357-378.

Smith, J. (2005). Globalization and Transnational Social Movement Organizations. In Davis, G. F., D. McAdam, W. R. Scott & M. N. Zald: *Social Move-*

*ments and Organization Theory.* Cambridge University Press: New York, p. 226-248.

Spar, D.L. & Mare, L.T. (2003). The Power of Activison: Assessing the Impact of NGO's on Global Business. *California Management Review.* Vol. 45 No. 3: 78-101.

Stacey, R. D. (2003). *Strategic Management and Organizational Dynamics – The Challenge of Complexity.* FT: Prentice Hall: Harlow England.

SustainAbility, The Global Compact & United Nations Environmental Programme (2003). The 21$^{st}$ Century NGO – In the Market for Change. Accessed at *www.SustainAbility.com*

The Nordic Partnership. (2002). Business Models for Sustainability. Accessed at *www.wwf.dk*

The Nordic Partnership. (2005). Press release: Unique NGO-business cooperation dissolved. Accessed at *www.wwf.dk.*

Tsoukas, H. (1999). David and Goliath in the Risk Society: Making Sense of the Conflict between Shell and Greenpeace in the North Sea. *Organization.* Vol. 6 No. 3: 499-528.

Weick, K. & Sutcliffe, K. M. (2001). Managing the Unexpected – Assuring High Perfromance in an Age of Complexity. University of Michigan Business School Management Series. Jossey-Bass: San Francisco.

## Notes

1. The Nordic Partnership conducted studies on: the potentials for sustainable supply chain management, the development of government policies in the Nordic countries conducive for partnering, assessing the potentials for partnerships in the Nordic countries, identifying the key actors within the realm of socially responsible investment, the possibilities for integrated product policies in the supply chain, and on NGO expectations of corporate CSR.

CHAPTER 10

# Communicating CSR issues in supply chains: Experiences from Asia

*Mette Andersen*

*The development towards a broader
definition of corporate responsibility for also
addressing contractor conditions has started to move
– and it is a development that will not be stopped.*

H. B. Jørgensen & A. Nielsen (2001)

## Corporate social responsibility along supply chains

Many Scandinavian companies embracing corporate social responsibility (hereafter referred to as CSR) have by now realised
that this concept is no longer confined to the domain of the individual company, but is increasingly encompassing their entire
supply chains (Business for Social Responsibility, 2001; Jenkins,
2001; Jørgensen & Nielsen, 2001; Pedersen & Neergaard, 2004).
Thus, a growing number of corporate stakeholders believe that
companies should be held responsible for environmental and labour practices of their trading partners – and in particular suppliers. In fact, many stakeholders do no longer differentiate between
a company and its suppliers with regard to environmental and social behaviour, and they do not hesitate to confront companies
with expressions such as *"tell me who your friends are, and I will
tell you who you are"* (Confederation of Danish Industries, 2003)
and *"you are not better than those you choose to cooperate with"*
(Jørgensen & Mogensen, 2003).

So far, the majority of the companies meeting these expectations
are the large brand-name producers and retailers, whose products
are subject to labour-intensive production processes, typically taking place in low-wage countries in the Third World or Eastern
Europe with poorly developed environmental and social traditions.
As a consequence of the developments in global communications
and technology, the transmission of information to the general public about working and environmental conditions at factories in low-
wage countries has increased considerably in recent years (Bakker
& Nijhof, 2002; Jenkins, 2001; Jenkins, Pearson & Seyfang, 2002;
Jørgensen & Nielsen, 2001; Kearney, 1999), thus making it almost
impossible for companies to hide from the public unsound environmental and social supplier practices (Welford, 2000). Also non-
governmental organisations and the media have contributed to
raising the public awareness about and concern for unsound environmental and social practices at factories in low-wage countries
(Welford, 2000; Klein, 2000; Barrientos, 2002; Jenkins, Pearson &
Seyfang, 2002).

Realising that working actively with environmental and social
issues towards suppliers may provide them with a competitive ad-

236

vantage and reduce the risk of damaging their brand or reputation, many large brand-name companies and retailers have created strategies and visions addressing poor social and environmental standards at their Third World or Eastern European suppliers (Barrientos, 2002; International Labour Organization, 2003; Jenkins, 2001; Jenkins, Pearson & Seyfang, 2002; Jørgensen & Nielsen, 2001; Oxford Research, 2003;). However, turning such strategies and visions into actual environmental and social improvements along the supply chain is often a long and time-consuming process. Ensuring that a product is produced in an environmentally and socially sound manner at suppliers requires that the strategies and visions are followed by not only the suppliers, but also by the company's own employees. While the suppliers must be geared to live up to the buying company's environmental and social expectations and values, the buying company's employees must be geared to work with environmental and social issues extending the border of the company (Cramer, 1996; Rocha & Brezet, 1999; Lippmann, 1999; Kolk, 2000; OECD, 2001; Schmidt, Christensen & Øllgaard, 2001; Jørgensen & Pruzan-Jørgensen, 2002; Bakker & Nijhof, 2002). These tasks typically require a high degree of coordination on the part of management, and such coordination in turn requires communication efforts. Thus, without external communication aimed at suppliers and internal communication aimed at own employees, a company's supply-chain related CSR strategies and visions are likely to remain flowery rhetoric.

Many Scandinavian companies addressing CSR in their supply chains have so far not finalised the above process. As long as this process is not finalised, many of the companies tend to be quite wary of communicating to the customers in the stores that the conditions under which their products have been produced do not harm workers or the external environment. Thus, it will in this chapter be argued that before a targeted communication effort downstream in the supply chain is initiated, a company should focus on making sure that its suppliers and own employees conform to its strategies and visions.

While both external and internal communication seems to be one of the main challenges related to working with CSR matters in supply chains in general, we might argue that this communication task is likely to constitute an even bigger challenge when we look at companies' activities in less developed countries in particular. Many large retailers and brand-owning companies from the industrialised countries – including Scandinavia – typically establish purchasing offices in several less developed countries, which purchase finished products from their local area. The employees at these purchasing offices are typically local people (Mamic, 2004). In many of these countries, CSR issues have traditionally not been part of the corporate agenda, and both the employees at the companies' own purchasing offices and at their suppliers may therefore not be so familiar with these issues.

This chapter sets out to explore the nature and role of external and internal CSR-related communication at an Asian purchasing office of the Scandinavian retailer, IKEA. The chapter will discuss the communication means involved in the company's supply-chain CSR activities as well as point to the main challenges related to the various means of communication.

IKEA is an interesting company to study for various reasons. Firstly, this company has several years' experience from working systematically with CSR in global supply chains. Secondly, it holds a leading position in its supply chains enabling the company to exercise governance and exert influence in the chains. Thirdly, IKEA is a brand-owning company and is therefore particularly vulnerable to bad publicity. It should be noted, however, that IKEA may not be considered representative of the wider population of Scandinavian companies due to its enormous size, which puts it in a rather advantageous position vis-à-vis its supply-chain partners, and due to its status as a family-owned company which is not accountable to shareholders. It may therefore not be easy to apply the findings of the IKEA case directly to other companies. The findings from the study should rather be seen as examples of how CSR in global supply chains is communicated by a front-runner company, which in turn may be used as inspiration for companies wishing to engage in this field.

Data have been collected at IKEA's purchasing office in Thailand, where nine interviews have been conducted. IKEA has various purchasing offices around the world, and the reason for focusing on the office in Thailand is that handling CSR in supply chains constitutes a particular challenge in Asian countries. However, as only one office was visited, the communication means will be described according to the observations of the employees at this particular office. An examination of the same field made at another purchasing office might therefore have produced other findings.[1]

The remainder of the chapter is divided into three main parts. Firstly, we will take a brief look at the literature dealing with the communicative aspects of CSR in supply chains. Secondly, we will look at the way in which supply-chain related CSR communication is unfolded at IKEA's Thai purchasing office. Based on the statements in the existing literature as well as the specific experiences made by IKEA, the chapter will round off by highlighting the most important aspects related to communicating CSR within own organisation and to suppliers.

## The communicative aspects of CSR in supply chains

Various scholars argue that working effectively with environmental and social issues towards suppliers requires systematic communication *both* between the company and its suppliers *and* within the company's own organisation. For example, Preuss (2002) argues that once a company has established its own CSR-related values into a policy, the company must communicate these values to both its own employees and its supply-chain partners. Moreover, Jørgensen & Pruzan-Jørgensen (2002) distinguish between internal and external embeddedness as important elements in working with CSR along supply chains. They argue that it is not enough for a company to communicate a set of ethical requirements to the suppliers. The company itself also needs to fulfil these requirements, which in turn requires – among other things – effective communication within the organisation. Bakker & Nijhof (2002) distinguish between internal and external processes necessary for working with CSR in a supply-chain perspective. These processes include, among other things, a communication dimension. Finally, (Cramer, 1996) argues that firms striving

239

to implement a life cycle-oriented strategy typically encounter two organisational bottlenecks. Firstly, they need to cooperate and communicate with other members in the supply chain to realise potential improvements. Secondly, they need to incorporate a chain-oriented mindset into other related activities within their own organisation, and such incorporation includes a large communicative aspect.

Having clarified the need for both external and internal communication, we now turn to the *role* of such communication. The supply-chain CSR literature provides various examples of the importance of *external* communication between the buying company and its suppliers. Research within the field indicates that suppliers are generally more apt to accept and fulfil their responsibilities if they are clearly informed about as well as able to understand the elements of the buying company's supply-chain CSR processes, e.g. the criteria on which they are selected, the reasons behind the buying company's CSR requirements, the values of the buying company, etc. (CIPS, 1999; Preuss, 2002; Bakker & Nijhof, 2002; Mamic, 2004). In communicating the process, Carter & Jennings (2000) point out that it is particularly important for the buying company to provide the suppliers with a clear explanation for why it works with environmental and social issues towards suppliers as well as to communicate to the suppliers that it perceives CSR as more than window dressing. Doing so is likely to enhance the probability that the suppliers embrace the requirements they are presented with and hence to reduce resistance by the suppliers. Besides increasing the general awareness of CSR matters on part of the suppliers, communication may also take the form of guiding and assisting the suppliers about how to undertake specific improvements (Preuss, 2002; Bakker & Nijhof, 2002; Mamic, 2004).

If we direct our attention towards *internal* communication, much of the literature argues that the role of internal communication in relation to supply-chain CSR activities is primarily to establish a recognition, support and understanding among the organisational members about the importance of working with CSR initiatives beyond the company's formal boundaries (Carter &

240

Jennings, 2000; Mamic, 2004; Andersen, 2005). Such recognition, support and understanding seem important, since the implementation of supply-chain CSR initiatives is likely to depend on how the employees perceive the notion of supply-chain CSR. While many companies develop CSR values and policies, several studies point to the importance of supplementing these values and policies with communicative means with the purpose of making the employees conform to them (Carter & Jennings, 2000; Mamic, 2004; Andersen, 2005). Such communicative means may serve the purpose of providing the organisational members dealing with purchasing or supply chain activities with a clear explanation of the importance of implementing a specific CSR activity, encouraging the employees to embrace the CSR activities, and guiding the employees in how to undertake the implementation of the activities (CIPS, 1999; Carter & Jennings, 2000). Several studies reveal that communication about supply-chain CSR matters is most likely to be successful if these issues are integrated into already established management systems. The most common examples hereof are the integration of CSR issues into employee training, performance appraisals, recruitment, etc. (Mamic, 2004; Andersen, 2005). In addition to the more or less formalised systems, Andersen (2005) has found that effective supply-chain CSR communication may also take place in the form of encouragement provided by the most enthusiastic organisational members. Such organisational members can be referred to as 'change agents' since they may succeed in making their colleagues embrace the notion of supply-chain CSR, identify opportunities and initiate action on their own. Finally, part of the literature points to the different needs for communication of different organisational groups (Lenox & Ehrenfeld, 1997; Carter & Jennings, 2000; Preuss, 2002). Whereas the CSR responsible staff may not need so much encouragement and knowledge about the importance of working with CSR issues towards suppliers, purchasing personnel are likely to need more change of mindset if they are to treat CSR issues on equal terms with other parameters such as price, delivery time, quality, etc.

241

In the next part of the chapter, we will explore the role of the external and internal communication efforts adopted by IKEA's office in Thailand, which handles purchasing from all Thai suppliers.

## Communicating CSR issues in supply chains at IKEA

*Introducing the company*

IKEA is a Swedish home-furnishing retail chain. Its products are designed by in-house or external designers and are produced by 1,300 suppliers in 53 countries. Almost 2/3 of the suppliers are located in Europe and 1/3 in Asia. Only 3 % of the suppliers are from North America. Purchasing is handled by 46 offices in 32 countries. Each of these offices has a purchasing team for each type of material they source. The purchasing teams monitor the production of suppliers, which includes testing of new ideas, negotiating prices and checking quality while keeping an eye on environmental and social conditions. Moreover, the purchasing offices have at their disposal specialists who conduct environmental and social audits at suppliers (www.ikea.com).

*CSR in supply chains*

Since the end of the 1990s, IKEA has been witnessing an increasing focus on the conditions under which its products are produced. Attention to these issues emanate from consumers as well as the media and non-governmental organisations. Even though many of IKEA's suppliers are located in countries where environmental and social issues are well taken care of, IKEA also cooperates with many suppliers in countries where the environmental and social agenda is just developing. This is particularly the case for Asian as well as Eastern European suppliers. The company has for several decades had a vision of creating a better everyday life for its customers, its own employees and the employees working for its suppliers, which – combined with the risk of receiving negative publicity due to unsound environmental or social conditions at the suppliers – led the company to develop a set of ethical requirements, i.e. a code of conduct, which all suppliers worldwide are expected to fulfil. The code of conduct cov-

242

ers 19 different areas divided into more than 90 specific issues. The areas covered by the code of conduct are listed in Figure 1.

- General legal requirements
- Emissions, discharges and noise
- Ground contamination
- Chemicals
- Hazardous and non-hazardous waste
- Environmental improvements
- Fire prevention
- Worker safety
- Provided housing facilities
- Wages and working hours
- Child labour
- Forced and bonded labour
- Discrimination
- Freedom of association
- Harassment, abuse and disciplinary practices
- Routines for procurement of wood
- Protected areas, intact natural forests and high conservation value forests
- Plantations in tropical and sub-tropical areas
- High value tropical tree species

**Figure 1:** Areas covered in code of conduct

Besides writing up the code of conduct, the company's top management also developed a set of external and internal procedures to be followed at all purchasing offices for ensuring implementation of the code at the suppliers. Communication constitutes a central element in these procedures, and the following sections describe the nature and role of communication to suppliers and own employees at the Thai purchasing office. Since the 46 purchasing offices undertake almost identical functions, many of the

243

findings from the Thai office will also apply to other purchasing offices.

*External communication*

To facilitate fulfilment of the code of conduct requirements by the suppliers, IKEA puts great efforts into *preparing suppliers* for the importance, which it attaches to its code of conduct. Thus, when visiting potential suppliers, the purchasing teams make it clear that the firms will not be able to conduct business with IKEA unless they – within a given timeframe – are able to fulfil all the requirements of the code of conduct. The teams also put an effort into explaining to the suppliers why it attaches so much importance to social and environmental issues. In this way, the suppliers become familiar with the ground rules of working with IKEA right away. And even though a potential supplier may seem promising from a purely business-oriented point of view, the supplier will not be pursued in the selection process if it seems unlikely to treat environmental and social matters as equal to other aspects of business.

Once a supplier has been chosen, IKEA's internal auditors conduct an on-site audit of the supplier before the first delivery with the aim of mapping out the extent to which the supplier fulfils the code of conduct. The audits are typically announced beforehand, but IKEA also reserves the right to perform unannounced audits. No Asian suppliers have been able to fulfil the requirements by the first audit. However, IKEA does not break off relations with a supplier due to non-compliance with the requirements as long as the supplier demonstrates a willingness to improve its conditions. Thus, for all the non-compliance issues IKEA requires that the supplier prepares a written action plan detailing how these issues will be rectified. All non-compliance issues should be rectified within 24 months.

Whereas many of the requirements are rather easy to comply with or correct, other requirements are more difficult and time consuming to correct. The more difficult requirements relate to the following areas:

244

- Personal protection equipment
- Working hours
- Wages (piece rate workers' compensation, overtime compensation)
- Workers' rights (employment contracts, pension funds, right to form unions)
- Hazardous waste
- Handling of chemicals

During the 24-months period, IKEA's purchasing teams carry out *regular supplier visits*. During these visits, the teams follow up on whether the suppliers complete the necessary corrective actions according to the action plan. This follow-up process contains a considerable communicative element. Many Asian suppliers lack knowledge about environmental and social issues, particularly when it comes to local regulative requirements and long-term benefits. Even if top management and the personnel in charge of implementing IKEA's and other customers' code of conduct requirements understand the importance of such implementation, they may find it difficult to motivate the workers at the factory floor to carry out the necessary changes. Moreover, implementation is likely to be further complicated by the suppliers' lack of financial resources. Therefore, in order to enhance the ability of the suppliers to undertake the necessary corrections and improvements, the purchasing teams face the great challenge of explaining to the suppliers the rationales behind IKEA' code of conduct as well as assisting them in how to make the corrections and improvements. Among the means used by the purchasing teams are PowerPoint presentations about the code of conduct concept as well as pictures taken from other suppliers, showing both good and bad examples of how to do things. Through such communication, the purchasing teams have indeed managed to change the mindset of many suppliers about the importance of improving environmental and social conditions as well as to equip them with specific knowledge to undertake the corrections.

When the purchasing teams find that a supplier has corrected all the non-compliance issues, the internal auditors conduct a fi-

245

nal audit. If the auditors are able to verify correction of all deviations, the supplier becomes code of conduct approved.[2] Once a supplier is approved, the purchasing teams follow up continuously on the maintenance of the code of conduct issues to ensure that environmental and social issues remain a high priority for the suppliers. This task often constitutes a great challenge for the purchasing teams, since many Asian suppliers find it difficult to understand why it is important to maintain the code of conduct standards after they have achieved code of conduct approval. In this process, the purchasing teams therefore put great efforts into communicating to the suppliers that IKEA does not only require maintenance for its own sake, but also for the sake of the continuous wellbeing of the suppliers' workers and their external environment.

Besides the on-going dialogue with the suppliers as part of the follow-up process, IKEA also communicates its high priority to the code of conduct through *formal training of the suppliers.* Twice a year, the purchasing office in Thailand invites the suppliers to a so-called Supplier Day with the aim of providing the suppliers with an overall understanding of IKEA's general business and priorities, of which the code of conduct constitutes a considerable element. One of the clear advantages of such a Supplier Day is that the suppliers are typically represented by persons from management. This is in contrast to the regular supplier visits paid by the purchasing teams, where the teams mainly talk with the personnel responsible for environmental and social affairs as well as the workers at the factory floor. Being able to communicate the code of conduct concept to management representatives is of great importance to IKEA, since these persons are often able to pressure and encourage employees further down the organisation to cooperate with IKEA on code of conduct issues. Moreover, Supplier Day is a good opportunity for the suppliers to meet each other and exchange opinions about the code of conduct and other issues.

The members of the purchasing teams find that the effects of the communication means described above have increased over time concurrently with their own increased knowledge and understanding regarding code of conduct issues. This finding indicates that the ability to communicate environmental and social issues to suppliers is to a large degree dependent upon the way in which these issues are communicated within IKEA's own organisation. In the following section, we therefore turn to the internal communication at the Thai purchasing office.

*Internal communication*

IKEA's Thai purchasing office has several communication means in place, which over the years have served to increase the level of knowledge and understanding of the purchasing team members.

When the code of conduct was introduced in 2000, the purchasing teams at the Thai office – as well as many other Asian purchasing offices – did not possess much knowledge and understanding of environmental and social issues. This lack of knowledge and understanding was owed partly to the low priority traditionally given to environmental and social issues in Asian societies and partly to the fact that most purchasing team members have a technical background and had therefore not been used to think about environmental and social aspects of production. When the code of conduct was introduced, the purchasing teams therefore faced difficulties understanding the importance of and their role in the code of conduct process, and they were inclined to look at the task as an extra burden. This situation was unfortunate, because if it starts off with a bad attitude towards the code of conduct inside the walls of IKEA, it is difficult to sell the idea to the suppliers. It therefore became clear to management that clear communication to the purchasing teams about the code of conduct was needed. Some of the most important communication means adopted at the Thai office will be described in the following.

IKEA has quite a long tradition of providing environmental training, and following the introduction of the code of conduct, the company's top management therefore decided to establish *worldwide training courses aimed specifically at the code* as well. The training courses have increased the Thai employees' knowledge about the reasons behind the adoption of social and envi-

247

ronmental requirements towards suppliers, why and how it is important for IKEA's business, the contents of the code of conduct and the consequences of non-compliance with the code. Thus, these courses aim at providing the purchasing teams with a fundamental understanding of why IKEA works with a code of conduct at all as well as at enhancing their ability to follow up on and support implementation and maintenance of the code of conduct at the suppliers. The management at IKEA has particularly found it relevant to focus on the purchasing teams' fundamental understanding of social and environmental requirements based on the assumption that without such an understanding, it is difficult to change the mindset of the suppliers.

Another central means of communication, which aims at increasing the purchasing team members' CSR-related knowledge and understanding considerably, is *frequent interaction with the internal auditors*, who are experts on technical and regulatory aspects of CSR. The purchasing team members may join the auditors on audits, during which the auditors share their knowledge and experiences. Likewise, the auditors may join the team members on their regular supplier visits and assist the members in their follow-up efforts.

IKEA's Thai office also has in place communication means in the form of appointment of *'change agents'*. Thus, the purchasing team leaders have by the management at the office been given the day-to-day responsibility of code of conduct implementation and maintenance. This implies – among other things – that they are expected to encourage the other team members to continuously staying committed to code of conduct-related issues. A particular challenge related to this task is to keep the team members focused on the maintenance of the environmental and social standards at the suppliers after code of conduct approval. Typically possessing a technical background, several team members tend to somewhat relax their attention to code of conduct-related issues after code of conduct approval of suppliers and instead focus more on the tasks within their main area of competence, e.g. product development and quality issues. Therefore, the encour-

248

agement efforts by the team leaders have proven to be an important communication means.

The importance of supply-chain related CSR matters is also communicated through the *evaluation system*. Among the dimensions on which each purchasing team is evaluated is the number of code of conduct approved suppliers in a team's supplier portfolio. By including this dimension in the evaluation criteria, management seeks to signal to the employees that the code of conduct work is of great importance to the company, and the teams are accordingly encouraged to put a great deal of effort into code of conduct issues.

Owing to the various means of communication just described, the purchasing team members have experienced that their understanding and knowledge level regarding code of conduct-related issues has been raised from almost non-existent in 2000, when the code was first introduced, to quite high today. Besides benefiting the purchasing team members themselves, their enhanced knowledge and understanding have made them better capable of changing the mindsets and improving the knowledge of the suppliers. Whereas many of the purchasing team members initially felt quite uncomfortable talking to the suppliers about code of conduct-related issues because they themselves did not know much about this, they feel quite confident to talk about these issues with the suppliers today. Finally, the various means of communication have served to establish a working environment at the Thai office in which working with CSR matters in relation to suppliers is increasingly becoming a natural way of working and is no longer considered a burden by the employees. CSR matters are now handled on an equal basis with other business areas such as quality, product development etc., thus making them a consolidated part of the supplier relations.

An overview of the external and internal means of communication at IKEA's Thai purchasing office is provided in Figure 2.

249

**Figure 2:** External and internal communication means at IKEA

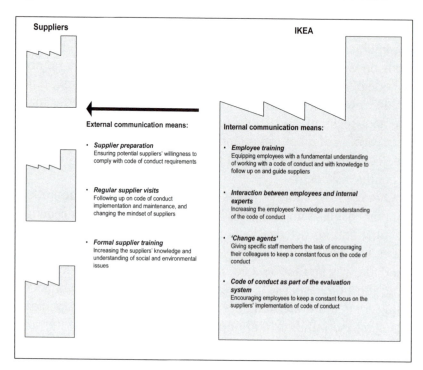

## The role of internal and external communication for practicing CSR in supply chains

This chapter has argued that inter-organisational and intra-organisational communication constitute important elements in working with CSR in supply chains, particularly when sourcing from less developed countries where CSR issues have traditionally not been part of the corporate agenda. The chapter has shed light on the nature and role of supply-chain CSR communication at IKEA's purchasing office in Thailand. Combining the findings from IKEA with the arguments in the existing literature, we are able to point to a number of aspects of relevance for CSR-related communication in supply chains:

250

- *It is important to make own employees understand the importance of working with social and environmental issues in supply chains.* Internal communication needs to include a great emphasis on understanding. It appears to be a great advantage that e.g. employee training not only provides the employees of the buying company with specific techniques and tools for following up on and supporting the implementation and maintenance of the CSR requirements at suppliers, but also provides them with a fundamental understanding of why working with CSR in supply chains is important for the company's business. Providing the employees with a fundamental understanding serves two purposes in particular. First of all, the employees, who traditionally may not have been concerned with CSR issues, are more likely to embrace the CSR initiatives if they understand why it is important that the external environment and factory workers are taken care of. Secondly, once a company's own employees understand the reasons for working with a code of conduct, it becomes much more easy and comfortable for them to make the suppliers understand the importance of working with social and environmental issues.

- *The employees' knowledge and understanding can be increased through formal and informal management systems.* When CSR issues are integrated into already established formal management systems such as training, evaluation systems, etc. within the buying company, the employees are constantly reminded about their importance. In this way, CSR issues are not treated as an 'add-on' to other business activities but are likely to become a natural part of the day-to-day business operations. However, whereas training and performance evaluations may only take place a couple of times a year, more informal systems may contribute to an increase in employee knowledge and understanding on a day-to-day basis. The appointment of 'change agents', who have the role of encouraging their colleagues, may serve to keep the organisation constantly focused on environmental and social issues. Also, the willingness of internal CSR experts to share their knowledge with their col-

251

leagues is likely to increase both knowledge and awareness of the latter.

- *It is important to make suppliers understand the importance of working with social and environmental issues.* Just like a fundamental understanding of the buying company's own employees is important for the way in which CSR in supply chains is managed, a fundamental understanding on part of the CSR responsible personnel and ordinary workers at the suppliers is likewise crucial for changes to take place here. Thus, when suppliers are located in countries, where the general understanding and awareness of social and environmental matters tend to be limited, it seems imperative that the buying company builds up an understanding as well as a positive attitude at the suppliers. It is particularly important to make suppliers understand the importance of working with social and environmental matters on a continuous basis. Having not been used to work with such issues, many Asian suppliers tend to focus mainly on implementing the specific code of conduct requirements so as to satisfy the various buying companies – and less on maintaining their CSR standards or initiating new activities by themselves. An increased understanding at the suppliers can be achieved through proper preparation of potential suppliers as well as through formal training of key personnel at existing suppliers.
- *Suppliers should be guided and assisted on a continuous basis.* Besides providing the suppliers with a fundamental understanding of CSR-related issues, Asian suppliers will often benefit from communication in the form of practical guidance or assistance concerning how to fulfil the buying company's requirements. In the course of time, an increasing number of Asian suppliers will be more familiar with CSR issues and hence do more things on their own, but until then it seems essential that the buying companies continuously assist them.

### Where do we go from here?

As the above paragraphs have served to illustrate, the role of communication aimed at suppliers and own employees should not be underestimated when practicing CSR in supply chains, which extend to remote areas of the world. A third type of communication, which has not been dealt with in this chapter, is communication to those who purchase the products in the stores. So far, many Scandinavian companies practicing CSR in supply chains seem to have been quite reluctant to publicly communicate their efforts, and when they do communicate, they tend to do so in a rather modest way. The reason is often quite simple; working with CSR towards suppliers is an on-going process, and it may take many months – or even years – for the necessary improvements to be carried out. As long as this process is not finalised, the companies are generally not very keen on demonstrating their good efforts to the public. However, once the communication efforts directed at suppliers and own employees have become well established and effective, a natural next step for companies would be to focus more targeted on communicating their endeavours and outcomes to their customers.

Main questions to be answered in this context are:

- Which procedures should be employed to ensure that suppliers behave in accordance with a company's own CSR standards and values?
- How can managers ensure that their own organisation is geared to communicate social and environmental matters to suppliers?
- How far back in the supply chain does an organisation's social and environmental responsibility extend?

253

## References

Andersen, M. (2005). *Corporate Social Responsibility in Global Supply Chains. Understanding the uniqueness of firm behaviour.* Copenhagen Business School.

Bakker, F. G. A. d. & Nijhof, A. (2002). Responsible Chain Management: A Capability Assessment Framework. *Business Strategy and the Environment, 11,* 63-75.

Barrientos, S. (2002). Mapping codes through the value chain: from researcher to detective. In R.Jenkins, R. Pearson, & G. Seyfang (Eds.), *Corporate Responsibility and Labour Rights. Codes of Conduct in the Global Economy* (pp. 61-76). London: Earthscan Publications Ltd.

Business for Social Responsibility, E. F. (2001). *Suppliers' Perspectives on Greening the Supply Chain* San Francisco, CA: Business for Social Responsibility, Education Fund.

Carter, C. R. & Jennings, M. M. (2000). *Purchasing's Contribution to the Socially Responsible Management of the Supply Chain* Centennial Circle, AZ: Center for Advanced Purchasing Studies, Arizona State University Research Park.

CIPS (1999). *Ethical Business Practices in Purchasing and Supply* The Chartered Institute of Purchasing & Supply.

Confederation of Danish Industries (2003). *Globalt engagement – lokal handling.*

Cramer, J. (1996). Experiences with Implementing Integrated Chain Management in Dutch Industry. *Business Strategy and the Environment, 5,* 38-47.

International Labour Organization (2003). *Business and Code of Conduct Implementation. How firms use management systems for social performance* International Labour Office.

Jenkins, R. (2001). *Corporate Codes of Conduct. Self-Regulation in a Global Economy* United Nations Research Institute for Social Development.

Jenkins, R., Pearson, R., & Seyfang, G. (2002). Introduction. In R.Jenkins, R. Pearson, & G. Seyfang (Eds.), *Corporate Responsibility and Labour Rights. Codes of Conduct in the Global Economy* (pp. 1-10). London: Earthscan Publications Ltd.

Jørgensen, H. B. & Mogensen, B. (2003). Hvor langt rækker ansvaret? *Sustainability Quarterly.*

Jørgensen, H. B. & Nielsen, A. (2001). Responsible Supply Chain Management. *Revision & Regnskabsvæsen: Tidsskrift for erhvervsøkonomi og skatteforhold.*

Jørgensen, H. B. & Pruzan-Jørgensen, P. M. (2002). Ansvarlig leverandørstyring. *Træ & Industri* 11-13.

Kearney, N. (1999). Corporate Codes of Conduct: the Privatized Application of Labour Standards. In S.Picciotto & R. Mayne (Eds.), *Regulating International Business. Beyond Liberalization* (pp. 205-220). Basingstoke: MacMillan Press Ltd.

Klein, N. (2000). *No Logo.* London: Flamingo.

254

Kolk, A. (2000). *Economics of Environmental Management.* Essex: Pearson Education Limited.

Lenox, M. & Ehrenfeld, J. (1997). Organizing for Effective Environmental Design. *Business Strategy and the Environment, 6,* 187-196.

Lippmann, S. (1999). Supply Chain Environmental Management: Elements for Success. *Environmental Management, 6,* 175-182.

Mamic, I. (2004). *Implementing Codes of Conduct. How Businesses Manage Social Performance in Global Supply Chains.* Geneva: International Labour Office/ Greenleaf Publishing.

OECD (2001). *Making Codes of Corporate Conduct Work: Management Control Systems and Corporate Responsibility.* Organisation for Economic Co-operation and Development.

Oxford Research (2003). *Bæredygtighed i supply-chain – hvordan omsættes markedets krav?* Copenhagen: Oxford Research.

Pedersen, E. R. & Neergaard, P. (2004). Virksomhedens Samfundsmæssige Ansvar (CSR) – en ny ledelsesudfordring. *Økonomistyring & Informatik, 19,* 555-591.

Preuss, L. (2002). Green light for greener supply. *Business Ethics: A European Review,* 11, 308-317.

Rocha, C. & Brezet, H. (1999). Product-oriented environmental management systems: a case study. *The Journal of Sustainable Product Design* 30-42.

Schmidt, K., Christensen, F. M., & Øllgaard, H. (2001). Product Orientation of Environmental Work. *Corporate Environmental Strategy, 8,* 126-132.

Welford, R. (2000). *Corporate Environmental Management 3. Towards Sustainable Development.* London: Earthscan Publications Ltd.

www.ikea.com

## Notes

1. The data, on which this chapter is based, were conducted for the purpose of a PhD thesis.
2. If a supplier is not able to fulfil the code of conduct requirements within 24 months, but shows a positive attitude towards implementation of the requirements, he is put on a 'risk register' and given additional time to fulfil the requirements. When a supplier is on the 'risk register', IKEA does in principle not press new orders. If a supplier, on the other hand, does not show an interest in complying with all requirements, IKEA will typically terminate the relationship with that supplier.

255

# Investor Relations and CSR Communication:[1] Conversing with the Forgotten Stakeholder

*Kai Hockerts*

*I believe that Corporate Social Responsibility (CSR) will become increasingly part of the mainstream investor unit. We will see a coming together of the community of Socially Responsible Investors (SRI) and the mainstream investor community.*

Mark Smith, Investor Relations Manager, British Telecom, Interview 2002

In an attempt to manage Corporate Social Responsibility (CSR) risks most multinationals make systematic consultation of stakeholders a key element of their communications strategy (Morsing, 2003). A considerable amount of firms also include CSR elements in their marketing messages – be it through ethical labeling of specific products or corporate branding around a theme of responsibility. However, one element of corporate communications has lagged behind on this new trend; communications with investors has remained stubbornly focused on traditional financial issues. One may thus see the shareholder as a somewhat "forgotten" stakeholder, at least as far as it concerns CSR communication.

It is only recently that CSR has entered into the domain of investor relations: Firstly, a growing number of investors are adopting socially responsible criteria for their investment decisions. Although, so far socially responsible investing (SRI) is still a niche interest it is nonetheless commanding a considerable amount of attention from firms. Consequently investors, analysts, and rating agencies flood companies with surveys and questionnaires about corporate social responsibility (Kahlenborn, 2002; Nelson Sofres, 2001; O'Rourke, 2002).

Secondly, investor relations officers (IRO) increasingly see CSR as an element of their firm's competitive advantage and attempt to include it in the models of mainstream analyst (Hockerts & Moir, 2004). The second trend responds to a growing interest among investors to widen their assessment of companies from purely financial indicators towards non-financial aspects. Among the intangible factors considered, CSR has received a particular amount of attention.

CSR is by no means a new phenomenon (e.g. Ackermann & Bauer, 1976; Carroll, 1979; Davis, 1973; Frederick, 1994; McGuire, Sungren, & Schneeweiss, 1988; Sethi, 1975; Vogel, 1986; Wood, 1991). However, it is only in the past decade that CSR has returned forcefully on the corporate agenda (AccountAbility, 1999; Dyllick & Hockerts, 2002; Gladwin, Kennelly, & Krause, 1995; Kapstein, 2001; Moir, 2001; Shell, 1998; SustainAbility, 1999; Tepper Marlin, 1998; WBCSD, 1999; Zadek, Pruzan, & Evans, 1997). The extent to which this rebirth of CSR has impacted

258

corporate communications with investors will be at the core of this chapter.

The outline of the chapters follows two general themes:

1. The first subsection presents the *interaction between the investor relations (IR) community and specialized social rating.* This part analyses the perceived professionalism and the value created by such agencies. While IR officials agree that social rating agencies have become more professional they continue to see room for improvement.
2. *The interaction between IR officers and investors* is analyzed in the second subsection. While respondents identified a growing interest in CSR among certain investors they did, however, see a need for further education of most mainstream investors.

**Scope of this Study**

This chapter is based on a research study (Hockerts et al. 2003) as part of which investor relations professionals were interviewed in companies with diverse backgrounds. A total of 20 companies from the UK (4), Germany (3), Switzerland (3), the Netherlands (2), France (2), Belgium (1), Italy (2), Norway (1), and the U.S. (2) have participated in the study. These firms were chosen so as to increase variety of country, sector and attitude towards corporate responsibility. We have thus covered industry sectors as diverse as Aerospace & Defense, Automobiles, Construction, Energy, Engineering, Financial services, Food, Retail, IT, Pharmaceuticals, Services, Telecoms.

In order to allow variation in the attitude towards corporate responsibility three different ways were chosen to identify contacts. We approached members of CSR Europe, members of the UK Investor Relations Society, and alumni from a leading European business school now working in Investor Relations. As a consequence interview partners had different levels of experience with corporate responsibility. A small number of respondents were designated specialists for corporate responsibility within the IR department while the majority were general IR officers for whom corporate responsibility made up only a very small part of their work. To avoid a bias towards large multinationals and the so called "Sustainability Leaders", we included smaller-capitalized companies as well as firms that were not represented on any sustainability indices. Furthermore, we included two firms headquartered in the U.S.

## Communicating with Social Rating Agencies

Unsurprisingly, given the large number of questionnaires and surveys they receive on the topic of CSR, investor relations officers stressed the role of social rating agencies and SRI analysts in shaping the firm's CSR reputation among investors. The respondents resented particularly filling in a multitude of surveys with similar and yet slightly different questions. They also doubted the expertise of many of the smaller rating boutiques. These sentiments were equally strong among respondents with high or low social ratings. At the same time most IR officers lauded analysts for providing detailed feed-back. They also appreciated the opportunity to benchmark against its competitors.

*The Quality of Rating Agencies and Analysts*

Nearly all firms interviewed reported to have been rated by a screened fund or a dedicated rating agency. Most SRI analysts were contacting companies routinely once per year with additional interviews (in person or by telephone) as needed. Many IR officers mentioned that the questionnaires received have been getting longer and more demanding. As one respondent remarked: "It's actually a considerable investment in time to fill them in and to do it properly."

There were divergences between the *data gathering techniques* employed by SRIs – some relied heavily on questionnaires, some more on face-to-face meetings. A small number of analysts hadn't even contacted the firms at all and instead rated them on what they found in the public domain. Such a go-it-alone approach was generally not received well as it did not give firms a chance to set the record straight. However, on the other hand IR officers were also complaining about the growing number of questionnaires. One respondent put it as follows:

260

> "I think there is a little bit of resentment of having to answer [so many questionnaires]. It'd be nice if we could just give a standard set of answers and move on. But of course, they're all slightly different, so it does become quite time consuming. It is difficult for us at the moment to see the value of all of them."

Interviewees noted differences in the *types of questions* they received. They also felt that the motivations behind asking questions differed. Questionnaires from pension funds were seen to be more politically geared and more difficult to understand than surveys by rating agencies. Differences between the rating systems were also noted when companies received different results: "There is no generic standard across. You can be AA on one and DD on another."

IR officials also commented on the differing *expertise within the SRI( rating teams.* One welcomed when rating agencies deliberately rotated their analysts so as to give more depth to the ratings. However, others stressed that in order to evaluate a company fairly the analyst needs a good understanding of the industry as well as the firm at hand. They also diagnosed a general lack of trained analysts. Interestingly some firms outlined a participative process of the ratings in which they often ended up teaching the analysts how to improve their own processes. A notable trend was that companies increasingly asked analysts to fill out the questionnaires based on information provided in the social or environmental reports. Only then would the IR staff engage in questions on gaps and further dialogue.

Only three interviewees had a definite positive response to the question *"Do SRI ratings adequately reflect the company?"* One, for example, felt that:

> "[SRI analysts] are doing good work. We are sending all the details and they are checking them carefully. They have a lot of additional questions and often have to speak to the experts responsible for this in the firm. They know what they are asking."

261

Others gave a qualified yes, stating that they thought it was very difficult for an individual analyst to understand everything in a company, especially when rating particular businesses that have no real industry benchmarks and quite specific environmental or social concerns. One investor relations professional commented that analysts were dealing with huge amounts of information from various companies. In many cases they did not have the resources to actually engage with each firm and carry out a proper analysis.

Two companies noted an improvement in the quality of the ratings over time:

> "Now we're pretty satisfied with them, but a lot of it I think has to do with our engagement and knowing exactly what they're asking and what we're willing to give them, then letting them tailor it."

Many negative responses on the quality of the ratings were picked up in the interviews. For example one interviewee hinted at some differences in opinion on the results of the ratings, feeling that it has been a fairly combative dialogue leaving the firm unsatisfied. He also raised concerns about the fact that ratings improved with the amount of reporting and engagement: "It's an awful lot of spin if you're not careful".

The administrative process of evaluation also troubled IR officers. One case was noted wherein the questionnaire was inappropriately addressed and by the time it found its way to the relevant persons, it was too late to be included on that Index. Also the quality of the external information the SRI's used was sometimes perceived to be out of date or simply incorrect.

Interviewees were also critical of the *scope and focus of the questions posed* by the SRI analysts. For example, the recent increased quotient of questions on corporate governance did not appear to be very well thought through and appeared to be jumping on the public issue bandwagon. Others complained that the focus of the rating questions sometimes missed the point of the business by being, for example, too fixed on manufacturing or the impacts of production processes rather than services. One re-

262

spondent went on to state that the criteria were too loose and not tailored to the industry sectors: "You get put into very big boxes [which do not always] recognize the improvements that have been made".

There were some complaints that the SRIs did not integrate economic or financial considerations into their social and environmental criteria. Furthermore, respondents felt that questionnaires were "obviously written from a very Western standpoint which might not be applicable in other cultures".

Partly because of the divergence in quality and also workload, many companies are now selective about which rating agencies they will answer. One interviewee stated that their selectivity was also based on the perception that:

> "we don't want to spend lots of time filling in questionnaires which ultimately are really about helping someone else market a product, which doesn't actually make a huge difference to us".

The list of answered questionnaires nearly always included the *SRI Indexes*, which appeared to be gaining in influence. Many IR officers perceived inclusion in an SRI index, such as the Dow Jones Sustainability Index (DJSI) or the FTSE4Good, as important. "It's quite tangible for investors, whereas the reports are less so". One investor relations director saw the indices as a catalyst for creating interest. However, he guessed that "eventually people are going to look out for themselves and the interest in these indices may be diluted."

*Usefulness of the feed-back from Rating Agencies and Analysts*
Most of the companies interviewed stated that they were happy to receive feed-back from the rating agencies once they had finished their investigation. However, the *format and quality of the feed-back* differed widely. A selected few provided detailed reports of ten pages or more highlighting perceived strengths and weaknesses of the firm. Most analysts, however, did not provide more than a one or two pages summary. One respondent qualified this

feed-back as "very obvious [and even] boring". In other cases the feedback given was simply the final 'score' of the rating or notice of inclusion in an index:

> "You're just told if you're included or excluded, and if you're lucky you'll get some sort of generalized reason why".

One respondent judged that analysts working on behalf of ethical groups provided rather poor and limited feedback. Higher quality feedback, he felt, could be gained from rating agencies offering in-depth assessment against a fee. Interviewees also noted cases where they received no feedback whatsoever. "The list of questionnaires that we receive is definitely longer than the list of reports we get back."

Once the feed-back was received, analysts often provided firms with an *opportunity to comment on the feedback given by the analysts.* Agencies usually allowed companies to suggest additions and to correct mistakes. But in some cases the rating process was more participatory. "Because of the relationship we have with most of these folks over the years," stated one respondent, "we help them [..] craft their surveys and give them feedback [on their methodology]."

Many of the companies interviewed invested time to understand why they were given a particular rating, especially if it was a bad score. One interviewee noted that a negative rating can be due to the lack of the information. "[Sometimes] they can't make a judgment and hence down rate us someway."

Interviewees varied in their perception of the *usefulness of feedback from rating agencies and analysts.* The less usefully results turned out to be nothing more than a regurgitation of the data provided in the questionnaire. However, by engaging in a dialogue with the analysts firms were able to benefit more from the rating process.

> "For a while we were just getting data back that was ours. And it was difficult for us to know, was it good, was it bad

and what were our benchmarks? What we started to do about two years ago is really sit down and have separate meetings with them and ask, what is it you guys are ranking and rating on? We've learned a lot and turned it into some internal improvements. [Sometimes these changes have let to] quantum leaps because we now know exactly what these groups are ranking and rating us on."

Often ratings were perceived as useful for identifying emerging issues stakeholders might be interested in as well as monitoring the company's external image. Others have used the feed-back to benchmark their firm's performance against other companies in the same sector and to get general information about best practice in other industries.

"What's great about the [Business in the Environment Index] is that there is comprehensive feedback to companies of the results. [It provides a] benchmark for how we compare with other companies and makes some sensible comments about our approach."

The *distribution of the rating results within the firms* varied amongst the companies interviewed, from full public disclosure of the rating results on the website or in the environmental report, to internal distribution only. Many stated that the feed-back from ratings was distributed to the CEO, the CFO, and IR, as well as the dedicated environmental or social responsibility function. Some companies even provided the rating results to their Board of Directors. Not all feedback from the rating agencies was equally distributed. Whether a rating was communicated usually depended on the perceived quality of the rating agency and not the outcome of the rating per se.

Rating results were used proactively to *attract interest from SRI fund managers.* Being included in an SRI index or fund was even felt by some IR officials to be useful in approaching mainstream investors. Inclusions in a SRI index or fund was a signal to main-

265

stream investors that the firm was "not involved in any scandals and that [it was] aware of these important issues".

Identifying limits as well as opportunities of SRI ratings one respondent summed up his perception as follows:

> "Do these ratings add to our shareholder value? Probably, but some value that's not measurable. Is it of value to us, our employees and to a growing investor base? Absolutely!"

## The Role of the Investor Relations Function

So how does the rise of CSR impact the investor relation's function? Six main findings emerge from the research project underlying this chapter (see also Hockerts and Moir, 2004). One respondent likened the recent changes in the IR function to the move from one-way broadcasting towards two-way relationship management. As part of this transition he saw IR becoming "the eyes, ears and mouth of the organization". On the one hand IROs communicate firm strategy and firm performance to the external community. On the other hand they feed back the reactions of the marketplace to management. The engagement with CSR issues, it was felt, exposes IR increasingly to a broader audience including the NGO community or even government and thus broadens their role.

**Figure 3:** The Role of Investor Relations in Communicating CSR Performance

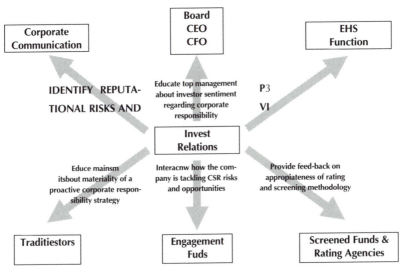

While corporate responsibility broadens the IR function's duties it has also driven the integration of IR with other departments in the firm. A large majority of respondents said that the answering of SRI questionnaires was a collaborative effort carried out together with the environmental function or with corporate communications. Most respondents had instituted systems to handle SRI issues by dividing up responsibilities between IR and other departments. At one firm the task of filling in questionnaires has, for example, evolved from IR towards the corporate environmental and social function, itself a new function.

> "In the past, we used to deal with [questionnaires] directly but as of two to three years ago, we started to direct these questions to the people working in [the appropriate] department, which was established at this time."

Although the work of filling in questionnaires was increasingly delegated to the experts IR officers kept close tabs on the relationship with SRI analysts and investors. Of those interviewed, most had met with an SRI group in person at least once. Some were meeting regularly – up to once per month, while for others it was between two or three times per year. In general, yearly meetings with the larger SRI investors as well as the bigger rating agencies were encouraged.

Meetings which started out as one-on-one (company to individual SRI) have increasingly become multi-stakeholder. Part of this shift is due to corporate leadership (ie by organizing question sessions) and partly by SRIs who want to maintain good relations with the companies and not overload them with too many get-togethers. One respondent described meetings with stakeholders that included investors as follows:

> "In the past, you could say the company would be having a conversation with investors over here and NGOs over there, but increasingly those conversations are getting more integrated. Indeed, we run sessions over the year with both interested investors and NGO groups in the room together. So we can look at issues more holistically."

Typically engagement with SRI analysts or investors starts with a presentation by the IRO, but would be continued by more specialized environmental or social managers. Corporate responsibility issues have also begun to enter meetings with mainstream investors. However, as described by one respondent corporate responsibility remains far from being completely integrated in such meetings:

> "[When we meet a large investment fund] there would be a lead analyst who takes the meeting from their point of view, plus 6 or 7 fund managers and there'll probably be somebody who is SRI. We will answer the normal questions about the business, business performance, and that sort of thing. Then right at the end the analyst will turn to the SRI person and say 'you can ask your question now'. Then he will ask questions about safer chemicals or whatever it is.

> You give an answer and then that's it. So it's a little bit of paying lip service."

Estimates of how much time IR officers spend on social and environmental issues (including dealing with SRIs) varied. Most IR officers said that they dealt with corporate responsibility issues for less than two to three hours per week. However, all agreed that the amount of time spend on the topic had increased over the past five years. In a few firms IR officer had been particularly designated as the responsible person for corporate responsibility issues on the IR team.

IR officers spend much of the time dedicated to SRI by filling in surveys as well as responding to enquiries from pension funds and lobby groups. Dealing with surveys was felt to be particularly time consuming as information had to be sourced from a variety of areas. "And you need to get very top level sign off for any external communication," adds one IR officer.

Many IROs expect to take on more communications functions relating to the social and environmental dimensions in the future, resulting possibly in a convergence of what used to be segregated communications.

> "CSR will become increasingly part of the mainstream investor unit. We will start to see a coming together of the SRI and the mainstream investor community and therefore my role will be less separated."

Some companies already note that their meetings with investors are increasingly integrated, with both mainstream and SRI investors in the same room, and even on occasion with other stakeholders like NGOs present as well. Another respondent points out that relations between companies and external parties have up to now been dominated by shareholders. "But other stakeholders are important for shareholders too. The value of a company is more than just its profit," he adds. As such, he expects IR communications to widen to encompass stakeholder relations as well.

*Educating Management*

The findings from the study indicate that the role of IR in relation to CSR issues is changing from a broadcasting mode towards more interactive relationship management (Hockerts et al., 2004). Several IR officers reported the wish to educate their constituents about corporate responsibility issues related to their firm. On the one hand they wanted to alert analysts and investors to the value potential of their firm's proactive behavior. On the other hand they played a key role in identifying emerging issues and forewarning management about potential risks to the firm's reputation in the market place.

In their role as the relationship manager between a firm and the financial markets IROs emerged as an important driver of corporate transformation. A first contribution was to point out gaps in corporate responsibility policies or programmes as identified by the SRI's ratings. Examples of gaps that were identified through SRI ratings and later acted upon include: introduction of a social policy, adaptation of the corporate governance structure, as well as the implementation of a policy on ethical trading. Companies were also using engagement with SRI experts to monitor the emergence of social and environmental issues in the public domain.

Respondents stated that improved corporate communications was a major learning point: "We've learnt that we probably get better results if we're out there, if people can see what we're doing and what we're not doing". The process of filling in SRI questionnaires was seen as a useful education in itself: "If you are able to answer the questionnaire, it means you are well on track on that issue". Many IRO's mentioned benchmarking as one of the key drivers for organizational learning outcomes from the SRI's ratings and engagement process.

> "We look at the ratings that are done on us very carefully and we benchmark against other companies"

Interviewees mentioned that they learnt more in the informal, off-line engagement process with investors and analysts than they did in the rating or questionnaire process. It was usually in these in-

270

formal settings that analysts talked about an emerging issue and asked the IR staff how they dealt with that. A big driver for organizational learning seems to be the down-rating of a company.

> "Once you get on top of these lists, everybody wants to stay there. It gets competitive among our peers and it's all healthy improvement."

### Educating Investors and Rating Agencies

Apart from internal learning processes it also emerged that IR officers have a role to play in educating investors and analysts about corporate responsibility issues. One point of learning that emerged from the interviews was that companies were often teaching investors on how to approach social or environmental issues. Some companies were actively communicating their social or environmental performance to investors, whether questioned by analysts or not. This was not limited to the SRI funds. Several respondents saw a role for educating mainstream investors as well.

> "We as the IR department should inform mainstream investors and hopefully they will include this in their investment decision."

In this quest IR officers were egged on by SRI analysts in the large asset management companies. Being often smiled upon by their mainstream colleagues these analysts welcomed the unexpected help in educating their own non-SRI inclined peers. Those IR officers that did pro-actively communicate on social and environmental issues to investors found that some of their audience became very interested in the issue and wanted to know more – while others merely "listened politely". Some IR departments went further by offering investor events outside of normal reporting and schedule dates wherein investors spend one or two days with the company learning about the vision, the strategy and the 'real issues' of the company. Part of these meetings was a discussion of pro-active management of environmental and social risks.

271

## Conclusions

This chapter has studied two issues in relation to investor relations and CSR. These were the perceptions investor relations professionals held of social rating agencies and the role of IROs in communicating CSR. Expectations regarding the latter are first and foremost for greater reporting requirements in general and for communications with investors. IR officials also expect the process to become more transparent and more wide-ranging. This development may mean that as mainstream investors become used to receiving CSR information from some firms, they will expect all firms to explain their stakeholder approach.

In this regard, IROs expect mainstream investors and analysts to increasingly integrate social and environmental criteria into their assessments – but only gradually. A starting point for such integration is likely to be with risks, especially material risks that are quantifiable and which have a direct financial impact. Companies can expect to come under scrutiny as to how they manage the different risks they face not just in terms of sales and earnings and costs but also in terms of the risks from their impacts on the environmental and on the social front.

The profession of investor relations is relatively young. As such, the scope for greater development of the role IR plays is significant. The communications function for IR, for example, can be expected to become more two-way in nature. IR is what one respondent called a "window to the capital markets". There is plenty of potential for IR officers to communicate the investment community's concerns and perceptions of the company back to management on a greater scale than is currently being done. And from IR officers' reflections on what they have learnt, there is increasing awareness for more effective and impactful communications with mainstream investors.

This chapter has also clear implications for the practice of socially responsible investing. Social rating agencies and analysts face an increasing challenge of legitimacy towards the firms they are analyzing. Unless they can convincingly demonstrate their understanding of the CSR challenges faced by firms, and the rationale they use in analyzing them, analysts risk losing one of the most important sources of data collection they possess – namely the firms themselves.

## Where do we go from here?

Based on the above analysis and reflections, it becomes clear that the integration of CSR confronts investor relations managers with a number of challenges. Three questions stand out in particular:

1. What information do investors need from the IR function in order to evaluate the potential impact CSR can have on business performance?
2. To what extent do IR managers have to tailor their CSR message depending on the type of investor (institutional or retail) or the region (North America, Europe, Asia)?
3. What role can social rating agencies play in providing CSR related information to investors?

## References

AccountAbility. 1999. *AccountAbility 1000 (AA 1000). A Foundation Standard in Social and Ethical Accounting, Auditing and Reporting*. London: AccountAbility.

Ackermann, R., & Bauer, R. 1976. *Corporate Social Performance: The Modern Dilemma*. Reston: Reston Publishing Co.

Carroll, A. 1979. A Three-Dimensional Conceptual Model of Corporate Performance. *Academy of Management Review*, 4: 497-505.

Davis, K. 1973. The Case for and against Business Assumptions of Social Responsibility. *Academy of Management Journal*, 16: 312-322.

Dyllick, T., & Hockerts, K. N. 2002. Beyond the Business Case for Corporate Sustainability. *Business Strategy and the Environment*, 11(2): 130-141.

Frederick, W. 1994. From CSR1 to CSR2. *Business & Society*, 33(2): 150-165.

Gladwin, T., Kennelly, J., & Krause, T.-S. 1995. Beyond Eco-efficiency: Towards Socially Sustainable Business. *Sustainable Development*, April 1995(3): 35-43.

Hockerts, K. N., Hinderer, A., Leng, S., & O'Rourke, A. 2003. *Corporate Responsibility and the Role of Investor Relations, From Switchboard to Catalyst*. Brussels: CSR Europe.

Hockerts, K. N., & Moir, L. 2004. Communicating Corporate Responsibility to Investors, The Changing Role of the Investor Relations Function. *Journal of Business Ethics*, 52(1): 85-98.

Kahlenborn, W. 2002. *The Social and Environmental Impact of SRI – Results of Past Research ' in Summary Report of the EUROSIF Conference April 2002*. Chapter presented at the EUROSIF Conference, April 2002, Frankfurt.

Kapstein, E. 2001. The Corporate Ethics Crusade. *Foreign Affairs*, 80(5): 105-119.

McGuire, J. B., Sungren, A., & T. Schneeweiss. 1988. Corporate social responsibility and firm performance. *Academy of Management Journal*, 31: 354-372.

Moir, L. 2001. What do We Mean by Corporate Social Responsibility? *Corporate Governance: The International Journal for Effective Board Performance*, 1(2): 16-22.

Morsing, M. 2003. Conspicuous Responsibility: Communicating Responsibiilty – to Whom? In M. Morsing, & C. Thyssen (Eds.), *Corporate Values and Responsibility – the Case of Denmark*: 145-154. Copenhagen: Samfundslitteratur.

Nelson Sofres. 2001. *European Survey on Socially Responsible Investment and the Financial Community*. Brussels: CSR Europe.

O'Rourke, A. 2002. *A New Politics of Engagement: Shareholder Activism for Corporate Social Responsibility*. 2002/129/CMER. Fontainebleau: INSEAD.

Sethi, P. 1975. Dimensions of Corporate Social Resposnibility. *California Management Review*, 17(3): 58-64.

Shell. 1998. *Profits or Principles: Does There Have to Be a Choice?* London: Royal Dutch/ Shell Group of Companies.

SustainAbility. 1999. *The Social Reporting Report*. London: SustainAbility.

Tepper Marlin, A. 1998. *Visions of Social Accountability: SA 8000*. London: Financial Times Management.

Vogel, D. 1986. The Study of Social Issues in Management: A Critical Appraisal. *California Management Review*, 28(2): 142-151.

WBCSD. 1999. *Corporate Social Responsibility*. Geneva: WBCSD.

Wood, D. J. 1991. Corporate Social Performance Revisited. *Academy of Management Review*, 16: 691-719.

Zadek, S., Pruzan, P., & Evans, R. 1997. *Building Corporate AccountAbility – Emerging Practices in Social and Ethical Accounting, Auditing and Reporting*. London: EarthScan.

## Notes

1. I would like to acknowledge the financial support of CSR Europe (www. csreurope.org) for the study underlying this research. I am also indebted to Sunita Leng and Anastasia O'Rourke at INSEAD and Adeline Hinderer at CSR Europe for their role in data collection and analysis.

# CHAPTER 12

# Reporting consistently on CSR – Choosing appropriate discourse strategies

*Anne Ellerup Nielsen & Christa Thomsen*

*In our financial annual report we will start commenting on things that do not only have a financial impact on our company. We will highlight issues that represent a challenge to industry and to our company; in case these issues are not taken properly into account, they risk being a financial problem for the company... In the future, we will increasingly integrate our reports, which means that we will no longer operate with separate financial, environmental and sustainability reports. The integrated report will instead give an overall account of the company.*

Interview with Lars Rebien Sørensen, CEO, Novo Nordisk.
*Jyllands-Posten*, September 2nd. 2004.

## Introduction

CSR reporting serves different purposes depending on contextual and corporate characteristics (Gray et al., 2001). Companies report their activities "in order to be accountable to their constituents – their stakeholders, or those agencies that fall within the company's sphere of influence" (Holland & Gibbon, 2001, p. 279). In some European countries, including Denmark, stakeholders such as governments and legislators explicitly recommend that companies report on their social and environmental activities in their general annual report (cf. the Danish law on Organisational Annual Reporting of 2002). However, the motivation to provide an account of a company's actions is driven not only by external but also by internal factors including the improvement of the company's image and the positive effect on the bottom line through an improved market share, both of which will have a positive impact on shareholder value. It may also be driven by a wish to reduce risk, particularly for those companies whose business activities are perceived to be environmentally or socially damaging (Holland & Gibbon, 2001). CSR reporting thus can be considered as a tool that allows companies to respond to stakeholders who increasingly claim transparency and accountability from companies in order to find out if they are trustworthy and reliable (Gao & Zhang, 2001). However, CSR reporting may also be considered as a tool that allows companies to initiate the dialogue with stakeholders, i.e. as part of a more proactive strategy, as proposed by the CEO of Novo Nordisk.

As the introductory quotation illustrates, companies such as Novo Nordisk no longer find it sufficient to *inform stakeholders about* financial aspects and risks related to finances in the annual report. They also want to *comment on* or *highlight* ethical problems or dilemmas such as medical prices in developing countries. If they don't take these kinds of initiatives, they risk being victims of political regulation, for example on the initiative of the World Trade Organisation (WTO) – a regulation that may have long-term economic consequences for a company. The initiatives can be visible in annual reports, social reports, sustainability reports, environmental reports, and the like. Hence the communication or

278

the dialogue with stakeholders can be characterised as proactive and goal-oriented, which means that strategies such as argumentation and persuasion play an important role. As there is no established legislative framework, only principles and guidelines (e.g., the triple bottom line, the Global Reporting Initiative, AA1000) that go beyond financial accounting and include social and environmental reporting, many companies are more or less 'left on their own'. The lack of a common understanding and terminology in the area of CSR has given rise to a debate about how companies should demonstrate their CSR (Zadek, Pruzan & Evans, 1997), whereas a debate about which discourse strategies companies should adopt for reporting on CSR has been given less priority. How can companies for instance develop appropriate strategies for reporting on CSR in terms of elements such as topics, discourse types and rhetorical strategies (Nielsen & Thomsen, forthcoming), and what are the implications for managerial practice which is the theme of this chapter? Companies need to know how to develop consistent strategies in order not to nourish the debate about whether many CSR activities described in annual reports are perceived as corporate spin only concerned with reputation management, instead of being regarded as a values-led ethical approach to business (Jackson & Bundgård, 2002).

To increase our understanding of how companies can report consistently on CSR, we argue that it is necessary to understand CSR reporting processes. We further suggest that the theory and literature on CSR on the one hand and Critical Discourse Analysis (CDA) on the other hand prove to be a fruitful method for a better understanding of these processes. Theory on CSR raises some important questions for understanding what organisations are responsible for and motivated by, whereas CDA raises some important questions for understanding the discourse of CSR. In particular it highlights two key issues: firstly, identifying the way in which a discourse selectively translates events around it, and secondly, examining why a particular interpretation and discourse has gained predominance (Burchell & Cook, 2006).

This chapter first outlines theory and literature on CSR and Stakeholder Relations focusing on the different perspectives and

279

the contextual and dynamic character of the CSR concept. CSR reporting challenges are discussed and a model of analysis is proposed. Next, our chapter presents the results of a case study showing that companies use different and not necessarily consistent strategies for reporting on CSR. Finally, the implications for managerial practice are discussed. The chapter concludes by highlighting the value and awareness of the discourse and the discourse types adopted in the reporting material. By implementing consistent discourse strategies that interact according to a well-defined pattern or order, it is possible to communicate a strong social commitment on the one hand, and to take into consideration the expectations of the shareholders and the other stakeholders on the other hand. The focus is on the use of discourse types representing different perspectives or argumentation strategies.

## CSR theory

In the theoretical literature three different perspectives or approaches typically dominate the question of what organisations are responsible for and motivated by. According to the classical approach, "the social responsibility of business is to increase its profits" (Friedman, 1970). Decisions are in the hands of the company owners who are driven by profit maximization. Social responsibility is considered to be primarily the responsibility of the government.

In the stakeholder approach companies are not only considered as being accountable to the owners of the company, but also to the stakeholders. It is assumed that stakeholders influence the activities of the company and/or are influenced by the activities of the company (Freeman, 1984).

The most comprehensive approach to social responsibility is the societal approach in which companies are considered to be responsible to society in general. "Good corporate citizenship" (Waddock, 2004) is a means to obtain a "licence to operate" from society (Committee for Economic Development, CED, 1971).

Carroll (1991, 1999) compresses the essentials of the three approaches. He suggests that the mission of companies today includes four dimensions, i.e. an economic, a legal, an ethical and a

280

philanthropic dimension: "The CSR firm should strive to make a profit, obey the law, be ethical, and be a good corporate citizen" (Carroll, 1999, p. 43). Carroll's definition focuses on the stakeholders of the company. The problem with this definition is that it is very broad. A more useful distinction is proposed by Van Marrewijk (2003) who describes five different ambition levels for social responsibility related to the different stakeholders of the company: "compliance-driven", "profit-driven", "caring", "synergistic" and "holistic". A "stakeholder" is "any group or individual who can affect or is affected by the achievement of the firm's objectives" (Freeman, 1984, p. 25). Freeman considers the primary stakeholders as those who have a legitimate interest in the company, i.e. investors, employees and customers. Competitors, distributors, local society, interest groups, media and society are considered as secondary stakeholders. The Stakeholder Management concept can be used to understand and manage internal and external changes (Freeman, 1984, p. 52). Freeman distinguishes between three different perspectives or levels: the rational level, the procedural level and the transactional level, and he gives several examples that demonstrate how the lack of coherence between the goals, strategy and processes, and the lack of consistency in the messages sent out by the organisation internally and externally, causes troubles for the interaction and communication with stakeholders.

Freeman emphasises with reference to Peters and Waterman (1982) that Stakeholder Management is a voluntary concept. However, organisations with an expressed Stakeholder Management Capability develop and implement communication processes with many different stakeholder groups, negotiate with stakeholders about critical issues and aim to sign voluntary agreements. They try to understand the needs of their stakeholders, involve the different functions or departments in the development of the strategy, act proactively, allocate resources in a way which takes into consideration stakeholders' expectations, and in general think in "stakeholder-serving" terms.

The stakeholder model can be used to describe the company, but it can also be used as a means to obtain economic results, stability, and growth. Finally, the model can be used normatively

– morally or ethically – as it shows how companies should treat stakeholders (see for example Donaldson & Preston, 1995). According to Freeman companies must establish good relations with their stakeholders as part of the strategic management. The company and its stakeholders form a network of resources of which the purpose is to create win-win-situations or synergy. Stakeholders may have values other than purely economic ones, and they may be disappointed or even angry with the decisions made by the company. The task of the leaders is to handle the dilemmas and conflicts that arise by understanding the expectations and values of the stakeholders and by building up a sense of confidence and loyalty. In order to understand stakeholders' expectations the company must be in a dialogue with them.

The European Commission also links CSR to the stakeholder concept. CSR is "a concept whereby companies integrate social and environmental concerns in their business operations and in their interactions with their stakeholders on a voluntary basis" (EU Commission 2001, p. 6). The definition is used by leading companies in Europe and is considered fundamental in European CSR policy. Danish companies tend to focus on the social dimension. Rendtorff (2003, p. 43) explains that ideas about social responsibility are not as developed in Europe as they are in the USA where there is an ethical legislation. However, in Denmark there is a strong tradition for social responsibility and individual concerns, which is seen as a result of the cultural and historical heritage and the structure of the labour market. In this respect, the trade unions – more than the American NGOs – play an important role as they make certain that companies take into consideration their employees and other stakeholder groups. Employees in Denmark and in Europe have greater influence on the decisions made by companies than employees in the USA. In general, the decision process is top-down in American companies whereas the socially oriented European – and especially Danish – companies historically tend to invite their stakeholders to participate in a dialogue. According to Rendtorff this aspect has led to a situation where the focus is no longer solely on shareholder value and the bottom line. The different perspectives on CSR are certainly a big

282

challenge for companies – and CSR reporting is a good example of this challenge.

## CSR reporting challenges

The emergence of non-financial reporting can be seen as an attempt to increase transparency with respect to corporate actions concerning social and environmental issues. However, CSR and CSR reporting are voluntary concepts, and corporate self-selection of indicators may weaken the impact of CSR reporting. In general, much time and effort are spent selecting indicators and producing non-financial reports. In this context it becomes relevant to investigate what companies actually say and how they say it (Nielsen & Thomsen, forthcoming), and to assess whether companies choose appropriate discourse strategies.

As stated above, CSR is a contextual concept that fundamentally is a question about the relations between the company and its environment. The concept becomes operational when it meets the specific stakeholders and their expectations. This meeting opens up for a potential conflict as the concept of social responsibility is about ethics and values and contains an implicit demand for a solution (Thyssen, 2002, p. 127). One question raised is for example: Is this new agenda beneficial for society and who should set priorities (Knudsen, 2005)? Knudsen states that from a societal perspective it is beneficial that corporations and civil society participate in solving problems that governments may be unable to handle. Without active involvement on their part, core problems might not be addressed. However, a key issue to address from a societal perspective is: Who sets the priorities? A general assumption is that to the greatest possible extent, democratically elected representatives should set the overall priorities concerning corporate responsibility initiatives with respect to the environment, human rights, and the like. How else can one ensure that priorities reflect the priorities of the electorate? Another question is how much it is reasonable to ask of companies (Knudsen, 2005)? Which perspective on CSR is dominating and what is the ambition level (see also CSR analysis model in 5)? Having this scenario in mind it is important to see how companies cope with

283

this dilemma when reporting on CSR (Nielsen & Thomsen, forth-coming).

In principle there are no limits to social responsibility. Therefore the main challenge for the organisations is to manage the mutual expectations. On the one hand, organisations must be able to cope with the internal expectations. On the other hand, the company must be able to meet the external expectations as well. The company can manage the mutual expectations by entering into a stakeholder dialogue and by adopting for example specific rules or guidelines for the communication with the stakeholders. These rules may include reporting standards and deadlines. The form and content of the communication depends on contextual elements such as the size of the company, the specific stakeholder groups, the complexity of the issue, the ambition level, and the nature of the engagement specified by the company.

Another challenge consists in motivating CSR initiatives, which in practice means that the company must be able to explain to internal and external stakeholders why it is logical or necessary for the company to assume social responsibility. Being socially responsible is not evident to companies that operate within ordinary market terms. This explication is important in order to be credible. If, for example, CSR initiatives are particularly expensive, the company must be able to explain to the stakeholders – especially owners and investors – why these initiatives are necessary and in which way they will lead to business privileges and competitive advantage.

According to common CSR theory, companies are motivated by different drivers that are not all equally compatible. Consequently, companies face different challenges when reporting on CSR, the main challenge being to adopt discourses (and discourse types) that are consistent with the purpose of the company. We draw on CDA in order to understand the discourse of CSR. As we shall see in the following, CDA allows us to identify the way in which a discourse selectively translates events around it. Secondly, CDA allows us to examine why that particular interpretation and discourse have gained predominance (Burchell & Cook,

284

2006). The question we ask is 'why this particular selection and reduction, why here, why now? (Fairclough, 2005, p. 5).

## CDA – a means of understanding the way we talk about things

CDA (Fairclough, 1992, 1995) is a framework allowing us to study how the social practice of an activity and the language conventions we use when we speak about this activity interact. In terms of CDA, social practice cannot be considered in isolation from language use and vice versa. Through our language use (vocabulary, grammar and meaning relations between sentences) we construct *discourses* (particular ways of constructing particular domains of social practice) shaping into structures of discourses or *discourse types* (configurations of genres and discourses articulated in particular communication situations) which reflect a specific social order or *discourse order* embedding a set of ideological assumptions and power relations which control the social practice of an area of activity (Fairclough, 1995, 76). Given the strong interaction between the social practice of doing things and the discourse practice of talking about these things, the analysis of discourse practices can contribute to uncover to which extent the members of a particular discourse community tend to reproduce the way things are or initiate a way to social change.

CSR may be seen in the light of the above-mentioned dynamic interrelation between reproduction and change. On the one hand, CSR communication may be seen as reproducing the competition paradigm innate to business in the post-modern sense where communication and branding to a great extent have invaded the arena as uniqueness parameters on behalf of functional and technological product performance. On the other hand, CSR is an important indicator of social change proving that businesses wish to reshape their role by adopting a discourse of being socially and environmentally responsible actors. A quick glance at companies' reporting and corporate web sites seems to indicate that businesses all over the globe are adopting the language of CSR, citizenship and ethics within their business plans. As stated by Burchell and Cook (2006, p. 125): "The language of the "business case", and the development of social and environmental re-

285

porting places a central emphasis upon socially responsible practice being a necessary part of a successful business strategy. The picture presented in this context is that CSR is naturally and inevitably ingrained within core business values."

Using the approach of CDA, Burchell and Cook (2006) thus illustrate how a CSR hybrid discourse has been shaped from recent social changes (governments' withdrawing from areas of social provision, emphasis on voluntarism and transparency, companies' ethical exposure in media and advertising material, their responses to anti-capitalism and anti-corporate campaigns of the 1990's, etc.). In terms of CSR, companies are thus on their way to construct a social and environmental discourse universe in which they seek to gain credibility as respectable and responsible actors.

## CSR reporting: a two-fold discourse
In a study of Danish companies' CSR reporting from May 2006 (Nielsen & Thomsen, op.cit.) the approach of CDA was used in order to illustrate that specific social and ethical issues such as *diversity management, employee satisfaction, sponsorships* and *environmental sustainability*, have come to set the agenda in postmodern organisations. This approach also allowed us to gain insights into the way these issues are interpreted and manoeuvred by the companies and their stakeholders. The analysis was based on a case study of selected Danish large and medium sized organisations' (Grundfos, Pressalit Group, Falck A/S, Novozymes, ISS, DSB[1]) CSR reporting (extracts from annual reports, social reports, sustainability reports, environmental reports, and the like). The organisations are members of the Danish Network of Business Leaders[2] and are known as CSR pioneers in Denmark. Thus, they may be said to represent "best practice" companies that by having close relationships with governmental and local institutions play a particular proactive role in implementing CSR and in integrating ethical and social commitment into their overall strategic intent.

In order to uncover the discourse strategies embedded in the CSR reporting of the companies, we designed an analysis model

286

which takes into account the contextual environment of the companies as well as their CSR perspectives and ambitions (model 1).

According to the model below, discourse is a result of the above-mentioned four types of challenges related to 1) globalisation and market situation, 2) the role of business in society (people, planet, profit), 3) the relations with stakeholders and 4) the CSR ambition level of the company.

**Model 1:** *Analysis Model*

The CSR reporting discourse universe in the inner circle of the model is understood as the result of our interpretation of how CSR is practiced, presented and staged in companies' reporting with

287

due respect to their CSR scope, ambition level, stakeholder relations and the contextual environment in which they operate.

Using the model outlined above, we examined the discourse strategies adopted by the six companies in their 2004 annual reports following a three step analysis. The first step of the analysis resulted in a survey of CSR issues, illustrating the priority the reporting companies gave to presenting information on their *employees, local community, environment, society, corporate governance and accountability, business strategy* and *measurement.* The second step of the analysis located the discourse strategies adopted by companies in relation to the four CSR challenges of our model: the companies' CSR perspective, ambition level, contextual environment and stakeholder priority. The first two steps of the analysis enabled us to draw a narrative scenario of each of the companies' CSR profiles as for instance driven by *individual care and social commitment* (in the case of Grundfos) versus *globalisation, risk and compliance* (in the case of Falck). The third step of the analysis allowed us on the basis of the preliminary analysis results to discern two discourse orders representing two different ways of social acting and thinking: a discourse order of *profit maximization* and a discourse order of *social responsibility.*

The table below (Table 1) is an overview of how the CSR issues are staged in the reports of the reporting companies in terms of the two discourse orders of *profit maximization* and *social responsibility* respectively. The ideological impact of considering for instance the employees in a company as a working resource rather than as a group of individuals with personal aspirations and dreams says a good deal about the company's self-understanding and how internal power relations between top management and the workforce may unfold. Examples of text fragments from companies' annual reports allow us to further demonstrate the characteristics of the two different discourse orders.

288

**Table 1:** *CSR-discourse orders*

| Issue | Discourse order | |
|---|---|---|
| | **Profit Maximization** | **Social Responsibility** |
| | **Discourse types** | |
| Employees | Working Resource | Individual self-development |
| Local community* | - | Local partnerships |
| Environment | Compliance | Environmental-friendly |
| Society | Stakeholder commitment | Social commitment |
| Corporate Governance | Financial accounting | Ethical behaviour discourse |
| Measurement* | CSR measurement | - |

* Issues which have no counterpart in the annual reports of our study

If we select the first issue in table 1, *employees,* we note that the issue is staged fairly differently in the reporting of two of the companies of our analysis: ISS and Grundfos. In ISS *employees* are presented as a "dedicated and skilled workforce" and a "stakeholder" as representing "human capital" for whom the company has designed a specific motivation programme ("Strategy Encentivise TM") in which "substantial resources are invested in staff and management development...in order to enhance employee competence and upward mobility of staff". What we observe in this staging of the employees is that the discourse strategies used by ISS strongly support the profit maximization paradigm. We base this evaluation on the financial reasoning appearing in the use of language based on an in-put out-put reasoning in which human resources are considered in terms of "investment" and "reward" which bear fruit to the company in the future rather than in terms of the employees' individual prosperity and self-development. The ISS approach to employees as human capital is also strongly supported by the use of accounting terminology in the surrounding text such as "share of employees" and "employee turnover". In other words, employees are staged in a business

289

strategic context in which they are seen as a means to reach the company's expectations and goals. Their characteristics in terms of personal properties, individual wishes and aspirations are not part of the reporting strategies adopted by ISS. In Grundfos, the issue of employees is presented from the perspective of the employees as individuals in terms of their personal aspirations, desires and skills which they can choose to enhance and develop in order to improve their personal working life and not only with the aim of achieving the overall goal of the company: "Our employees are people – human beings – with ideas, a sense of commitment, needs, desires, a sense of responsibility, skills and competences and – sometimes – problems. Our employees are not just resources like machinery, buildings and capital – on the contrary; by virtue of its complexity, any human being has numerous potentials", "Mutual respect creates a sense of balance", "Our employees thrive and demonstrate their satisfaction because their jobs and working conditions provide them with great opportunities for professional and personal growth and development". In this example, employees are exposed as complex human beings with personal needs and resources as well as problems. They are presented with a focus on qualities which can be of interest to the company as well as to themselves as individuals, e.g. with the benefits which the working life offers employees in order to achieve personal satisfaction, so that at the end of the day human resource management becomes a win-win activity. Furthermore, we note that the whole idea of the profit maximization paradigm is explicitly rejected in favour of a discourse of human and individual care, which brings the entire discourse universe of Grundfos in accordance with the paradigm of social responsibility. If we look at the risk factors presented by ISS and Grundfos respectively, it is no surprise that they also tend to belong to different social orders. Whereas ISS is an international service industry with many competitors and public and private investors around the world, Grundfos is a Danish family owned industrial company that views the global market conditions as a challenge for innovation and change rather than as a threat. Furthermore, the geographic location of the company in one of the middle range

290

towns of Jutland, counting several local employees at Grundfos, creates a close and more intimate atmosphere between company owners and employees than in many global and decentralised organisations – which might explain the significant individual concern and sense of commitment of the company towards the employees. As for ISS, competitors, shareholders and financial analysts closely follow every activity of the company, and even professional customers are trying to put pressure on the company in order to negotiate better facility service contract conditions. Both companies, however, are equally exposed to corporate spin and press rumours like any other big national or international corporation across the world, but their overall contextual environment may be said to be different. Thus, the context of the organisation, its market situation, CEO profile and reputation, its particular stakeholder relations and their claims and wishes are all parameters which together with the strategic intent of the organisation in all respects influence it's CSR strategy and discourse universe.

**Implications for managerial practice**
If, according to CDA, discourse practices not only tend to reproduce the way things are but also initiate a way to social change, and if we accept to see CSR reporting under these circumstances, as the companies in our case study seem to do, it has serious implications for managerial practice. A number of decisions have to be made regarding CSR reporting.

From a modern organisational and corporate communication perspective, first, the future – and the success – of any one company in today's society, depends critically on how it is viewed by key stakeholders (Cornelissen, 2004, p. 9). Thus companies need to build and nurture relationships with stakeholders, and they must know how to strategically manage and organise activities aimed at their stakeholders. Reporting is one of the activities used by companies for strategic and operational aims, and it may be considered a tool that helps companies to be judged as 'legitimate' by most, if not all, their stakeholders in order to survive and prosper. Conceived as such, annual reports and other reports must focus on the organisation as a whole and on the task of how

291

an organisation is presented to all its key stakeholders, both internally and externally. In this light, companies must decide whether they want to issue a stand-alone CSR report or whether they want to integrate the CSR report in the annual report, which is more in line with corporate communication thinking. In this case companies must also decide under which heading they want to include their report on CSR. The practices are multiple, ranging from very sophisticated and well-established systems to a "brief mention of CSR" in the annual report (Idowu & Towler, 2004).

Secondly, companies should be aware of different CSR discourses and discourse types, and they will have to decide whether they want to reproduce the discourse of shareholders or the discourse of other stakeholders (such as e.g. government and/NGO's) and/or whether they want to and are able to shape their own CSR discourse in an attempt to dominate, control and determine the parameters of the relationship between business, the state and civil society regarding CSR. This decision demonstrates whether a company chooses a reactive or a proactive strategy. The future direction of CSR may in fact be strongly influenced by the ability of different actors to assess and influence these complex processes of interaction and negotiation evolving between business and stakeholders (Burchell & Cook, 2006).

Thirdly, reporting consistently about CSR presupposes that companies and organisations have a clear idea not only of how far they can and want to go in assuming social responsibility in terms of investments, costs and allocations, but also which particular CSR profile their business and strategic intent can adopt without creating gaps between action and vision. Not all organisations have the capacity and the potential to massively support education in third world countries, get rid of foreign suppliers who do not observe every single environment protective measure of the EU, build corporate kindergartens, establish recruitment and retaining policies, and so forth along with complying with the general requirements of innovation and change of the global market place. However, by linking a clear cut and down-to-earth strategy for their CSR profile, which takes into account their specific contextual environment, to an appropriate rhetorical style

292

which is congruent with their own limits and goals, organisations' chances to be taken seriously by suspicious stakeholders will increase.

However, one of the crucial problems of CSR communication is that instead of improving the reputation of businesses as good corporate citizens amongst stakeholders, the incorporation of social and ethical concern into their business strategy and reporting policies have created more suspicion and resistance about their doings and intentions. To quote Burchell & Cook (2006), "companies are entering into a discourse in which they are not necessarily viewed as the most credible actors". Their ability to control the discourse is threatened by stakeholders who contribute to the debate with their own interpretations and who are considered more trustworthy by the public such as environmentalists, consumers, health organisations and NGO's. Therefore, part of improving the discourse work of companies and organisations will be to collaborate and enter into a dialogue with these stakeholder groups in order to gain a platform for better mutual understanding and a consistent CSR discourse universe.

**Conclusion**
Our chapter has discussed the implications for managerial practice of a case study showing that companies use different and not necessarily consistent strategies for reporting on CSR. The value of the discourse and the discourse types adopted in reporting material is highlighted. We have argued that by adopting consistent discourse strategies that interact according to a well-defined pattern or order, it is possible to communicate a strong social commitment on the one hand and to take into consideration the expectations of the shareholders and the other stakeholders on the other.

The focus is on the use of discourse types representing different perspectives or argumentation strategies, e.g. the perspective represented by *the discourse order of profit maximization* and the perspective represented by *the discourse order of social responsibility*. Discourse types consistent with the discourse order of profit maximization are for example *working resource, compliance, stakeholder commitment, financial accounting* and *CSR measurement.* Discourse types consistent with the discourse order of social responsibility *are individual self-development, local partnerships, environmental-friendly, social commitment* and *ethical behaviour.*

### Where do we go from here?

If, according to CDA, discourse practices not only tend to reproduce the way things are but also tend to initiate a way to social change, and if we accept to see CSR reporting under these circumstances, it has serious implications for managerial practice. A number of decisions have to be made by CSR reporting managers and others related to questions such as:

1. Should we issue a stand-alone CSR-report or should we rather integrate the CSR report in our annual report, which is more in the spirit of corporate communication thinking?
2. Should we only reproduce the discourse of our stakeholders or should we rather shape our own CSR discourse in an attempt to dominate, control and determine the parameters of the relationship between (our) business, the state and civil society regarding CSR?
3. Which CSR discourses are important to us, and how do we link strategy with rhetorical style?

Companies find the best answers in their own contexts. Thus the main question they should ask at a strategic and operational level may very well be "why this particular selection and reduction, why here, why now?" (Fairclough, 2005, p. 5).

## References

Burchell, J. & Cook, J. (2006). "Confronting the 'corporate citizen'. Shaping the discourse of corporate social responsibility." *International Journal of Sociology and Social Policy*. Vol. 26. No. 3/4, pp. 121-137.

Carroll, A. B. (1991). "The pyramid of corporate social responsibility: Toward the moral management of organizational stakeholders." *Business Horizons, 34*, pp. 39-48.

Carroll, A. B. (1999). "Corporate Social Responsibility. Evolution of a Definitional Construct." *Business & Society*, vol. 38, nr. 3, pp. 268-295.

Cornelissen, J. (2004). *Corporate Communications. Theory and Practice*. London: Sage Publications.

Donaldson, T. & L. E. Preston (1995). "The stakeholder theory of the Corporation: concepts, evidence, and implications." *Academy of Management Review*. Vol. 20. No. 1, pp. 65-91.

EU Commission (2001). *Greenchapter on Corporate Social Responsibility*.

Fairclough, N. (1995). *Critical discourse analysis*. London: Longman.

Fairclough, N. (2005). "Critical discourse analysis, organizational discourse and organizational change", downloadable chapter, available at: *www.ling.lancs. ac.uk/staff/norman*

Freeman, R.E. (1984). *Strategic Management: A Stakeholder Approach*. Boston, MA: Pitman.

Friedman, M. (1970). "The Social Responsibility of Business is to Increase its Profits", *The New York Times Magazine*, September 13.

Gao, S.S. & Zhang, J.J. (2001). "A Comparative Study of Stakeholder Engagement Approaches in Social Auditing. In: Andriof, J. & McIntosh, M.: *Perspectives on Corporate Citizenship*. Sheffield: Greenleaf Publishing, pp. 239-255.

Gray, R., Kouhy, R. & Lavers, S. (1995). "Corporate social and environmental reporting. A review of the literature and a longitudinal study of UK disclosure." *Accounting, Auditing & Accountability Journal*. Vol. 8. No. 2, pp. 47-77.

Gray, R., Javad, M., Power, D.M. & Sinclair, C.D. (2001). "Social and Environmental Disclosure and Corporate Characteristics: A Research Note and Extension." *Journal of Business Finance & Accounting*. 28 (3) & (4), pp. 327-356.

Holland, L. & Gibbon, J. (2001). "Processes in social and ethical accountability. External reporting mechanisms." In: Andriof, J. & McIntosh, M.: *Perspectives on Corporate Citizenship*. Sheffield: Greenleaf Publishing, pp. 278-295.

Idowu, S.O. & Towler, B.A. (2004). A comparative study of the contents of corporate social responsibility reports of UK companies." *Management of Environmental Quality: An International Journal*. Vol. 15. No. 4, pp. 420-437.

Jackson, C. & Bundgård, T. (2002). "Achieving quality in social reporting: the role of surveys in stakeholder consultation." *Business Ethics: A European Review*, pp. 253-259.

295

Knudsen, J. S. (2005). "The Global Reporting Initiative in Denmark: Emperor's New Clothes or Useful Reporting Tool?". Downloadable chapter, available at: *www.copenhagencentre.org.*

Nielsen, A. & Thomsen, C. (2007). Reporting CSR – what to say and how to say it? *Corporate Communications. An International Journal.*

Peters, T.J. & Waterman, R.H. (1982). *In search of excellence: Lessons from America's best-run companies.* New York: Harper & Row.

Rendtorff, Jacob Dahl (2003). "Værdibaseret ledelse og socialt ansvar. Aspekter af virksomhedernes gode statsborgerskab." *Økonomi og Politik,* nr. 3. København: Jurist- og Økonomforbundets Forlag.

Thyssen, O. (2004). *Værdiledelse: om organisationer og etik.* København, Gyldendal.

Van Marrewijk, M. (2003). "Concepts and Definitions of CSR and Corporate Sustainability: Between Agency and Communion". *Journal of Business Ethics* 44, pp. 95-105.

Waddock, S. (2004). Parallel Universes: Companies, Academics, and the Progress of Corporate Citizenship." *Business and Society Review* 109:1 pp. 5-42.

Zadek, S., Pruzan, P. & Evans, R. (Eds.) (1997). *Building Corporate Accountability: Emerging Practice in Social and Ethical Accounting and Auditing.* London: Earthscan.

## Notes

1. Grundfos: *http://www.grundfos.com/* – Pressalit: *http://www.pressalit.com/pressalit/en-GB* – Falck A/S: *http://www.falck.com/index-uk* – Novozymes: *http://www.novozymes.com/en* – ISS: *http://www.issworld.com* – DSB: *http://www.dsb.dk/*

2. Network established in 1996 by the Minister of Social Affairs, belonging today to the Ministry of Employment. The networks counts 16 business leaders in large and medium sized companies and is a forum to discuss the development of corporate social responsibility and public-private partnerships towards establishing an inclusive labour market, cf.: *http://www.copenhagen centre.org/sw661.asp*

# About the Contributors
# Strategic CSR communication

**Name · Title / Position · Primary research interests**

**Mette B. Andersen** · Ph.D. · Corporate social responsibility, corporate social responsibility from a supply-chain perspective, environmental management systems, eco-labelling

**Suzanne C. Beckmann** · Dr.rer.soc. / Professor · Integrated communications management, brand management, strategic planning and market orientation, consumption studies and consumer behaviour, corporate social responsibility and methodological development in market research

**Susse Georg** · Ph.D. / Professor · Corporate environmental reporting/communication, institutionalization of environmental management, organization theory

**Eric Guthey** · Ph.D. / Associate Professor · Social identity studies, mana-gement and photography

**Kai Hockerts** · Ph.D. · Corporate social responsibility, social entrepeneurship, environmental management

**Peter Kjær** · Ph.D. / Associate Professor · Media and organization, strategic communication, management knowledge, institutional change, public sector organization, health management

**Roy Langer**  Ph.D. / Professor · Organizational and marketing communications

**Mette Morsing** · Ph.D. / Associate Professor · Organisation theory, communication and corporate social responsibility

**Anne Ellerup Nielsen** · Ph.D. / Associate Professor · Corporate communication, corporate social Responsibility, marketing communication, new popular management communication and web mediated corporate communication

**Lucia Reisch** · Dr. oec. / Visiting Professor · Consumption studies and consumer behaviour; consumer policy, sustainable consumption and social corporate social responsibility; communication of sustainability issues

**Majken Schultz** · Ph.D. / Professor · Strategic management, identity-image studies and reputation management

**Christa Thomsen** · Ph.D. / Assistant Professor · Corporate communication, cross-sector communication (social partnerships),  corporate social responsibility, dialogue analysis

**Steen Vallentin**  Ph.D. / Associate Professor Corporate social responsibility (including stakeholder management and values-based management), media and communication theory (particularly public opinion theory), organization theory and corporate communication

# Index

299